THE VAGABONDS

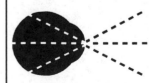

This Large Print Book carries the
Seal of Approval of N.A.V.H.

THE VAGABONDS

THE STORY OF HENRY FORD AND THOMAS EDISON'S TEN-YEAR ROAD TRIP

JEFF GUINN

THORNDIKE PRESS
A part of Gale, a Cengage Company

Farmington Hills, Mich • San Francisco • New York • Waterville, Maine
Meriden, Conn • Mason, Ohio • Chicago

LIBRARY OF CONGRESS CIP DATA ON FILE.
CATALOGUING IN PUBLICATION FOR THIS BOOK
IS AVAILABLE FROM THE LIBRARY OF CONGRESS

ISBN-13: 978-1-4328-7214-4 (hardcover alk. paper)

Published in 2019 by arrangement with Simon & Schuster, Inc.

Printed in the United States of America
1 2 3 4 5 6 7 23 22 21 20 19

For Jon Karp, who suggested the subject.
And for James Ward Lee,
Carlton Stowers, Anne E. Collier,
Jim Fuquay, and Ralph Lauer,
the friends who were with me
on many of the miles.

CONTENTS

PROLOGUE: PARIS, MICHIGAN —
MID-AUGUST 1923 9

Chapter One: 1914 29
Chapter Two: 1915 74
Chapter Three: 1916 115
Chapter Four: 1918 159
Chapter Five: 1919 214
Chapter Six: 1920 252
Chapter Seven: 1921 290
Chapter Eight: Interlude: November
1921–June 1923 342
Chapter Nine: 1923 363
Chapter Ten: 1924 397
Chapter Eleven: Jep Bisbee Is
Famous 430

NOTES 457
BIBLIOGRAPHY 503
ACKNOWLEDGMENTS 529

PROLOGUE:
PARIS, MICHIGAN
MID-AUGUST 1923

Bad weather plagued much of Michigan during the late summer of 1923. Unseasonably cool temperatures combined with near-constant rain, trapping residents indoors and tamping down what had been, for the last fifteen years or so, an ever-increasing influx of tourists eager to enjoy the state's bracing mix of sprawling woodlands, arching hills, and sparkling lakes.

This was especially true in the tiny, unincorporated township of Paris, named in the 1850s for early settler John Parish. Somewhere along the line the "h" was dropped. If most of Michigan eerily resembled a palm-down left hand, Paris was located at approximately the lowest joint of the ring finger. Grand Rapids, the nearest city of any consequence, was sixty-five miles to the south, several hours' hard driving given the poor quality of the roads wending their way through that part of the state.

Paris, like most of its neighboring villages in Mecosta County, was a stop for the Grand Rapids and Indiana Railroad to take on water and load timber and other goods after its tracks were laid across the state in the late 1860s and early 1870s. Paris residents, rarely numbering above the mid-hundreds, were mostly farmers. Others worked at the state fish hatchery in town — the wide Muskegon River flowed nearby. The hatchery was the town's crown jewel. When the train left town, it always carried containers of brown trout "fingerlings" to stock lakes and rivers all over the region. Many of the humble houses in town were still fairly new. A fire in 1879 had decimated much of the early settlement, and cash-strapped locals took almost a generation to completely rebuild.

Early in Paris's modest existence, outsiders usually arrived as passengers on a Sunday-only "picnic train" from Grand Rapids that made one of its stops near the hatchery. These visitors frequently purchased drinks, snacks, and notions at Montague's store. The Montagues were among the area's first settlers. In 1923, Charlie Montague ran the shop. To attract a new generation of customers, he'd installed gas pumps out front. In only two decades, the number of automobiles in America had swelled from approximately eight thousand to about ten million. Highway 131, a bumpy dirt/gravel hybrid that frequently tore tires, chipped paint, and cracked windshields, ran through the middle of town. In Michigan as everywhere else in the country, Americans increasingly used cars for weekend or extended holiday travel as well as day-to-day work- or errand-related driving. "Gypsying" was an early, popular term for such outings. Participants were known as "vacationists," or, if extended trips involved pitching tents at night, "autocampers." Many drove through Paris on their way to somewhere more interesting, often Traverse City further to the northwest, which offered ferry services to whisk passengers and their cars to the frequently spectacular climes of Michigan's Upper Peninsula across Lake Michigan.

The first full-fledged gas stations had begun springing up around the country, but most of these were located in cities or else along the nation's more improved major highways. Backcountry drivers generally depended on mom-and-pop grocery pumps like those at Montague's for fuel replenishment. As out-of-town traffic through town increased, so did Charlie Montague's income from sales of gasoline and motor oil. Some Paris residents owned cars, too. Like their fellow field-tillers across the land, Mecosta County farmers initially opposed the car gypsiers, who frequently camped overnight on their land without permission and left behind mounds of trash. But the farmers eventually realized the time-saving benefit of hauling crops to market by car rather than horse-drawn wagon and joined in automobile ownership themselves. There were still a lot of horses and wagons in Paris. At about 25 cents a gallon, Charlie rarely sold more than $100 worth of gas in a busy week. Thanks to the inclement weather so far in August that restricted driving for town residents and gypsiers alike, he'd lately been hard-pressed to sell that much.

This made what happened in mid-month all the more surprising. On a drizzly afternoon, Paris townsfolk were out and about, puttering in gardens, visiting on stoops with neighbors, or shopping at Montague's, when they heard the purr of powerful engines. Then out of the mist on Highway 131 there appeared from the southeast a fleet of very grand automobiles, six in all, Lincolns and Cadillacs and two other vehicles that looked like nothing anyone in

Paris had seen or even imagined before, hulking squarish metal wagons clearly built for hauling bulky loads.

The impressive caravan glided to a stop outside Montague's. The driver's side doors of the passenger vehicles opened, and from them emerged strapping men outfitted in matching khaki uniforms that resembled military garb. A small crowd gathered as these uniquely dressed fellows took turns filling their cars with gasoline. The onlookers, too intimidated to ask outright, whispered among themselves: Who *are* these people? After a few moments, their collective gaze switched to the windows of the passenger cars, staring at the men and women who still sat inside the automobiles, keeping out of the drizzle. Then a few locals felt sufficiently emboldened to move forward, and someone blurted loudly, "That guy in the back seat looks like Henry Ford!"

It was.

For any number of reasons — his outspoken pacifism prior to the recent world war, speculation about his prospects for the U.S. presidency in the upcoming 1924 election, constant print and photographic coverage that made his name and hawklike visage familiar, his widely perceived championing of the working class with high wages and shortened workdays, and, above all, for his modestly priced Model T that, for the first time, made car ownership possible even for people of limited means — Henry Ford had become perhaps the most famous man in America. He was certainly the most famous ever to show up unexpectedly in Paris, Michigan, and everyone in the crowd pushed forward to see him for themselves. Ford obligingly got out of his car. He offered no wave of greeting or any other theatrical gesture — he was deservedly renowned as a singularly undemonstrative man who in particular eschewed speeches. But with that exception Ford generally accepted the responsibilities of his celebrity — he'd worked diligently to cultivate it, realizing early on that his personal fame heightened demand for Model Ts — and so Ford stood in the dampness, nodding and smiling pleasantly, letting the crowd have a good look. The gawkers were only momentarily satiated. Then their excitement escalated, for if this was Henry Ford with an accompanying fleet of luxury cars, then it surely must mean . . .

Most summers for approximately the last decade, Henry Ford set out on auto trips that often extended two weeks or more, visiting remote towns and small communities, camping sometimes in parks and more frequently on private land, always asking permission first from owners and if required compensating them generously. On every trip, Ford was accompanied by friends — sometimes other business magnates or else government officials, high-ranking Ford staff members, once the now recently deceased president Warren G. Harding. His road companions always included two stalwart Ford pals, tire tycoon Harvey Firestone and much beloved inventor Thomas Edison, the only living American whose fame rivaled Ford's own. After a few such trips, the trio, together with a fourth friend, the late naturalist John Burroughs, fancifully dubbed themselves "the Vagabonds," and each year the announcement of their latest summer excursion sparked endless speculation about where they might venture next. A general region was always cited in advance, but not a specific route. They might pop up anywhere — speculation was rampant. In 1923, it was known that the Vagabonds would attend Harding's funeral in Ohio, then motor on into the Upper Midwest, possibly through Wisconsin and undoubtedly parts of Michigan. Town newspapers throughout the region were full of wishful speculation — wouldn't it be wonderful if they stopped *here*? Paris residents, who mostly read either the *Battle Creek Enquirer* or the more local *Big Rapids Pioneer,* would have held little hope that the celebrity troupe would motor their way. One of the Vagabonds' avowed goals on this summer's trip was to visit Ford lumber interests in Michigan's Upper Peninsula, most easily reached from Ohio by driving due north through eastern Wisconsin. Yet here was Henry Ford, rain dripping off the brim of his hat, and if Ford was present that must mean somewhere in one of those passenger cars sat Thomas Edison, and there he was, the great head topped by messily flopping silver hair making him easy to recognize as well. But Edison didn't get out; he was in the early stages of a nasty cold and the weather was too severe. Harvey Firestone, his last name far better known than his genial, generic face, was identified inside several of the cars, and always in error. Firestone and his family, traveling in yet another fine car, were many miles away because their driver had gotten lost. This happened frequently on the Vagabonds' summer trips. One car or another would take a wrong turn on a poorly marked road, and someone on the trip's support staff would eventually be tasked with tracking down the missing

16

vehicle and guiding it back on route.

Meanwhile, here were Ford and Edison and (supposedly) Firestone in Paris, apparently making a brief stop to refuel, but then Henry Ford had a question for the crowd: Did anyone know the way to Jep Bisbee's house? They all did — everybody in Paris knew where everybody else lived — and Ford's inquiry further ratcheted up their sense of speculative wonder, for eighty-one-year-old Jep was the closest thing tiny Paris had to a hometown celebrity. For all of his lengthy adult life, Jep variously earned his daily bread as a store clerk, drugstore and grocery store manager, house painter, and farmer. In the most current edition of *The Farm Journal Illustrated Directory of Mecosta County,* an ad-saturated directory of who lived where locally, Jep was identified as a shoemaker. But his real talent, and true professional love, was playing his handmade fiddles at area dances and festivals. Jep had a family to support, so he couldn't fully embrace the itinerant, constantly hand-to-mouth career of a country musician, but Sarah Bisbee, his wife of forty-four years, and their now grown kids were good musicians, too, and quite often the entire Bisbee family performed onstage, fiddle and piano and second fiddle and clarinet and bass

17

fiddle and sometimes even a bass drum. Set lists always featured old-fashioned favorites like "Turkey in the Straw" and "The Girl I Left Behind Me," the kind of tunes that set toes a-tapping and lent themselves perfectly to square dancing. All of which was fine for hardscrabble folks in Mecosta County, and in other neighboring parts of their sparsely populated region. By local standards, Jep's music career was a considerable success. But how could an important big-city man like Henry Ford have even heard of old Jep Bisbee?

In front of Montague's, Ford offered no explanation. He simply asked directions to the Bisbee home and waited through the beat or two it took for the crowd to digest the question and respond. A parade of volunteers stepped up to lead the auto caravan a few hundred yards to Jep's. The cars rolled slowly along and stopped in front of a nondescript residence with a small barn out back. As town residents continued staring, Ford got out of his car again, marched to the front door, and knocked. A second man came with him. When Mrs. Sarah Bisbee emerged, she was naturally taken aback by the sight of Henry Ford on the stoop, with a fleet of cars and apparently half the town right behind him. Ford politely introduced himself and the second man, Edward Kingsford, who managed one of Ford's lumber businesses in the Upper Peninsula. Ford asked if Mr. Bisbee was home. Later, as witnesses added embellishments, Mrs. Bisbee was described as calmly ushering her famous visitor and his companion right in, acting for all the world as though celebrities appeared on her doorstep all the time, but the reality was that she needed to gather herself before mumbling that Jep was out in the barn. Instinctive good manners compelled her to invite them in while her husband was fetched — a number of townsfolk, eavesdropping for all their ears were worth, heard Ford's question and gleefully hustled to the barn on his behalf — but shock prevented Mrs. Bisbee from fully embracing her sudden role as hostess to the great and asking Ford to bring along all the other people who remained in the cars outside.

Mrs. Bisbee seated Ford and Kingsford in her modest parlor. When Jep hustled in, Ford, never one for unnecessary chitchat, immediately asked him to get his fiddle and play. As a lifelong musician for hire, Jep was accustomed to performing on demand. This circumstance was certainly different — Henry Ford appearing out of nowhere in his home — but the request itself was normal enough. Jep got his fiddle and Kingsford explained why they'd come. Some years earlier, Kingsford heard Jep play at a dance. It was well-known among Ford associates that their employer loathed modern music — he found jazz particularly detestable — but thoroughly enjoyed traditional tunes and the square dances, waltzes, and polkas associated with them. When Kingsford learned that Ford was coming up through southwest Michigan on this summer's trip, he suggested a stop in Paris so that the boss could savor some of Jep's fiddling in person. And now, here they were.

Jep enjoyed the story and started to play, with his wife accompanying him on piano. No account exists of the songs they played, but whatever they were, Ford was enchanted. He toe-tapped right along, and when the Bisbees paused for a moment between numbers Ford sent Kingsford to summon the rest of the party. In came Thomas Edison, wide-bellied and clad as usual in rumpled clothes that looked like they'd been slept in, which they probably had — on Vagabonds trips, Edison was notorious for curling up for naps underneath trees, beside babbling brooks, or across car seats. Behind him were two ladies, Clara Ford and Mina Edison. As grande dames fully aware of their exalted social status, they were appropriately dressed to appear in public, in long flowing dresses that covered them from neck to instep with armorlike corsets beneath — nothing about an upper-class woman must appear to jiggle — and fashionable bonnets that remained pinned to their finely coiffed hair even indoors.

This was a moment when true country hospitality might have required the offering of refreshments, and how was Mrs. Bisbee to know what, in her limited larder, would be deemed acceptable by such American royalty? But Henry Ford rescued her from such a delicate decision. He'd come to hear music, not snack, and asked politely but firmly for the Bisbees to play some more. They did, and two unexpected things happened. First, Edison moved his chair directly beside where Jep stood, and bent so that his ear was almost directly over the fiddle's ringing strings. It was widely known that Thomas Edison was exceptionally hard of hearing, and here was proof. He clearly didn't want to miss a single note or nuance. Even more astonishingly, Henry and Clara Ford stood and began dancing together, right there in the Bisbee parlor, just like a country couple at a Mecosta County barn dance. The Fords had obviously danced to folk tunes before. They moved with grace and precision, smiling as they swayed, and when the Bisbees' fingers ached so much that they had to stop playing, Ford was positively garrulous. Afterward, when neighbors badgered Jep for details, he said Ford kept repeating how hard it was to hear such fine music nowadays. The Bisbees played the *right* music, the great man said, real *American* music and not that awful-sounding jazz. In between paying compliments, Ford made an offer: He wanted to buy Jep's fiddle. It turned out that Ford had a whole collection of them, Stradivariuses and other fine violins, and he believed Jep's modest homemade instrument would fit right in. (Ford himself enjoyed sawing away on a Stradivarius, but the resulting sounds were more correctly identified as noise rather than music.) Jep had no attachment to this particular fiddle — he made, played, and sold them all the time. Likely he would just have given the thing to his very distinguished guest, but never got the chance. Instead of offering a modest amount as a preliminary step in negotiation, Ford slapped $100 down on a table as payment and of course Jep took it, that sum surely being five or even ten times more than he'd previously made on a handmade fiddle.

All that — the Vagabonds coming to town, them asking for Jep Bisbee, the Fords dancing in the Bisbee front room, Ford forking over a century note for Jep's fiddle, miracles beyond proper description — and then Thomas Edison topped them. He'd let Ford do the talking, but now he flashed that wide wonderful smile familiar from all the newspaper photos and, in a voice made croaky by his cold, instructed Jep to prepare for travel. Once his summer trip was done and he was back home in New Jersey, Edison explained, he wanted Jep and the whole Bisbee family to board a train at the Paris depot and head there, too. Once arrived, Jep would make recordings right in Edison's private studio, just like famous opera singers and symphony orchestras sometimes did. Edison, who'd invented the phonograph way back in the 1870s, also had a company that sold recordings everywhere. They'd make Jep's music available to the entire nation. And while Jep was out east, Edison promised to introduce him to the New York City press, who'd write all kinds of stories about him. Edison pointed out that other musicians he'd recorded became so popular that they headlined extended tours around the country. His offer gave Jep not only the chance to make a national name for himself, but maybe a lot of money, too. Jep hardly knew what to say. Just hours earlier, such things would have been as far beyond belief as the elderly fiddler sprouting wings to fly.

It was at this point that Ford had a final surprise. He told Jep that he was so pleased with his music, he was going to give him a new Model T with all the extras right off the Ford assembly line downstate. It'd be delivered soon, right here in Paris, so Jep could drive himself to jobs at dances and festivals in style. And then, while Jep and Sarah stood there stunned, the Fords and Edisons and Kingsford bid them rather abrupt goodbyes, got in their cars, and the whole caravan whooshed off north in the rain. One moment Henry Ford and Thomas Edison were in the parlor, making all kinds of dazzling promises, and the next they were out of sight.

Afterward, the Vagabonds' visit naturally dominated talk in Paris. Those who couldn't believe their own eyes were reassured in print that they hadn't been mistaken. Reporters must have been among the passengers in the fancy cars, because over the next few days articles about the visit to Jep and the pledges made to him appeared in newspapers as far away as California and New York. That was certainly fine, but then came subsequent stories about the Vagabonds' further summer adventures, and none of these mentioned Jep, reporting instead how Ford put out some small wildfire in a park upstate and Edison's cold got worse — at least one newspaper declared that he might die, which he didn't — and how Mrs. Ford got into it with some young lady sunbathers by a lake, criticizing their too-revealing short-shorts and refusing to give them her autograph. Then came stories announcing the trip was over, that Ford was back home in downstate Dearborn and Edison in New Jersey.

The Bisbees and everyone else in Paris were left to wonder — did Ford and Edison really mean what they'd said? In the weeks after they passed through town, no further word was received from them, let alone train tickets to New Jersey or a spanking new Model T. Sure, Jep had his $100 for a fiddle, and Charlie Montague couldn't stop crowing about making $100 on gasoline sales in a single hour, what with all the gallons those drivers pumped into the Vagabonds' fancy cars. These things alone would have been historic for the small town, events endlessly described to future generations. But the larger question remained. It was likely that these two great men made all kinds of promises as they drove about the country, perhaps too many to remember every one when they got back home and resumed making cars and inventing things. It seemed possible — and, as more days passed, even probable — that amid the ongoing great doings of their famous lives, Ford and Edison simply forgot Jep Bisbee.

The rest of August and then all of September passed, and by early October there was still no word, no summons to New Jersey or the delivery of a car. People in Paris settled in for the approaching winter. They sympathized with poor Jep, whose hopes had been raised so high. At least he remained spry enough to continue playing for a few dollars here and there at local gatherings. His reputation benefited from the Vagabonds' visit — it wasn't every country fiddler who could claim he'd played as Henry and Clara Ford danced, impressed Thomas Edison to boot, and had copies of newspaper articles to prove it.

But the great men had encouraged him to expect so much more. As the weather turned colder, as the first snow fell on Paris, Jep Bisbee could only continue hoping that

Henry Ford and Thomas Edison were not only great men, but truthful ones, too.

CHAPTER ONE:
1914

On February 23, 1914, nine and a half years before Henry Ford and Thomas Edison dropped in on Jep Bisbee in Paris, Michigan, two thousand people swarmed around the train depot in Fort Myers, a small but growing town on Florida's west coast. The crowd, comprising virtually the entire area population, included quite a few people toting homemade banners and a small brass band ready to strike up celebratory tunes. Everyone sweated in the warm sunshine. The Atlantic Coast Line train they awaited was almost a half-hour late, and as they milled impatiently their excitement became increasingly mixed with concern. Thomas Edison, by far Fort Myers's most famous — if only part-time — resident, was scheduled to arrive for his annual months-long escape from the winter cold and business cares of New Jersey, and if newspaper reports from up north were to be believed, he was bringing along not only his wife and three youngest children, but also two prominent friends. One, naturalist John Burroughs, was a well-known author-lecturer who both charmed and instructed readers and audiences with fact-filled tales of countryside rambling. Town leaders, eager for economic growth from tourism, had hopes that Burroughs might commemorate his visit with magazine articles or even a book extolling the wonders of colorful area plants and wildlife. Previous Burroughs writings had inspired many readers to visit the author's native New York state and also Yellowstone National Park. If sufficiently impressed, he might bestow the same priceless favor on Fort Myers. The seventy-six-year-old Burroughs must be made welcome from the moment he stepped from the train.

This was even truer of Edison's other well-known guest. In 1908, Henry Ford introduced a car that transformed American consumerism and travel. Previously, automobiles were exclusively for the rich, costing thousands of dollars just for purchase, and considerably more for upkeep — the country's rough roads pounded dents into heavy chassis, ripped hoses, shook loose valves, and punctured overburdened tires at staggering, expensive rates. But Ford's

Model T changed everything. Thanks in great part to Ford's innovative assembly line, Model Ts were mass-produced on a previously unimaginable scale. In competitors' factories, it took workers several hours to assemble an individual car. At the Ford plant, a completed Model T rolled off the line every two and a half minutes. It was America's first real family car. Various styles had room for as many as six passengers (one publicity photo showed parents and nine children crammed in), with a five-passenger model the most popular.

One feature of the Model T was to impact all other American cars. Prior to 1908, there was no set placement for steering wheels — they might be placed on the right or left side of the front seat, pretty much at the manufacturer's whim, with right-side steering prevalent. But Ford insisted that the Model T wheel be on the left because he intuited a change in car passengers. Automobiles were used more and more for family transportation, with, of course, men always driving but with wives, mothers, daughters, sisters, or girlfriends seated beside them. Most American roads remained rough, with many composed of dirt that could deteriorate to mud or dust depending on weather. U.S. cars were driven on the right-hand side of the road. If the steering wheel was on the left, and female passengers were seated on the right, then the driver could pull up to sidewalks and the ladies could step out of the car and onto pavement without soiling their shoes.

Model Ts were also utilitarian — fancy body styles, pots for plants, and other gewgaws that traditionally prettified automobiles (and drove up the price) were conspicuously absent. Ford passed on the savings to his customers. At the time of its market introduction, the Model T sold for as little as half what other cars cost, and from there Ford continued tinkering with the manufacturing process, aggressively seeking ways to cut production expenses and Model T prices even more. The best example fostered a popular joke that you could buy any color Model T that you liked, so long as the color was black. Few realized that Ford insisted the cars come in that color because black paint dried quickest, meaning Model Ts could be whipped through the assembly line and off to dealerships at an even faster pace, saving additional time and labor-related dollars. Thanks to these and other innovations, in the last few years the car's average price gradually dipped from $850 down to the $500s.

Model T savings for owners only commenced with the initial purchase. Ford's engineers — he employed only the very best and brightest — copied certain European auto manufacturers who utilized vanadium steel, a much lighter metal that allowed Model Ts to skim over rock-rutted, pothole-clotted roads that routinely shook heavier cars into pieces. An Oldsmobile Model S tipped the scales at 2,300 pounds; a Pierce Great Arrow weighed in at a hefty 2,700. At 1,200 pounds, the Model T weighed half as much, and the cost of body repairs and replacement tires was accordingly less. Suddenly, members of the expanding American middle class could afford not only to own a car, but to drive it inexpensively wherever there was any semblance of a passable road. They responded enthusiastically. In 1908, as Ford introduced the Model T, Americans owned approximately 194,400 cars. Just six years later, as the crowd gathered at the Fort Myers train depot, that number had increased to about two million, and Ford controlled almost half the automobile market.

The Model T alone would have established the fifty-one-year-old Henry Ford as a household name, but just three weeks before his anticipated arrival in Fort Myers, he'd further cemented his reputation as a friend of the working man with a stunning announcement. In an era when factory line workers were lucky to earn $2 a day for their labor and toiled through ten-hour shifts six days a week, Ford pledged to pay $5 a day, and to reduce workdays to eight hours. More pay for less work — this was largesse almost beyond comprehension. Everyone in America was talking about it, and at this very moment when his popularity had reached a new zenith, Henry Ford was due to arrive in Fort Myers — that is, if the blasted train ever came, and if, this time, Thomas Edison actually kept his word. Yes, he'd promised Yankee reporters that he was bringing Henry Ford and John Burroughs south to Fort Myers, but the man had broken promises, and trusting Fort Myers hearts, before.

Edison first arrived in Fort Myers in March 1885, on vacation with business partner Ezra T. Gilliland and mourning the recent death of his first wife. There was nothing unusual with a rich, well-known man from the Northeast escaping some of the winter cold with a Florida trip, but what was different about Edison was that he shunned the state's far more populous and cosmopolitan east coast. It was impossible, at that time, to reach much of Florida's west coast except by rickety train across the northern part of the state and then south by boat. No roads linked the coasts in mid- or lower-state. The vast Everglades formed a natural, forbidding barrier. Fort Myers itself was mostly populated with a few hundred cowboys and untold thousands of cattle, raised on local ranches to be shipped off to far-flung markets. But trail drives and railroad cattle cars in other places had pretty much eradicated the local beef industry, and tiny Fort Myers's existence was to some extent in jeopardy. Edison's visit, and subsequent decision to buy property and build a vacation retreat, was an unexpected godsend. As the inventor of the phonograph, the kinetoscope, and flexible film rolls that comprised important steps in the movie industry, and of the incandescent light bulb, the first to burn long, bright, and inexpensively in homes and offices (and, perhaps more critically, of generating systems that made connecting electrical power to these bulbs commercially possible), at present Edison was unquestionably the most famous man in America. If he vacationed annually in Fort Myers, surely some of that fame would attach itself to his new part-time hometown.

Things got off to a promising start. Edison and Gilliland built adjacent homes, and Edison added a laboratory adjoining his. He said that he would tinker and invent even on his Florida vacations — what great new *thing* might be birthed right in Fort Myers, with all the attending publicity? The world waited breathlessly for whatever he would conjure next, and now, hopefully for months at a time on a yearly basis, that global gaze would fix squarely on Fort Myers.

Edison soon made an announcement that thrilled his new Florida neighbors. For his Fort Myers laboratory to function properly, it must have electricity and lights. Accordingly, he would import a massive dynamo/generator system and electrify the entire isolated community. To this point, Fort Myers homes were lit with kerosene lanterns and candles. Outside of a few major cities, this was true all over Florida. By this one act of its new favorite son, a tiny backwater would leap forward in both reputation and self-respect. A town with electricity *mattered.* In early 1886, Edison returned with a new wife in tow, and as they honeymooned Edison informed the local newspaper that he'd get his home and laboratory set up for electric lights first with a small generator, then the rest of the town would have electricity immediately afterward, or as soon as the necessary equipment (which he would pay for himself) could be shipped from the North. On the night of March 17, 1887, most of Fort Myers's other 349 residents lined up outside the Edison estate and gasped with wonder as its lights went on. The local newspaper speculated that a date would soon be announced for the rest of the community to be properly wired and illuminated. But the anticipated shipments didn't arrive, and Edison returned to New Jersey. Everyone in Fort Myers assumed that their leading citizen would return and electric service would commence the following year, but neither happened. Edison and Gilliland had a nasty business falling-out that ended up in court and shattered their personal relationship. Edison had some health issues, and various other personal and business affairs claimed his attention. He didn't return to Fort Myers in 1888, or the next year, or the next, and the townspeople decided that Thomas Edison had either forgotten or never meant his promise to bring electric light to them. A few more years passed without Edison returning to town. At one point he neglected to pay taxes on his Fort Myers property, and nearly lost it. Some construction work continued on the property, and various Edison relatives, including the inventor's aging father, occasionally spent time there, but never the man himself or Mrs. Edison or their children. In 1897 another rich resident — even without Edison, Fort Myers managed to attract a small coterie of wealthy snowbirds — paid to import a sufficiently powerful generator to light the town.

Then, in 1901, Edison and his family returned, offering no explanations for their extended absence. The inventor praised Fort Myers's progress: "It is the prettiest place in Florida and sooner or later visitors . . . will find it out." Edison was accepted rather than warmly welcomed back. Though he was no longer expected to personally perform miracles for the town, his presence would still attract attention and, hopefully, more visitors. In 1904 the railroad finally reached Fort Myers. Permanent town population swelled to more than one thousand. Tourists on boat trips stopped to fish and shop. Things were definitely on the uptick, and then in 1907 the Edisons unexpectedly stepped forward again. They invested $250 in a community drive to build a country club and donated $150 to help found a town library. Best of all, they volunteered to line Riverside Avenue, the town's main street, with attractive palm trees — in a letter addressed to the Fort Myers town council, Edison pledged to buy the trees, provide sufficient fertilizer, and replace any trees that died for a period of two years. After that, the town would be responsible for all costs and upkeep. The offer was quickly accepted, and Edison returned to local good graces to such an extent that plans were made to rename Riverside Avenue for him.

But the palm tree plan proved just as unreliable as Edison's promise of electric lights. Too busy to oversee the process himself, Edison authorized two locals to acquire the trees and get them in the ground. It was expected to take only a matter of months. Some palms would come from the Everglades, others from Cuba. But a temporary quarantine delayed delivery of the Cuban trees, and most of the Everglades palms didn't survive uprooting and replanting. Things sputtered along for several years. One of the local men tasked with buying and planting the trees was W. H. Towles, who also chaired the town council. Towles kept acquiring and planting more trees, but most wilted and died. He asked for and believed he received Edison's approval for this additional expenditure. When Towles submitted a bill for $3,993.55, Edison was willing to reimburse only $1,500. The disagreement between them raged until the town council voted to pay Towles the difference between what he'd spent and what Edison paid him. Edison in turn was encouraged to "complete his gift to the city." He didn't — so far as Edison was concerned, he'd satisfied his obligation. As a rich, famous man, he was constantly badgered for donations to good causes, and even in a case like this when he'd been the one to make the original offer, limits had to be observed or else everyone would feel free to take advantage. Resentment festered on both sides. Soon afterward when a wealthy widow underwrote other improvements along the road, plans for "Edison Street" were scrapped and Riverside Avenue was renamed McGregor Boulevard in memory of her husband. In 1913, Edison donated some replacement palms, but, as Florida historian Michele Wehrwein Albion notes, "the relationship between the town and the Edisons remained somewhat strained."

Which was why, at the Fort Myers depot in February 1914, there was an escalating degree of uncertainty whether Edison was going to step off the train with Ford and Burroughs, or else arrive without them or any explanation for their absence. Edison himself might not be on the train. There was no way of knowing until the arrival. Then came the sound of a whistle somewhere up the track, and finally the train pulled into view. Everyone pressed forward to see who emerged.

The train was late because several Fort Myers civic leaders had boarded it in an unscheduled stop outside town. The town mayor, the Booster Club leader, and the Fort Myers Board of Trade president all wanted to share in the adulation when Edison, Burroughs, and Ford stepped out onto the depot platform. The famous visitors were taken aback, and not especially pleased at the impending hoopla that the boarding party described. Besides the banners and band, every automobile owner in Fort Myers waited to participate in a grand parade from the railway depot to Edison's home — that meant thirty-one cars in all. Madeleine Edison, the inventor's twenty-six-year-old daughter, later lamented in a letter that all she wanted to do was "get home and wash my face." There was nothing to do but go along — Ford, for one, had established a dealership in town, and sharing some smiles and handshakes might sell an additional Model T or two. The three famous men, trailed by Ford's wife, Clara; his son, Edsel; Mina Edison and children Madeleine, Charles, and Theodore, were greeted on arrival by raucous cheers, then escorted to waiting cars for the ceremonial procession. The parade wended its way along, banners waving, and eventually the crowd left and Edison was finally free to welcome the Fords and Burroughs into his home. Host and guests settled in for a relaxing vacation, and an extended chance to get to know each other better.

The friendship between Thomas Edison and Henry Ford was relatively new, though Ford's personal attachment to the inventor went back almost eighteen years. As a young engineer working for one of Edison's Detroit companies, in 1896 Ford was introduced to the man he previously admired from afar at a corporate banquet in New York. Ford had dreams of building affordable cars powered by gasoline engines and worked tirelessly on designing one during off-work hours. Recently he'd street-tested his first prototype called "the Quadricycle," a light wagon mounted on four bicycle wheels and powered by a small gas engine. As Ford gingerly steered the contraption around a few city blocks, a friend on a bicycle rode ahead to move aside pedestrians. Ford used this moment with Edison to describe his fledgling achievement. The older man, as was his custom with all would-be innovators, was encouraging, even though he himself believed that electric-rather than gasoline-powered cars would be the wave of the future. One of Edison's areas of post-incandescent-bulb research was the attempted development of a car battery that could hold sufficient electrical charge to propel a vehicle more than a few miles.

Over the years, as Ford founded and failed with two auto manufacturing companies before succeeding with his third, he endlessly reminisced about the meeting and Edison's words of encouragement: "Young man, that's the thing. You have it. Keep at it." Sometimes Ford described even more than that — he'd spent a long time at the banquet, talking with Edison; the two of them sketched things on napkins and shared a short train ride afterward. Ford was almost certainly exaggerating. But no matter how brief or extended this initial contact, his admiration for Edison blossomed into virtual worship as a result. Throughout his own business successes, as his hard work and belief in himself culminated with the Model T and subsequent automobile industry dominance, Ford warmed himself with memories of that encounter with his hero.

In April 1911, one of Edison's business offices in Orange, New Jersey, received a letter from a high-level staffer for Henry Ford requesting, on Ford's behalf, an autographed photo of Mr. Edison. At this point, Ford's reputation as an innovator (if not inventor — though it wasn't true, many assumed he'd actually invented the automobile) made him almost as well-known as Edison, and, because Ford was a cannier businessman than his hero, much wealthier. A few days later, one of Edison's sales managers sent along a photo of Edison, which, besides a signature, included the inscription "To Henry Ford: One of a group of men who have helped to make [the] U.S.A. the most progressive nation in the world." The sales manager added a note: "I assure you that Mr. Edison was only too glad to do this for Mr. Ford and he wished me to write you expressing his pleasure in doing so, and also inviting you and Mr. Ford to come to Orange at your convenience as he would be very much pleased to meet Mr. Ford." To Ford, his interaction with

Edison in 1896 was inspirational and life-changing. To Edison, it had been a brief encounter with an ambitious fan, not at all unique and instantly forgotten.

It took some time to arrange a date suitable to Edison's schedule, but in January 1912 Henry Ford and Thomas Edison met in New Jersey. Ford relished the opportunity to once again trade shop talk. Edison, impressed with Ford's booming car sales and resulting wealth, had an additional agenda. Though he was far from broke, Edison suffered financial setbacks on some of his own recent endeavors, notably in mining and a plan to build inexpensive houses made entirely of concrete. He now envisioned a monetary comeback by allocating enormous resources to the development of a storage battery so efficient that it would power electric cars up to the distances enjoyed by gas-burners. Edison charmed Ford as he would any potential investor, but at another level he found that he simply enjoyed the automaker's company. Edison had few close friends; he always suspected that anyone seeking friendship had ulterior motives. But Ford was already far richer than Edison, and almost as famous. There were other things in common — during this visit, they found themselves in complete agreement about the evils of Wall Street and the crass men there who cared only for profit and not for the public. Both were poor boys who made good. Ford was the son of a farmer. Edison left school and went to work on the railroad at age twelve. Neither had a college degree, and both were disdainful of those who believed classroom education was superior to hands-on work experience and common sense. When Edison shared his plans to develop a better storage battery for electric cars, Ford was impressed and willing to partner in the effort. His belief in the ongoing dominance of his gas-powered Model T was strong enough that he didn't fear competition from manufacturers of electric vehicles.

Later, Edison followed up the meeting with a letter to Ford. Usually he had business correspondence typed, but this time he wrote in his own flowing, even elegant hand:

Friend Ford . . . [thank you for] doing a little gambling with me on the future of the Storage Battery. Nothing would please me more than having you join in, it looks as if it had a large future. Of course I could go to Wall Street, but my experience over there is as sad as Chopins Funeral March, [so] I keep away. Yours, Edison

Ford's gamble was far from little — some estimates pegged it at anywhere from $750,000 to $1.2 million. In the end, nothing came of it. Edison never perfected a storage battery that fully energized electric cars or created market demand for them, and Ford's investment was lost. Ford wasn't upset. He considered it an honor to partner with Edison professionally, and even more to count the inventor as a friend. Like Edison, he didn't have many. Ford was a prickly man and also a complicated one, burning to make the world better for humanity as a whole while not enjoying personal contact with most individuals. Ford realized that no one other than Edison carried a comparable or even greater burden of public attention and expectation. They understood each other and the pressures on them in a way that no one else could, even their wives.

The friendship between Edison and Ford blossomed. Though business obligations made it difficult, they were able to occasionally make time to meet in person, usually the Fords dropping in on the Edisons while on trips to the East Coast. On one such occasion in January 1914, Ford and Edison granted a dual interview to a reporter from the *New York Times.* Ford announced that he and Edison were collaborating on plans

47

for an electric car that should enter production within a year. (It didn't.) Edison hinted at additional wonders to come from the new partnership, unidentified machinery that would allow workers to accomplish as much in hours as they currently did over several days. "The time is passing when human beings will be used as motors," he said. The normally reticent Ford concluded the interview with an uncharacteristically effusive tribute to his new, dear friend: "I think Mr. Edison is the greatest man in the world, and I guess everyone does."

Mina Edison and Clara Ford got on well, too. Both were fiercely protective of their husbands, and aware of their own presence in the public eye. It was natural, after a year or so of building the relationship, that the Edisons suggested the Fords should join them for a visit in early 1914 at their quaint retreat in Florida. Ford was pleased to accept. He even brought along another of his few close friends.

Unlike the near-immediate bond between Ford and Edison in Orange, Ford's friendship with John Burroughs took considerable time to form. The elderly, opinionated naturalist despised modern technology, cars especially. In speeches and in print, Burroughs predicted that automobiles and their drivers would eventually "seek out even the most secluded nook or corner of the forest and befoul it with noise and smoke." To him, the popularity of the Model T was the beginning of the end. He described Ford's brainchild vehicle as "a demon on wheels." Ford never doubted his own beliefs and decisions, forbidding disagreement from employees and ignoring any from outsiders. But he made an exception for John Burroughs. In general, Ford's hobby was work. He devoted almost every waking minute to it. But Ford loved birds all of his life and whenever possible set aside time to observe them — the sprawling grounds of his Michigan home included hundreds of birdhouses. Burroughs's evocative writings about feathered creatures enthralled him, a rarity for the reading-averse Ford.

In 1912, aware of the old man's contempt for cars in general and the Model T in particular, Ford wrote Burroughs a letter. In it he thanked Burroughs for all the pleasure his books had given him, and in return offered to send along a shiny Model T. Perhaps driving one himself would give Burroughs a different perspective. Burroughs grudgingly accepted, with the understanding that his ownership of the car would not be used for any publicity purposes. He initially insisted that his grown son Julian drive him about in it, then after a few weeks took the wheel himself. Burroughs had constant trouble maintaining control of the vehicle. Once he rammed the car into a barn, and Ford sent mechanics to make repairs. But if driving ultimately didn't suit Burroughs, Henry Ford did. Once the two men met, Burroughs was impressed by Ford's sincere interest in ornithology and, in fact, most things about nature. Ford, in turn, was starstruck by another person he'd previously admired from afar. They took nature hikes together, with Burroughs acting as all-knowing instructor and Ford proving an eager student.

In September 1913, Ford convinced Burroughs to take a car trip with him, from the naturalist's part-time home near Poughkeepsie, New York, to Concord, Massachusetts. Burroughs had introduced Ford to the philosophies (if not the printed words) of Emerson and Thoreau. Now the automaker wanted to see where these New England–based philosophers once lived and worked. Before they left, Ford invited Edison to join them, but the inventor was unable to break away from work in his laboratory. Burroughs, who'd previously roughed it on a well-documented wilderness camping trip in Yellowstone with then-president Theodore Roosevelt, expected more of the same. But Ford arrived with a fleet of cars loaded with servants and equipment. At their camping stops on the way there and back, they slept in large individual tents set up by staffers, enjoyed electric light from portable storage batteries, ate delicious meals prepared by a chef, and dressed each morning in freshly ironed clothes. They made frequent daily stops so Burroughs could point out interesting flowers, plants, and wildlife. Ford was enthralled.

Burroughs had a fine time, too. Afterward, each man got additional confirmation of how advantageous it was to be friends with the other. Simply by being seen out driving with Burroughs, or having newspapers take note of the outings, Ford sent a message to America. If old-fashioned John Burroughs loved to ride in them, how much more might younger, more progressive individuals savor the kind of outdoor adventures made possible by car ownership? As for Burroughs, he'd learned years earlier during his tramps with Roosevelt that having a famous patron greatly expanded audiences for his books and public lectures. There was more. Burroughs confided to Ford that he feared losing the family farm in Roxbury, New York, where he was raised. Relatives living there struggled to meet hefty mortgage payments. Ford bought the property outright and deeded it to Burroughs. Ford's generosity toward his few close friends was boundless.

Edison knew Burroughs only through Ford, but he was pleased to host the naturalist in Fort Myers. Edison used some of his acreage to cultivate fruits and flowers. Burroughs, expert in matters of soil and weather conditions and appropriate care of growing things, made useful suggestions about gardening. Edison was also a budding ornithologist. Prior to departing for Fort Myers, he told the *New York Times* that while in Florida he expected to join Ford and Burroughs in studying bird life in the Everglades.

Ford and Burroughs believed that this outing was the main purpose of the trip. All eleven thousand square miles of the Everglades, comprising marshes, sloughs, ponds, and forests, offered tantalizing glimpses of indigenous plants and flowers, along with a varied bird population and innumerable animals and reptiles. The plan, it seemed to them, was to organize an immediate excursion after their Fort Myers arrival into the seldom-explored heart of the Everglades, with Burroughs pointing out and explaining much of what they discovered. They were vaguely aware of certain drawbacks. There were dangerous creatures lurking in the wet and wild, principally alligators and snakes. But if they brought along a few hardy local guides and a gun or two, that threat would be neutralized. Also, there were no roads of any sort plunging even partway into the Everglades, let alone cutting across the whole thing. But Ford was proud of his cars — he'd had several Model Ts shipped to Fort Myers for this very purpose — and felt certain that they could handle the potentially treacherous terrain. Camp conditions would fall far short of those he and Burroughs had enjoyed on their recent New England trip. Ford servants wouldn't be on hand to cook, clean, and set up and operate storage battery systems for electric lights. Since Model Ts were built with little storage space, equipment would either have to be strapped to the sides or loaded in beside passengers. But the prospect of actually roughing it, sharing some of the same limited road resources as the growing number of humbler Americans setting off on camping trips in their Model Ts or other cars, had its own appeal. Ford, Edison, and

Burroughs would be three aging but still physically capable men reveling in real, rugged adventure.

Ford and Burroughs were eager to set out and assumed that Edison shared their enthusiasm. They were dismayed when their host informed them that he wanted to rest a while first. Edison needed it — a few months earlier, worn down by business stress and his own night-owl work habits, he'd suffered a breakdown. Mina Edison made certain that this was known only to the immediate family. Even Ford may not have been aware of it. Now for several days in Fort Myers, Ford and Burroughs prowled restlessly around the inventor's estate while Edison lounged inside, listening to music recorded by one of his companies and played on a phonograph manufactured by another. He also leafed through some of the hundreds of books in his Fort Myers library. Edison finally pronounced himself sufficiently refreshed. Ford and Burroughs were ready to leap into the cars.

It wasn't that simple. First, local guides were engaged, and all three — Frank Carson, Les Hibble, and Sam Thompson — warned that the planned ramble was far riskier than the Northern men realized, even before the campers reached the massive Everglades. The region between Fort Myers and the 'Glades was prowled by panthers and bears. The panthers lurked in the brush and made sounds like babies crying. If you were fooled and went to look, you would be attacked. Once in the Everglades, you entered an entirely different world, where the customs and rules of civilization had no meaning. Outsiders had no idea how many gators and snakes really were submerged in pools or out of sight behind brush or tree stumps. In many places the trees and moss were so dense that it was easy to get turned around and lose any sense of direction. Even those familiar with the Everglades occasionally died in there. This was going to be difficult and dangerous.

Ford, Edison, and Burroughs believed themselves up to it. The guides might be exaggerating, trying to throw a scare into perceived Yankee rubes. Burroughs in particular had dared all kinds of wilderness, from the mountains of Yellowstone to those of New York state, and there were plenty of bears and other fanged, clawed menaces in both places. If you stayed alert, you were fine. They'd come to Florida to explore the Everglades, and that was what they would do.

At some point, it was determined that Edsel Ford and Charles and Theodore Edison should come along, too. Neither father was especially close to his offspring, and both considered their sons to be somewhat spoiled and unworldly. Edsel was twenty-one, Charles twenty-three, and Theodore sixteen — a rough-and-tumble trip might be just the thing to toughen them up. The young men were enthusiastic at the prospect. Theodore Edison, in particular, loved nature and even kept occasional baby alligators as pets. After some discussion, an area in the 'Glades known as Deep Lake was designated as the trip destination. It lay some sixty miles southeast of Fort Myers. The guides suggested driving about forty miles east to the town of LaBelle, then turning south into the Everglades itself. They'd camp for several days at Deep Lake, studying flowers and fauna by day and warming themselves by a campfire at night. It wasn't official hunting season in Florida, but in the isolated Everglades they could watch for deer and other edible game. Fresh meat for dinner was a pleasant possibility. This latter prospect wasn't mentioned to Theodore Edison, who was notoriously soft-hearted about four-legged creatures. With everything apparently decided, they prepared to depart.

Then came a complication.

Mina Edison was an educated, opinionated woman. At forty-seven she was twenty years younger than her husband, and while devoted to him and his career, she also respected her own abilities and place in the world. Mina never allowed herself to be described as a "housewife" — women staying at home to raise children and provide support to their husbands were doing important jobs, too. She insisted on being called a "home executive," and expected to be consulted by her spouse on all important nonlaboratory matters and included in anything she deemed interesting and appropriate. The Everglades trip qualified. It was a romp, not in any sense inventing or manufacturing work. Women deserved the opportunity to enjoy nature and learn about things from Mr. Burroughs just as much as men. Edison and Ford weren't pleased — part of their incentive for the trip was to temporarily escape the domestic scene. But Mina Edison didn't waver — the men could argue all they liked, but the ladies were coming, too. Daughter Madeleine Edison was thrilled at the prospect, Ford's wife, Clara, less so. She was deathly afraid of snakes. But Mina overruled any reptile-related objection — they would have *fun.*

Further, possibly with the intent to drive home the point of female equality to her husband and his male companions, she invited her friend Lucy Bogue and Madeleine's chum Bessie Krup to come along, as well. They were pleased to accept — going on an outing with the Fords and Edisons was such a privilege. All their friends would surely be jealous.

Early on Saturday morning, February 28, five cars — three Fords and two Cadillacs — set out from Fort Myers. Supplies were suitable for rugged exploring and camping — tents, guns, fishing rods — but not the clothing. With the exception of the guides, who knew better but apparently hadn't warned their employers, the gentlemen wore coats and shirts with stiff collars and ties. The ladies were fashionable in long dresses and bonnets. Adventure or not, this was still a public outing. The elegantly bedecked party set off gaily and rattled along for perhaps five or ten minutes before encountering the first obstacle to its merry agenda.

Directly outside of town, what locals described as "wish to God" roads commenced — roads only in the sense that they were dirt paths scored on each side by two deep ruts from wagon wheels and occasional car tires, and drivers wished to God that the going was easier. Maneuvering to drive in the ruts meant risking tires getting wedged tight. If the ruts weren't sticky with mud after rain, they were usually clogged with sand. Driving around the ruts kept cars bouncing over stones and semiexposed palmetto roots. Madeleine Edison, who kept a journal about the trip, compared the experience to enduring a wild carnival ride, only for many hours instead of a few measured minutes. But soon the jouncing became secondary. Recent rain in the area caused "ponding," standing pools of water that were deceptively deep. Dirt became gluey mud. Tires stuck. Charles Edison, at the wheel of one of the cars, asked a guide how to tell the spots of highest ground beneath the water. He was informed, "You just have to feel your way." Edsel Ford brought a camera, and several of his snapshots showed male passengers gallantly walking through the water and mud alongside the cars so the vehicles would be lighter and less likely to bog down. In some places the water reached to their knees. It took much of the day just to reach LaBelle. Along the way, they encountered other travelers making better time, and waved politely to the locals perched on the seats of their ox-drawn wagons.

But at least there was still some semblance of road. That ended when the five-car procession turned south just past LaBelle. A barely discernible trail reached the mushy curl of land that comprised the outer edge of the Everglades and then disappeared altogether. Openings appeared between clumps of trees. The three guides, who'd hunted and explored in the area, now had to move ahead and guide the cars from one safe spot to the next. Insects, many of them biting varieties, swarmed everywhere. There were flowers and plants that Burroughs identified, but it was difficult getting out of the cars to gather around him. Any misstep might result in sinking ankle deep in muck.

A sense of excitement remained. Everyone knew it was going to be hard going, and this place with its earthy smells and eerie shadows was certainly more exotic than anything everyone but the guides had ever experienced before. Clara Ford looked less at sights described by Burroughs than the ground immediately around her. She knew snakes were everywhere, even if she didn't see them. As the adventurers rode, the autos jostled along such uneven ground that Madeleine Edison feared "being suddenly dashed into all this loveliness over the back of the car, and not missed for several hours."

In the swamp, as on the waterlogged Fort Myers–to–LaBelle road, progress was far slower than anticipated. They barely reached the Deep Lake area that day and rushed to set up camp before dark. Though far from the luxury enjoyed by Ford and Burroughs on their earlier auto trip, there were still amenities. The guides put up tents, spreading palmetto leaves on the ground to keep blankets and sleeping bags dry. Mosquito netting was draped over tent flaps to keep sleepers as bite-free as possible. Madeleine Edison described "live oak trees by the side of a reedy little lake." Ford went exploring, taking along Charles Edison and a .22 target pistol. The automaker amused himself by blasting the heads off snakes — Charles counted three such decapitations. The guides flushed out and shot a pheasant, which was technically out-of-season poaching. Even though he wasn't in on the kill, Ford posed for Edsel brandishing the trophy, which the hired hands then cleaned and cooked for dinner. Theodore Edison, apparently less sympathetic to fowl than four-legged creatures, didn't object. Edsel snapped another photo of his father's friend Edison sprawled on the ground, sleeping with his head on Mina's lap. In all, it was a challenging but rewarding day. Everyone looked forward to the next morning when real adventures could begin. There would be so many sights to see, surely even more brightly plumed birds and dazzling flowers — despite its murk, the Everglades was proving such a colorful place — and also alligators sunning on riverbanks. These scaly monsters surely didn't represent any real danger. The guides had guns, after all.

But then the skies darkened from the presence of ominous clouds as well as night, and the croaking frogs and buzzing insects were drowned out by approaching thunder. Winter months in this area were the dry season, but there were occasional exceptions, and this threatened to be one. The ladies in their fine clothes feared getting drenched. Burroughs, Ford, and Edison anticipated a lingering storm would drive wildlife back into the Everglades depths, depriving them of opportunity for close study. The guides' concern was by far the most practical — they hoped they were camped on sufficiently high ground for their employers to survive flooding. Then the storm struck, unleashing a savage deluge that crashed down in sheets. Madeleine Edison, possessed of a descriptive bent, later wrote that "like rabbits before a hunting party the members of the expedition came hurtling one by one into the tent" initially reserved for the women. It was the biggest and most stout. A few others sheltered in a smaller tent intended for the men. All everyone could do was huddle under blankets and hope that rising water wouldn't gush over the tents' palmetto leaf carpets, which it did within minutes. Then a blast of wind blew the big tent over. There were valiant attempts to pin the sides to the ground while Charles Edison repositioned a critical ridge pole. But one side of the tent still waved loose in the gale and everyone was soaked from head to foot. Water rose inside, and it took little imagination to mistake floating branches for snakes.

The storm eased slightly, and the groundwater receded a little. After a while, everyone in the tent tried to lie down in the least damp spots. Madeleine wrote that Edsel "brought in one of the automobile cushions to act as a raft and after taking soundings all over the tent lay down where the water was shallowest." The sodden gypsiers fell into fitful dozes. They awoke to a gray morning and the possibility of more bad weather. All but one of the campers laughed at their bedraggled appearances — most were wrapped in dripping blankets. But Bessie Krup refused to leave the tent until she had dry garments to wear. No one had any spare items to loan her. Every stitch in camp was soaked. Ford strung a rope between some trees and hung Bessie's clothes and some of the blankets on it to dry. The guides managed to light a fire, and over breakfast the situation seemed less dire. They sang some songs. Charles Edison composed a limerick:

Consumption, pneumonia and grip[pe]
Will be the result of this trip.
We'll all die together
From the inclement weather
On the door mat of Heaven we'll drip.

But besides joking, there was little else to do on Sunday. Going forward in the cars was risky. So was setting out on foot to search for interesting plants and wildlife. To Clara Ford's dismay, snakes driven from their holes by floodwater slithered everywhere. Nearby splashing sounds might originate with small, harmless swamp creatures or alligators. The obvious alternative was to stay by the fire and gradually dry off. At some point the guides ventured out and shot a deer, but venison didn't become part of the day's menu. Instead, his family tried to keep the deer's death secret from Theodore Edison, who would have been horrified. It was an uncomfortable, frustrating day.

Either that night or on Monday morning, they voted whether to stick it out in the Everglades, hoping for better weather and the chance for drier adventures or else head home to Fort Myers. Only Charles Edison and Burroughs wanted to stay. Charles wrote later that the others "just couldn't see much of this camping life and these snakes. . . . [Burroughs and I] couldn't go on if the rest of them went back, so we finally had to give the thing up. But we did get quite a ways down in the big cypress, and it was wild country." The caravan straggled home to Fort Myers. Once they were fully dried off and rested, everyone looked back on the Everglades trip as less a debacle than a sort of slapstick hoot. They laughingly described each other's disheveled appearances following the Sunday night storm. Burroughs praised Edison and Ford as "good playfellows." Mina Edison worried that Clara Ford might not have had the same amount of good-natured fun as everyone else: "We talked of snakes too much of which she is mortally afraid." Edison and Ford discussed subjects of mutual interest, most business-related, some more general. Edison lectured on the dangers of smoking cigarettes — he claimed that the paper, though not the tobacco, was poisonous when burned. Ford was fascinated. The men fished off Edison's dock, and both families and Burroughs took a two-day boat trip up the Caloosahatchee River. The weather improved and everyone enjoyed the sunshine — Burroughs went so far as to favorably compare the local climate to Hawaii. Tellingly, though the men at least could have attempted a second Everglades expedition — they still had the cars, equipment, and guides available — they chose not to do so. Laugh at the memory of their first attempt as they might, they had no desire to risk another.

The Fords and Burroughs left Fort Myers by train on March 10. The Edisons stayed in Florida for another month. About a week before they returned to New Jersey, Edison received a letter from Ford thanking him for "the most enjoyable [vacation] that we have ever had." Ford also had a request: Based on what they'd recently discussed about cigarettes, he asked Edison to send "a special letter from you in your own writing" explaining the dangers of smoking them, which Ford would post in his factory for the edification of employees. Edison, who, though he avoided cigarettes, still chewed tobacco and smoked cigars, was pleased to comply. In part his letter read:

The injurious agent in cigarettes comes principally from the burning paper wrapper. The substance thereby formed is called "Acrolein." It has a violent action on the nerve centers, producing degeneration of the cells of the brain. . . . Unlike most narcotics this degeneration is permanent and uncontrollable. I employ no person who smokes cigarettes. Yours Thos. A. Edison

Everything Ford- or Edison-related attracted attention from the newspapers, and Ford's factory posting of Edison's letter was no exception. Spokesmen for cigarette companies read stories about it and protested vehemently. An advertising agent employed by Philip Morris Cigarettes bought ads in major newspapers, declaring that his client's customers should not "make the mistake of [believing] that just because Mr. Edison is a genius in ELECTRICITY, he is also infallible in ANALYTICAL

CHEMISTRY." The *New York Times,* previously generous in its coverage of all things Edison, suggested in an editorial that Edison had little scientific basis for his claim — the stinging headline read, "An Inventor Out of His Field."

Edison wasn't used to his opinions on anything being challenged. He doubled down on his original claim. In particular, he told a *Times* reporter, "Mexicans as a race are not clear-headed" because they all smoked so many cigarettes. Despite his stating otherwise to Ford in his letter, Edison routinely employed smokers. Now he banned cigarettes from all of his businesses, posting signs declaring, "Cigarettes Not Tolerated. They Dull The Brain."

The fuss didn't affect the friendship between Edison and Ford. In October 1914, the Edisons visited the Fords in Michigan. The wives continued to get along well, and the husbands envisioned endless business collaborations — for instance, while electric starters had been introduced in some cars manufactured by Ford's competitors, Model Ts still required cranking by hand. At some point Ford suggested that Edison should develop a starter system for him — of course, Ford would pay all development costs. There was certainly fond reminiscing about the Everglades adventure. They must do something similar again, getting in cars and *going,* though with better planning and less risk of catastrophe.

Then, in early December, Edison suffered a staggering blow. A raging fire destroyed his West Orange, New Jersey, laboratory and adjacent factory. Total damage to buildings and loss of equipment and materials was estimated at up to $5 million, and while Edison said publicly that $3 million of that was covered by insurance, his private correspondence indicated he received considerably less. Edison bravely claimed, "We'll build up bigger and better," but he faced considerable financial difficulty. Ford happened to be in New York at the time of the conflagration. He rushed to New Jersey to help. Edison later told a friend that Ford "didn't say much, just handed me a check, 'You'll need some money, let me know if you need more.' When I looked at the check, it was made out for $750,000. He didn't ask for any security, and of course over the years I repaid the principal, though he would never take a cent of interest." The facilities were rebuilt. No specific cause was ever determined for the fire, but Edison biographer Robert Conot offers a plausible suggestion. With employee smoking recently banned at the West Orange companies, "many of the men sneaked smokes in out-of-the-way places [on the property], and these were often full of combustible materials."

No matter how the blaze started, Ford came to Edison's rescue. In material ways, their singular friendship remained unequal. Ford not only subsidized their joint business ventures, he sent cars as gifts, not only for Thomas and Mina Edison, but sometimes for their children. Though Ford insisted that his dealerships be headed only by men of impeccable reputation and habits, he granted one to a son of Edison's first marriage even though Ford knew about the young man's dissolute past. Ford constantly sought ways to serve Edison and his family.

Though he was comfortable accepting all manner of tokens and tributes, Edison himself was not much of a gift giver. But he made clear his particular affection for Ford in another way. Like many of his prominent contemporaries, Edison ordinarily addressed other men by their last names, sometimes adding "Mr." as a sign of additional respect or at least recognition of some special standing or rank. But to Edison, who trusted so very few, the carmaker from Michigan was "Friend Ford," addressed as such in infrequent notes and sometimes in person. The appellation was perhaps the greatest compliment Edison could bestow.

Edison balanced his relationship with Ford in two other critical ways. First, in the earliest years of their friendship, he reignited Ford's sputtering ambition to continue achieving great things. In the time immediately following the massively successful market introduction of the Model T, Ford's innovative energy diminished. He spent far less time at Ford Motor Company, and twice came close to selling the business. Sometimes he talked of returning to the unassuming life of a farmer. It was as though Ford believed he had achieved what he could, and all that remained was extended, soul-draining ennui. But Edison's example convinced him otherwise. The great inventor could have decided in the 1880s that he'd contributed sufficiently to mankind, and taken his ease since. But Edison always sought the next great thing, and failures like mining innovation and concrete housing didn't deter him. He never lost belief in himself. Beginning in 1912 when he and the inventor quickly became the closest of friends, Ford felt energized again, thanks in great part to Edison's inspiration.

Too, for all of Ford's professional life he'd had to overcome skepticism from other successful men. He had always been the outsider, the one with the crazy ideas and clumsy social graces. Edison sympathized, because in his earliest years of prominence he was criticized for some of the same traits. The inventor not only accepted Ford for the rough-edged man that he was, he recognized in him the fine qualities that offset the carmaker's obvious flaws. In one undated, handwritten memorandum, Edison described Ford as "an ever flowing fountain of energy, a vivid and boundless imagination . . . instinctive knowledge of mechanisms, and a talent for organization. These are the qualities that centre in Mr. Ford. He is also to be admired for his very real solicitude for the welfare of the common people." Ford was aware that Edison was one of the very few who genuinely *liked* him, and was profoundly grateful for it.

Beyond the pleasure it brought to the men themselves, the Edison-Ford friendship also thrilled ordinary Americans, whose lives were radically changed, to great extent blessed, by the two men's inventions and innovations. Later in 1914 the outbreak of war in Europe, and America's potential entry into the conflict, began dominating the news. That made it even more refreshing to read about Edison and Ford in newspapers and magazines — they were among the country's most prominent celebrities, after all — and entertaining to wonder what future advancements the unique pair of friends would deliver. Only a generation or so earlier, electric lights in homes, phonographs, movies, affordable horseless carriages, substantial factory wages, and shorter workweeks would have been beyond public imagination. As individuals, Edison and Ford had already extended the boundaries of the possible. Now their genius was joined, and more miracles seemed certain.

CHAPTER TWO:
1915

On October 15, twenty months after their bedraggled adventure in the Everglades, Thomas Edison set off by train to meet Henry Ford in San Francisco, where the inventor would be celebrated with a gala day in his honor at the Panama-Pacific Exposition. As befitting a man of his stature, Edison didn't line up with other passengers to find an unoccupied seat on a passenger car. Instead, he and his wife and a few friends ascended from the platform into a luxurious private car outfitted by Ford especially for the trip. No detail was too small for Ford to fret over. The tobacco-hating carmaker went so far as to ask Edison's staff for their boss's favorite brand of cigars. The Edison party boarded the train near their home in West Orange, New Jersey, and the only complication Ford failed to anticipate was the presence of a pack of teenaged girls. For days in advance, newspapers had heralded the Edison-Ford trip; anything involving either of the men was considered important news, and the combination of the two merited special coverage. Edison's time and place of departure were accordingly well-known, and a wire service report noted that as he made his way to the train, "young women gathered about and some insisted on kissing him goodbye." Edison obliged — the story made no mention of Mina Edison's reaction to such forward behavior — and then took a moment to address the reporters on the scene.

"I feel like a prince," Edison told them, and, according to one story, "danced a few steps to prove it." He gestured toward the private car and added, "I'm going to travel to San Francisco like a prima donna." What Edison didn't add was that it had been touch and go whether he'd take the trip at all. Just weeks earlier, after months of repeated invitations, he still wouldn't confirm to Exposition organizers that he would come at all. The San Franciscans grew increasingly desperate. The purpose of the Exposition was twofold: to celebrate the completion of the Panama Canal, and to demonstrate that San Francisco had completely recovered from a 1906 earthquake that had devastated an estimated 70–80 percent of the city. Millions of dollars, including government grants and private contributions, were spent erecting a dazzling fairground of exhibitions and entertainments. Beginning with the opening days in February, celebrities of every stripe were featured as special guests, from former president Theodore Roosevelt to middle-American novelist Laura Ingalls Wilder. They did their part, drawing the national attention that the Exposition was intended to attract, but none had the same special appeal to American hearts as Thomas Edison.

Despite the war overseas, 1915 remained a time of wonder in America. Technology — *invention* — was the core of it. The earliest U.S. celebrities were military and political leaders. Now inventors held the ultimate spotlight. Rank-and-file citizens could at least grasp the basics of battlefield tactics and presidential campaigns, but it was delightfully beyond the imaginations of most how invisible forces like sound and electricity could be harnessed for the use of mankind. Edison wasn't the only inventor to achieve celebrity status. When Alexander Graham Bell completed the first transcontinental telephone call between New York and

San Francisco in January 1915, it made headlines in virtually all of the country's 2,500 daily newspapers and 16,000 weeklies. But Bell's fame paled beside Edison's, who was widely credited with inventing electric light, movies, and phonographs and recordings. This was a misconception — while the phonograph was solely Edison's brainchild, his landmark work with electricity and motion pictures advanced the earlier work of others. Besides his considerable achievements, Edison, with his rumpled clothes and good-natured grin, looked the part of a one-of-a-kind genius. He also had an innate sense of how to retain an air of mystery that reinforced public interest in and curiosity about him. When it suited him, Edison granted interviews, and even occasionally invited the public to the grounds of his laboratories, but he rarely made official appearances — usually citing work obligations — and adamantly refused to make speeches. That meant the public constantly read about Thomas Edison, often in stories speculating about what unimaginable wonder he might conjure next, but rarely saw him and virtually never heard him. That left them always wanting more and kept Edison at the very top of the celebrity ladder.

So the Exposition's offer of "Edison Day," including several appearances and culminating with a grand banquet during which the inventor would receive a special medal and make a speech in response, contradicted the way Edison preferred doing things. He didn't directly turn down the offer — there was, after all, obvious publicity benefit to being presented as the star of stars in San Francisco — but Edison kept citing work pressures that might not allow him to attend, and as the months passed and the suggested date of October 21 drew closer, Exposition officials tried another tack. The Ford Motor Company had an exhibition in place, a facsimile of the company's assembly line that actually turned out finished Model Ts before the stunned eyes of ticket-holders. Ford himself was scheduled to visit the Exposition sometime in October: a day in his honor was also planned. In mid-September, with Edison still dithering, they turned to Ford for help. Their telegram read:

The Exposition officials have set aside October twenty-first as Edison day we understand you contemplate trip to the coast to be here for day set aside in your honor October twenty second will you not use your good influence to induce mr Edison to accompany you so that he may be here in person on Edison day all coast states are anxious to have him with us at that time and we appeal to you as the one man whose influence with mr. edison is likely to have effect a committee to further Edison day plans consisting of representative of phonograph moving pictures storage battery incandescent light department working to make Edison day a success his presence very necessary toward that and Please wire collect.

A letter to Ford followed. In it, the officials promised that neither he nor Edison would be expected to make speeches or participate "in any programs which would be distasteful to you." Ford declined an entire day being set aside in his own honor — he wanted Edison, who remained his idol as well as his friend, to be the main focus of attention. But he agreed to try to convince Edison to participate, and on September 16 Ford's secretary wrote Edison's secretary that "Mr. Ford will go if Mr. Edison intends to be there," an indirect request that had a better chance of appealing to Edison than the direct suggestion he ought to go.

Edison replied via his secretary that "he cannot tell yet whether he will be able to go to San Francisco . . . if he can possibly get away he would be delighted to go with Mr. Ford, and he says that if Mrs. Ford goes, he supposes that he can also take Mrs. Edison." Ford knew Edison well enough to realize this was tantamount to acceptance. Exposition officials were thrilled and planning for Edison Day proceeded.

Then came further complications. When it was formally announced that the Panama-Pacific Exposition had Thomas Edison, other entities wanted their piece of him, too. Some were easily dismissed: invitations from virtually every major West Coast city for the great inventor to stop and be feted in their towns were politely declined due to time constraints on Edison's part. But a summons to Sacramento couldn't be ignored. It was the state capital, legislators there wanted and expected Edison to stop and be recognized, and since Edison had many business interests in the state, it behooved him to stop there on his way to the Exposition.

Another California stop proved necessary, this one to come after San Francisco. The Panama-Pacific wasn't the only exposition currently being held in the state. San Diego was hosting the Panama-California Exposition, and rivalry between the cities and their fairs was fierce. San Diego civic leaders were appalled to learn that San Francisco intended to hold a festival celebrating completion of the Panama Canal. As the first American port ships would reach passing west through the canal, San Diego assumed it had the exclusive right to stage such an event. San Francisco leaders disagreed — after all, compared to their city's fame, tiny San Diego was a mere flyspeck on beach sand. The towns went to political war, vying for government funding and official blessing. They agreed to cooperate only when New Orleans, sensing opportunity, began exploring the possibility of staging a canal-related exposition of its own. Still, San Francisco got the federal money. San Diego relied mostly on private contributions, but these were sufficient to build exposition grounds so beautifully designed and landscaped that they fully matched those in the larger, more famous city. Most of the same prominent people who appeared in San Francisco made subsequent appearances in San Diego. The failure of Thomas Edison to do likewise would have been an unforgivable insult and, to a somewhat lesser extent, the same would be true for Henry Ford. They chose to extend their trip. After all, people in Southern California bought light bulbs, phonographs, and cars.

As an added incentive for Edison to make the Sacramento stop, he was greeted in California's capital by Luther Burbank, the renowned plant geneticist from Santa Rosa. The two men had never met but were familiar with each other's work. Newspapers in California, eager to promote their home state genius, proclaimed "Wizard of the West to Greet Wizard of the East." They were obviously unfamiliar with Edison's determination that no one should in any way equate his accomplishments with magic. He frequently stated that the basis for any worthwhile achievement was hard work. Burbank, under considerable pressure from Santa Rosa boosters to persuade Edison to visit their town as well, made the overture. Edison, unwilling to offend his new acquaintance, apparently agreed to see if things could be worked out. At least ceremonies in Sacramento proved mercifully brief. Edison was formally received by the legislators, and, though he did not offer a speech in response to their florid welcoming remarks, still pleased them with a warm smile and bow. With that obligation satisfied, the inventor and his party, which now included Burbank, proceeded by automobile to San Francisco, where Ford was waiting.

As with the private railroad car, Ford took pains to make Edison's visit to San Francisco as pleasant and uncomplicated as possible. A frenzied public greeting for the inventor couldn't be avoided. A city newspaper noted that Edison arrived in town around 4 p.m. on October 18 and "as the inventor [appeared], flanked by Luther Burbank and Henry Ford, and with [San Francisco] Mayor Rolph leading the way . . . the cheers comingled in one great swelling chorus. It was a demonstration such as few arriving in San Francisco have been accorded." That was the last non-Exposition visitors saw of Edison. Ford whisked him and the rest of his party to the fair, where they were ensconced at the Inside Inn, an exclusive hotel on the grounds. Ford's family and guests were already there — besides Clara Ford, the group included Harvey Firestone, the automobile tire magnate from Akron, Ohio. Ford was always loyal to dependable suppliers, and Firestone was one of the very few who also became a personal friend. Besides providing tough, durable tires, Firestone made himself useful in other ways, cheerfully performing small, helpful tasks as needed. He and his wife were in San Francisco as guests of the Fords, but Firestone was also expected to remain ready to step in and handle whatever unexpected problems might present themselves.

On Tuesday, October 19, Edison and Ford toured the Exposition exhibits. Firestone was with them, but Burbank returned to Santa Rosa to prepare for an Edison-Ford visit there. Ford and Edison started early and walked the fairgrounds for nearly eight hours, taking in such sights as the first steam locomotive operated by the Southern Pacific Railroad. They were trailed all the while by reporters and photographers. The smallest details of their day made print, from what Edison ate for breakfast ("a wink at a teacup and a nibble of a rice wafer") to Ford's terse advice to a young man asking the key to success in life ("Work"). They clearly enjoyed the outing; every story concluded with the famous men being so enthralled with the Exposition's delights that they forgot a lunch appointment with their wives.

That night, San Francisco's telegraph operators hosted a dinner in Edison's honor. As a young man, he'd first made his living as an itinerant telegrapher, moving from city to city as work options dictated. Many of Edison's first inventions involved the telegraph — he revolutionized the industry by creating a handset enabling wires to carry as many as four separate messages at once. The dinner was a merry affair. An estimated four hundred city telegraphers attended. The menu was printed in Morse code, and all the speeches — none by the honoree himself — were tapped out on telegraphs. While everyone else dined elegantly, Edison asked to be served only a slice of hot apple pie and a glass of milk. It was explained to the hovering press that this was his favorite lunch "in the days when he pounded a brass key for a living." Afterward, everyone went outside to observe the lights in every downtown building burning in Edison's honor, while "electric flashes" from roofs spelled out another Morse code message welcoming Edison to the Exposition.

On Wednesday, Edison and Ford left the grounds when they accepted an invitation from Rear Admiral William F. Fullam, commander of the U.S. Pacific Reserve Fleet, to visit some battleships docked nearby. The *Oregon, South Dakota,* and *Milwaukee* were in training for America's possible entry into the war in Europe. With its illustrious guests on board, the *Oregon* set off on a short cruise around San Francisco Bay. Reporters noted that Edison smiled throughout the brief jaunt, and even made a point of walking over to one of the battleship's big guns and patting it "affectionately" before informing the press that, in his opinion, "preparedness" — bringing the U.S. military up to war footing — was wise. It made for an entertaining paragraph in the wire reports that went out to newspapers across the nation, but the stories were dominated by Ford. While Edison toured the ship, the automaker stayed "in the sheltering lee of the warship's funnel," and ardently contradicted all that his friend had said, starting with a threat to dismantle the Navy by giving every man currently in it a good job at a Ford plant, thus eviscerating the service. Considering where Ford was when he said it, this was not only controversial but rude. He didn't care.

Henry Ford was always a man of strong opinions, and one who absolutely trusted his own instincts. He especially disdained anyone identified as an expert: "If ever I wanted to kill opposition by unfair means, I would endow the opposition with experts. No one ever considers himself expert if he really knows his job." When prominent, better-educated men and their hired-hand experts insisted that the future of the automobile market was limited to manufacturing expensive cars for the wealthy, Ford believed that the real potential lay in sales of a modest but dependable vehicle to the growing American middle class; there would be less profit in individual transactions, but the sheer number of sales would yield greater cumulative returns. With the Model T, Ford was proved right, and he reveled in it. He also took great pride in the product he provided. Let competitors bring out new models year after year, tempting foolish consumers with bright paint and unnecessarily refashioned chassis. Ford stuck with the utilitarian Model T, offering only minor modifications like optional odometers, not only giving his sensible customers an inexpensive car, but one that would last indefinitely. He knew it was the perfect car and had no intention of changing it.

The Model T made Ford well-known, but for a product rather than his own personality. That changed in 1914, when Ford Motor Company introduced the $5 workday. Virtually overnight, Ford became renowned as a champion of the working man, especially when it was learned he planned to offer profit sharing to his workers in addition to their staggering daily raise. Ford was quoted everywhere as modestly taking credit only for doing the right thing — reliable workers for successful companies deserved their share of the profits.

What wasn't written about, or known beyond Ford Motor Company's corporate walls, was that the $5 workday was the brainchild of general manager James Couzens, not Henry Ford. Turnover among Ford factory workers had become rampant, as much as 300 percent in a single year. With line workers constantly missing or still in training, even the vaunted Ford assembly line sputtered. Ford's average daily wage of $2.34 was slightly above the national average of $2.09, but not enough to entice workers to stay. A salary that was more than double certainly would, but when Couzens broached the idea to his boss, Ford balked. He was willing to entertain a raise — perhaps $3 a day? Couzens insisted on $5. The additional cost in salaries would be more than offset by savings in training expenses and chronic absenteeism. A $5 day also guaranteed positive publicity. Every newspaper in the country would write about it, and it would appall Ford's competitors.

Couzens had been with Ford since the inception of Ford Motor Company. The

Model T was Ford's vision, but he was not temperamentally suited to overseeing daily operations. Couzens ran Ford Motor Company with an iron hand, and he was the only employee allowed to disagree, even to argue, with Ford. Their relationship nearly approximated one of equals until the Model T established inarguable market dominance, and then Ford began gradually to resent Couzens as only a glorified bookkeeper. The feeling was mutual — Couzens believed that Ford became so convinced of his own brilliance that he forgot others also made critical contributions to his company's success.

Matters came to a head in 1915. Ever since the rapturous public response to the announcement of the $5 workday, Ford felt encouraged to offer his opinion on all sorts of non-car-related subjects. He'd been right about the Model T, apparently determined in his own mind that the $5 day was really his idea, and had no doubt about his sagacity regarding everything else, the evils of war in particular. Ford had long believed that Wall Street bankers and investors were part of an evil cabal out to gain illicit financial control of America and the world. From there it was an easy step for him to decide that the conflict in Europe was part of this ongoing plot — munitions companies and their investors not only wanted but needed war, which created demand for their ghastly products. Too many gullible citizens were falling for Wall Street's "preparedness" propaganda. Ford felt it was his duty to inform Americans of what he considered obvious.

In April 1915, Ford granted an interview to the *New York Times,* telling the reporter, "Moneylenders and munitions makers cause wars. If Europe had spent money on peace machinery such as tractors instead of armaments, there would have been no war. The warmongers urging military preparedness in America are Wall Street bankers. I am opposed to war in every sense of the word." Two months later, Ford appealed to Middle America to join him in opposition: "New York wants war, but the United States doesn't. The peoples west of New York are too sensible for war." This was strong language, but Ford correctly knew or at least intuited that the majority of Americans agreed with him, if not with his condemnation of Wall Street and New York, at least in his hope of the U.S. avoiding war. President Woodrow Wilson advocated neutrality, though Germany made it difficult. In May, when the Germans sank the *Lusitania,* a British cruise ship that had more than a hundred American passengers aboard, Wilson warned Germany against any similar acts. Americans became more receptive to preparedness, though not entry into the war itself. Henry Ford, citing ads purchased in New York newspapers earlier in the year by the German government warning that all British vessels were subject to attack, said the dead Americans were "fools to go on that boat." In contrast, two weeks after the *Lusitania* sinking, Edison accepted a government request to chair a Navy "department of invention and development" comprised of the best civilian and military creative minds and tasked with creating new means of thwarting and, if necessary, fighting German aggression on the seas.

Couzens warned Ford about making controversial antiwar statements, which might offend potential customers and drive down sales. Ford paid no attention. In one interview he swore to devote his life and fortune "to prevent murderous, wasteful war in America and in the whole world." In another, Ford declared that "to my mind, the word 'murderer' should be embroidered in red letters across the breast of every soldier." Tension between Ford and Couzens grew, and in early October it boiled over. Couzens had always controlled the contents of the *Ford Times,* a company magazine distributed to employees and made available to the public at dealerships and through free subscriptions; at one point its circulation reached 600,000. Couzens was furious when a copy of the latest edition included two antiwar articles that he had ordered removed. Obviously, Ford had overruled him. Couzens confronted Ford, insisting that the owner's personal politics had no place in an internal company publication. Ford disagreed — it was *his* company. Couzens quit the next day. He went on to a distinguished political career, first as mayor of Detroit and later as a U.S. senator representing Michigan. But with Couzens gone, so was the only check on Ford's increasing proclivity to say exactly what he pleased, and damn the consequences.

Ford gloried in that freedom as he addressed the press during Wednesday's cruise. He joked that, to him, the battleships resembled extinct dodo birds: "The only [dodos] now [are] to be stuffed and exhibited in museums. That is where all the warships should be." He claimed he was ready to spend $1 million in antiwar efforts. Ford added that he had no hard feelings toward Admiral Fullam and the battleship commanders. His assembly line exhibit at the Exposition turned out a number of spanking new Model Ts every day. He invited the naval officers to come by the next day and see him there — each would receive a freshly minted car. All this was duly reported, but with coverage of Edison Day festivities following soon after, Ford suffered no immediate blowback. He may have assumed this was because everyone agreed with him.

Edison Day on Thursday was all that Exposition officials could have hoped. The honoree was driven to Festival Hall, which was surrounded by an estimated ten thousand admirers who'd been unable to get tickets to join him inside. They made up for it by cheering his arrival. According to the *San Francisco Chronicle,* "No hero fresh from a great war, a great statesman or any person ever elevated above his fellow-man ever before received such a sincere tribute. No celebrity thus far visiting the Exposition has been accorded such hearty homage." Edison, the story noted, responded to the cacophony "with rather a sheepish yet kindly smile." Once inside, Edison sat with Mina in the front row of a packed auditorium while fair officials took turns onstage paying him tribute. Reporters were conveniently allowed to sit directly behind the great man, so they were able to note that at one point the partially deaf Edison loudly whispered to his wife, "I'm glad I can't hear. I'd feel so foolish." Christine Miller, a soprano whose voice graced many recordings made at Edison's New Jersey studio, performed several numbers, and finally the president of the Exposition presented Edison with a bronze medal. As usual, the inventor did not deliver a speech. Afterward, as soon as it was dark, "one ton of rockets" and an additional "half ton of explosives" were set off in Edison's honor. The next day, it was announced that Edison Day attendance was the highest for the entire Exposition, topping tickets sold to see former presidents Theodore Roosevelt and William Howard Taft, "a demonstration that could not have failed to impress upon the inventor the place he holds in the hearts of his countrymen."

A few of the stories noted that during the afternoon before the Edison Day program commenced, Henry Ford put on overalls and worked for several hours on the Ford Motor Company's assembly line exhibit. At the end of his stint he gave newly assembled Model Ts to Rear Admiral Fullam and the captains of the *Oregon, South Dakota,* and

Milwaukee. Ford prided himself on never breaking a promise.

With their commitment to the Panama-Pacific Exposition complete and a few days in hand before they were expected in San Diego, on Friday Edison, Ford, and Firestone took a late morning train for a short trip from San Francisco to Santa Rosa and Edison's promised visit to Luther Burbank. Any hope they had of a quick, quiet meeting was disabused by a large crowd waiting for them at the depot about 1 p.m. They were escorted from there to Burbank's sprawling gardens, where the geneticist formally greeted them along with 1,800 cheering, chanting children; local schools were apparently emptied. The youngsters serenaded the visitors with "I Love California," and afterward Edison gamely posed for photos with them. Eventually the mob dispersed, and Burbank was finally able to show his guests around the grounds before ushering them into his combination workshop/laboratory. Edison was fascinated by everything and peppered Burbank with questions about fruits and plants. Ford was more specific. He wanted to know how peas could be genetically engineered to grow only to a certain size, making the canning process more efficient.

When Burbank and Edison fell into deep discussion about America's dependence on foreign rubber, and what plants might best be grown in the U.S. to meet the nation's growing demand, Ford excused himself and returned to the Santa Rosa depot, where he talked with railroad staff about their methods of scheduling arrivals and departures until Edison finally was ready to return to San Francisco on the 5:42 p.m. train. When asked how the visit had gone, Burbank said that Edison was "quick to catch [my] vision of what was being . . . attempted." But Burbank offered his highest praise to Ford, who "saw a different angle. . . . He wanted to know what was being done to increase production and develop new possibilities in plants. He is keen as mustard and has the longest view into the future of any man I have encountered out of the business world." Later, Ford sent Burbank a tractor in thanks for his hospitality, and also a telegram asking him to publicly back Woodrow Wilson for reelection in 1916. Ford was an avid Wilson supporter, so long as the president honored his campaign pledge to keep America out of war.

The weekend was supposedly reserved for rest. Ford used it to visit an old friend in Los Gatos, and afterward paid an informal visit to the Montezuma Ranch School for Boys. Edison wasn't as lucky. Demands continued for him to participate in special programs, and one couldn't be avoided. The president of Stanford University had once worked for Edison, and the inventor accepted a last-minute invitation from his former employee to make a Saturday morning appearance on campus. As usual, Edison avoided making a speech, but he still had to sit onstage for more than an hour while faculty members praised him to approximately 1,500 students, plus hundreds of additional people who'd learned Edison would be at the school and turned out to see him. That was supposed to be the extent of Edison's visit, but as Stanford officials escorted him through the crowd to his waiting car, a small girl slipped forward and asked to shake the inventor's hand. He naturally agreed. As the *San Jose Mercury Herald* reported, "That seemed to start the ball rolling." Everyone wanted a handshake, and Edison was obliged to comply. That took more time, during which the sixty-eight-year-old was constantly on his feet. It was a weary Edison who finally escaped to his wife and friends back in San Francisco.

There still seemed to be some time for Edison to relax away from crowds. He and

Ford were scheduled to appear at San Diego's Panama-California Exposition on Friday, October 29. It was decided that their combined parties would first take the train to Los Angeles. Though there was some advance publicity — the *Los Angeles Times* noted Edison's imminent arrival with a story headlined "Master Inventor Guest of Los Angeles: No One Has Brought World More Comfort" — everyone looked forward to visiting privately with friends and enjoying some peace before the final 120-mile rail trip to San Diego. And, at first, it happened almost exactly that way. At one point the Edisons were intercepted by a camera crew and reporters on their way to lunch with some longtime acquaintances, but the media was satisfied with Edison's brief observation that "You surely have some lights in this city. It isn't like New York, either, along one street."

Eventually the group was tracked down by owners of a film studio, who offered an invitation to come along and watch work on a movie currently in production. This interested everyone, Edison in particular. Almost thirty years earlier, Edison's seminal contribution to the motion picture industry was the filmstrip, a continuous flexible roll, and the kinetoscope, which projected moving images on tiny screens. It fell to other innovators to develop the projectors that allowed movies to be viewed on bigger screens by larger audiences, but Edison had provided a vital middle step and, so far as much of the public was concerned, he'd invented the movies. Beginning in 1903, Edison's movie production company actually dominated filmmaking, producing popular titles like *The Great Train Robbery; Camel Caravan; Pekin, China;* and *Uncle Tom's Cabin.* All were what was termed "two-reelers" with total running times of about twenty-five minutes. Competitors eventually countered with longer films, some lasting as long as three hours, but Edison, like Ford with the Model T, stubbornly stuck to the original product that was successful. Unlike Ford, his market share in the movie business soon declined. Here was a chance to see firsthand what another studio was up to, and, if nothing else, a pleasant way to spend an afternoon.

The invitation was a ploy. When the party arrived at the studio, instead of a working crew they found a pack of photographers (some sources suggest there was also a brass band) and a request for Edison to formally lay the cornerstone for a new studio building. Unwilling to seem a bad sport, Edison went along, smiling and posing. Afterward, he and his friends did get the promised tour of the studio. But their day was ruined, their spirits were down, and no one looked forward to more of the same in San Diego, where crowds would press them at the Exposition. Beyond that, their train departure and arrival times had proven to be widely known. More depot mob scenes loomed.

Harvey Firestone had a suggestion. They didn't have to go to San Diego on the train. The road there from Los Angeles was relatively smooth. Why not put together a fleet of cars and drive instead? That would make the trip more like an outing. To an extent they'd have to be open about the change of plans — it wouldn't do for Mr. Edison and Mr. Ford to appear to be shunning the public — but at least they'd be more in control of their own schedule. This idea had considerable appeal.

More Americans were making such trips by car. A jaunt of 120 miles in a single day was no longer daunting. Even fifteen years earlier, it would have been impossible, since there were very few cars (eight thousand as opposed to fourteen million horses) and fewer drivable roads. With the exception of train travel, the average American rarely ventured more than twelve miles from home, because that was the distance a horse and wagon could comfortably cover from there and back in a day. But as cars caught on, it became popular to spend a delightful day driving amazing distances to visit family or friends or some scenic spot, and still get back home in time for supper.

Certain parts of the country lent themselves to such recreation better than others. The Northeast had perhaps the best and most numerous roads, but Southern California wasn't far behind. The American Automobile Association, recognizing that car travel was gaining traction throughout the country, organized in 1902, two years after the Automobile Club of Southern California. The state was among the first to require car owners to register their vehicles — this cost $1 — and along with Connecticut, New York, and Massachusetts was among the first states to implement speed limits. Inconveniently for motorists, there was little uniform about these. States and cities picked and enforced various limits. In 1915, California's general speed limits were 10 mph "in built-up territory," 15 mph "in any city or town," and 20 mph outside these two areas. But Los Angeles restricted drivers to 12 mph in its central district, and San Diego prohibited speeds above 12 mph anywhere in the city. Speed traps enforced the laws. Cops sheltered behind shrubbery or buildings and timed cars with stop-watches.

For those whose cars boasted speedometers, it was relatively easy to stay within the speed limits. But many manufacturers offered speedometers only as an accessory; Ford Motor Company charged about $7 for one. That meant many drivers found themselves in newfangled traffic court, paying fines of $5 or $10. Henry Ford was caught speeding while driving in Michigan, and denounced speeding laws entirely. He argued that it was impossible to drive and constantly observe and obey speed limits.

Drivers in California and everywhere else in the country faced additional aggravations. Signs indicating local speed limits were rarely posted along roads. Neither were mileages to towns and cities along the way, or even the number or name of the roads themselves. Sometimes printed road maps were available — the Automobile Club of Southern California was among the first to offer these — but they were limited in the streets and roads that were identified within major cities, and even less help indicating where connecting roads should be taken outside of towns. Motorists were instructed to turn left just past a large red barn adorned with a tobacco sign, or right beyond a grove of trees on a high hill. Often, roadside businesses and attractions paid to be chosen as important markers, along with a persuasive description of why travelers should stop there along the way. ("Cawson Ostrich Farm: Your visit to sunny California is incomplete without a glimpse of these giant birds and their bristling, porcupiney chicks"; "Bimini Baths, [where] the water . . . contains mineral elements that render it highly beneficial as well as delightfully soft for bathing.")

Luckily for the Edison-Ford party, a recently improved California state highway ran between Los Angeles and San Diego. No poorly marked turns were required, and the ride would be a pleasure. Firestone arranged for cars to be provided. The Los Angeles media was informed about the switch from rail to road. The three obliged a *Los Angeles Times* photographer by posing in some of the vehicles. Sharp-eyed readers noticed that in one, Ford smiled behind the wheel of a hulking Kissel Kar, a powerful luxury vehicle manufactured by a competitor. The *Oakland Tribune* noted in a long article that Ford was enamored with the Kissel's superior speed. His confidence in the overwhelming popularity of his smaller, pokier Model T was such that he felt no threat in publicizing the advantages of another company's car. Ford probably chose the Kissel for the trip out of additional concern for the comfort of the ladies in the party. Had they been about to travel a typical rough American road, lighter Model Ts would have provided the best ride. But on the upgraded highway south to San Diego, the heavy, wide-based Kissel would provide a much smoother experience.

Sometime early in the morning of Friday, October 29, they set off in several cars — articles about the trip surprisingly don't mention how many, but at least three or four. The weather was sunny, and while the highway mostly ran out of the sight of the Pacific, ocean breezes still found their way through hilly gaps to cool drivers and passengers. The only timetable involved was the necessity of Edison and Ford arriving at the Panama-California Exposition by mid-afternoon. Speeds of 30 or even 35 mph were possible during long, flat stretches. That was nearly double California's noncity speed limit, but with considerable space between towns there was a corresponding scarcity of potential speed traps. Free of railroad timetables, with only 120 easy miles to drive, they could speed or lollygag at leisure. The trip was also thankfully free of additional publicity appearances. Only in Santa Ana were they forced to pause and greet the public. The town's schoolchildren lined both sides of the highway for more than a mile. Edison and Ford smiled and waved. It was relatively low-key and not at all taxing for the aging inventor. Just outside the Exposition's host city, they even managed a stop at Mission Basilica San Diego de Alcalá. Everyone found the architecture of the ancient church fascinating. For the better part of an exhilarating hour, they strolled the grounds like relatively anonymous tourists.

It was different when they arrived at their hotel. Exposition officials had kept careful track of Edison's and Ford's activities at the rival fair in San Francisco. The Panama-Pacific Exposition had the famous duo for several days — the Panama-California Exposition would host them only for an afternoon. It was necessary, then, to have a one-chance-only reception planned that would dwarf the cumulative events staged in San Francisco. In the minds of its organizers, the San Diego fair had far more potential significance than the one to the north. Both expositions celebrated the completion of the Panama Canal, but San Francisco's also attempted to glorify the rebuilt city itself. San Diego wanted civic recognition, too, but presented its fair as a means of regional advertising for tourism dollars — there was more to California than San Francisco. As one Panama-California publication noted, "The effort has been made to show the Eastern tourist that the American West has such an infinite variety that two great expositions can be held at the same time without . . . duplication of each other's efforts. The bigger, broader and better purpose is to assist materially in the development of the whole West — San Diego's back country, if that expression may be used . . . devotion to a cause bigger than the cause of any previous world's fair."

Edison Day had been acclaimed the highlight of San Francisco's Exposition, so San Diego was determined to top it with their own precious few hours with him. Edison and Ford were quickly disabused of any hope for some brief private time at their hotel. As soon as word of their arrival reached the Exposition, staff rushed to greet them and hustle them off. Every moment of their San Diego Edison Day was designed to outshine San Francisco. There, Edison arrived in a fine car, nice enough but not nearly as memorable as his fair entrance in San Diego. The entire Edison-Ford party of cars was grandly escorted in by a mounted squadron of the First United States Cavalry. The clip-clop of horses' hooves was easily drowned out by the cheering crowd. Edison, looking slightly stunned, found himself greeted by three lovely young women, each of whom "presented great bunches of flowers into his hands," according to the next day's *San Diego Union.* The inventor was described as "smiling his thanks."

As Ford discreetly moved to one side, Edison was led to a stage crowned by a massive flower canopy. Dignitaries greeting them there included the Exposition president and San Diego mayor Edwin M. Capps. Edison stood soaking in the cheers, and that was only the beginning of the reception. A massive line of children, more than ten thousand in all, filed past. Each child had a flower; every blossom was tossed at Edison until, the next day's paper reported, he was "nearly buried from view . . . [the flowers] permeated the air with their fragrance." Edison, as usual, declined to make a speech, though he was strongly urged by Exposition officials to do so — that would really show up San Francisco. Finally, Edison offered a brief comment: "I'm solid for children." He refused to say anything else, but those four words were enough. The crowd roared, and adults began lobbing full bouquets of flowers at Edison. An estimated four thousand bouquets had been brought onto the grounds for that purpose, and they formed a tottering pile atop the heaps of individual blooms tossed by the children. Then the throng pressed forward; everyone was determined to have a good, close look at the honoree. Many snapped photographs. Edison responded "with smiles and bows" until "the Kodak fiends [were] satisfied," according to the newspapers, which collectively concluded that there had never been such a greeting in city history.

The cavalry opened a passage for Edison and Ford to walk to a nearby exhibition building where "a tea and reception" awaited them. Only a narrow way could be wedged through the throng. They'd seen Edison, heard a few words from him, thrown flowers at him — now they wanted to touch him. But he kept moving, and the crowd turned its attention to the famous man at his side. They chanted, "Ford, Ford," and "the modest owner of the biggest automobile factory in the world was forced to step into the crowd." He declined demands for a speech, but as Mayor Capps looked on, Ford began shaking hands and chatting with some of the crowd. One of the first was a woman familiar with Ford's antiwar statements, who told him, "God bless you for what you have said."

No laudatory comment could have pleased Ford more. Edison was obviously ready to keep walking to the relative quiet of the reception, but he paused when Ford did, giving reporters a chance to cluster around the famous duo and begin shouting questions. Edison put them off, saying, "I always meet the newspaper boys and talk to [you] on the last day of my visit [to] a city. Not today. Tomorrow, perhaps," a clever misstatement since he was only obligated to the Exposition and San Diego for a few more hours. The reporters insisted he at least describe his reaction to the flowery reception, so Edison "swept his arm over the vast assemblage and looked his appreciation, apparently preferring to express it in this manner rather than in words." Then Edison turned and went in to the reception.

Ford, though, had plenty of words. When the reporters asked him to expand on antiwar comments he'd made in San Francisco — had he really promised to spend $10 million to oppose preparedness? — Ford was pleased to respond: "I did not say that. . . . I did say, however, that I would give $1 million in aid in the fight against preparedness, and I mean to fight it with all the power I can command. I mean literally that I will put all I have into a fight against it. I have been organizing for some time and the campaign will be systematically conducted. Money makes war. Nations have to make money to make war. It is our business to keep money away from them."

As had Edison, Ford swept an arm toward the crowd. "War brings these people nothing but crepe, hardship, starvation and taxes. I don't believe in rallying around the flag." He envisioned America entering the war, and Germany invading the U.S. in response: "How much . . . could you protect, even though for the next few years we devoted ourselves to building a navy, erecting forts, increasing the army? A foreign foe could land almost at will on our shoreline on either the Atlantic or Pacific. We couldn't begin to acquire enough equipment to protect our coasts. I would rather be with no protection at all."

The press frantically scribbled in their notebooks. City officials envisioned the next day's papers featuring front-page stories about Ford's antiwar diatribe rather than Edison's glorious reception. Mayor Capps was especially incensed. Within earshot of a reporter for the *San Diego Sun,* Capps hissed to Ford, "You may know all about a flivver car, but what do you know about war?" The newspaper reported the comment, but not Ford's reaction. Certain of his beliefs, he may simply have ignored Capps. Compared to vast national interest and respect for anything Henry Ford thought or had to say, what difference did quibbling from a mere mayor make? Ford continued on to the reception, and afterward he and Edison did not have the opportunity to make a grand tour of Exposition grounds because, as the newspapers explained, "the duration of the public reception . . . and the [private one] that followed it had taken more time than had been anticipated."

That night, Firestone hosted a dinner for the traveling party at an elegant hotel, arranging entertainment by a Hawaiian band and dancers whose performance Ford enjoyed so much that he later hired them to perform back in Michigan. The next day, the group dispersed. Firestone and Ford stayed on in California a little longer, while

Edison was anxious to return to his laboratory in New Jersey and took the first train east.

Before Edison left, he had a suggestion. The best part of the California trip had been the drive from Los Angeles to San Diego, free from any demands but their own whims. While Edison didn't enjoy public appearances, he did savor time spent with friends away from the crushing daily concerns at work. Surely Ford and Firestone felt the same. Why not embark on future car trips, picking a general rural area and route and then going along as they pleased? They could camp — perhaps John Burroughs would come along and point out all sorts of interesting plant life and birds, as had been the plan in 1914 during the aborted visit to the Everglades? Ford was immediately in favor. As he had during his earlier New England car and camping trip with Burroughs, he would supply tents and other camping equipment. Firestone would handle daily chores like food purchases and locating suitable nightly camping spots. If wives were consulted, they declined involvement. Mina Edison and Clara Ford probably remembered the Florida fiasco with less fondness than did their husbands. This would particularly have suited Edison — he always preferred the company of congenial men rather than women, who in his experience too often expected to be fussed over.

And besides recreation, the trips would suit business purposes, too. The three men were pragmatic enough to realize that they couldn't go anywhere, particularly as a group, without attracting constant notice. Their California adventures had just proven that newspapers couldn't get enough of Edison's and Ford's adventures. Everywhere else in the country, reporters would surely vie for an opportunity to write about local visits, and thanks to the recent development of wire services, their stories would appear in newspapers all over the U.S. — publications in cities as geographically disparate as Aberdeen, Washington; Austin, Texas; and Charlotte, North Carolina had just carried wire stories about Edison's and Ford's escapades in San Francisco and San Diego. But on these trips the coverage would be on their terms, going where and when they liked, not bound by commitments to fairs and avoiding the hubbub of major cities altogether.

Then or not long after, Edison and Ford and Firestone gave themselves a nickname: They would be "the Vagabonds," annually joining much of the rest of America in exploring the country by car, doing it perhaps in more cosseted fashion (they weren't about to set up their own tents or cook simple meals over sputtering camp-fires) but still, in spirit if not entirely in practice, joining with their countrymen's burgeoning enthusiasm for gypsying in automobiles. What better way for such rich, famous men to demonstrate their kinship with ordinary Americans? *We are really just like you.* They weren't venal; there was no intention of tricking anyone. Their main goal was to have a good time. But few business magnates in America had a shrewder understanding of marketing than Edison, Ford, and Firestone. If rank-and-file consumers liked what they saw and read about, as they surely would, then sales of cars and light bulbs and phonographs and tires would directly benefit, too. It seemed to be a plan without flaw.

CHAPTER THREE:
1916

Nineteen fifteen ended badly for Henry Ford.

Following his trip to the California expositions with Thomas Edison, Ford returned home to Michigan even more determined to pull America back from the brink of what he believed to be a senseless war. In November, he agreed to a visit from Rosika Schwimmer, a Hungarian activist whose antiwar beliefs rivaled those of the automaker for moral fervor. Under any other circumstances, Schwimmer would have been an unlikely Ford ally. She was a foreigner, and one of Europe's best-known and outspoken suffragists. (It would take until 1920, when three-quarters of the states ratified the Nineteenth Amendment, before American women gained voting rights.) Ford wasn't against women's rights. He just didn't think much about them. It showed in the factory salaries he paid. Women employed in Ford factories, though they received across-the-board raises in 1914, didn't qualify for the full $5 workday. That was reserved for male employees.

But Schwimmer quickly earned Ford's respect. In April 1915 at the International Congress of Women at The Hague, she'd helped craft a resolution calling for the European war combatants to lay down their weapons and engage in mediation with neutral nations. When Ford began making his widely reported promise to spend his entire fortune if necessary keeping America out of the conflict, Schwimmer, alert to the potential of unparalleled financial support, pressed for a meeting. When she succeeded, her persuasiveness was such that crusty Henry Ford, mistrustful of almost everyone, was spellbound. What was immediately needed, Schwimmer explained, was a great peace commission composed of America's best and brightest, which, with the blessings of the Wilson administration, would travel to Scandinavia and Europe, convene conferences with leaders there, and by sheer brilliance combined with common sense convince everyone to stop shooting and reason through their differences instead. Schwimmer said she had documents from European war leaders indicating their willingness to negotiate if only some responsible party could bring them to the bargaining table, and she showed some to Ford. There was subsequent speculation by critics of Schwimmer that these were forgeries, but they looked authentic enough to convince Ford.

Soon afterward, it was announced that Ford would charter a vessel, temporarily rename it the "Peace Ship," fill it with America's most prominent leaders, and sail to Europe to mediate the war there into an immediate standstill. Despite President Wilson's refusal to endorse the Ford-Schwimmer plan as an official mediation effort by the American government (a disappointed Ford called Wilson "a small man"), the carmaker, urged on by Schwimmer, moved forward. Invitations to participate were sent out to every state's governor and virtually every well-known clergyman, author, and educator in the nation. Ford, never comfortable speaking at formal public gatherings, unwisely predicted in a New York press conference that "We're going to try to get the boys out of the trenches before Christmas." Through Schwimmer and her overseas contacts, initial Peace Ship meetings were scheduled in Norway, Sweden, and Denmark, with the aim of winning over those neutral nations to the mediation cause. The ship's sailing date was announced as December 4.

Some newspaper editorials were mildly supportive, but more were skeptical. The *New York Tribune*'s snarky headline read, "GREAT WAR ENDS CHRISTMAS DAY: FORD TO STOP IT." The *Hartford Courant* claimed, "Henry Ford's latest performance is getting abundant criticism and seems entitled to all it gets." There were suggestions that Ford was only in it for publicity. Evangelist Billy Sunday compared Ford to circus impresario P. T. Barnum, who reportedly said that there was a sucker born every minute. These criticisms irked Ford — how could anybody misconstrue his motives when he was not only so obviously right, but sincere? He was hurt even more by the flood of polite refusals from almost everyone invited to participate. These included men he considered close friends. John Burroughs tried explaining in a warm but straightforward note:

I have such affection for you and admiration for your life and work that I hesitate to speak any discouraging word about any worthy scheme you may undertake. God knows we all want peace — a real endur-

118

ing peace and not a mere truce . . . to stop the war now would be like stopping a surgical operation before it is finished. The malignant tumor of German militarism must be cut out and destroyed before the world can have a permanent peace.

Burroughs and Edison came to the dock to see Ford and the Peace Ship off, but both turned down his last-minute entreaties to change their minds and join him. Ford even ignored his wife, Clara's, pleas to her husband to get off the boat — she felt certain that he faced imminent humiliation. Ford wouldn't be dissuaded — he *knew* that he was right. A band played "I Didn't Raise My Boy to Be a Soldier" and the Peace Ship sailed, with an undistinguished mishmash of mostly anonymous antiwar activists aboard, as well as reporters from several dozen major papers, all eager to send home colorful stories describing whatever happened next.

They didn't have to wait long. Ford's peace delegates soon began squabbling among themselves. The great man himself caught the flu and spent most of the Atlantic voyage shut up in his stateroom. In Ford's absence, Rosika Schwimmer emerged as the Peace Ship spokesperson. She immediately took offense at what she considered disrespectful coverage and became openly antagonistic toward the journalists. An anticipated warm, widespread reception in Norway turned out to be tepid and paltry. Within days, still claiming to be indisposed, Ford slipped away and sailed home. Peace Ship efforts went on without him, and there was some limited success — various talks and resolutions came out of Scandinavia for another year, though nothing of any substantial nature was accomplished. Ford complained that the real problem in Europe was that "citizens don't take enough interest in the government." Though Ford's pride was hurt, and his considerable fortune slightly dented — it was estimated that Peace Ship expenses, all borne by Ford, totaled just under $500,000 — if anything his reputation among rank-and-file U.S. citizens rose even higher. Most of the country, particularly the middle-American working class, still wanted the country to stay out of war if at all possible. Ford was saying what they believed. When big-city newspapers ridiculed him for it, they were mocking Middle America, too.

Ford himself was entirely unbowed. The Peace Ship, to his mind, wasn't entirely a failure — it had gotten people talking about peace, and that was the point. Despite their refusal to join him, Ford didn't lose affection for Edison and Burroughs; soon after New Year's he purchased an estate adjacent to Edison's in Fort Myers. Plans proceeded for a full-fledged Vagabonds auto trip sometime later in the year, summer or early fall. Ford also followed through on his annual tradition of sending Edison a new car; a mixup resulted in the dealer billing the inventor, who obligingly paid $482.75. Ford was incensed; the dealer not only had to return the check to Edison, he had to meekly request a receipt so Ford could be certain that Edison was reimbursed.

But friendship went only so far. In March 1916 Ford was nettled when Edison offhandedly told a reporter he expected to soon convert the automaker "to military preparedness." Ford's antiwar sentiments were strong enough to risk offending his hero. In a lengthy interview with the *Detroit News,* Ford recalled that "Mr. Edison once told me that it was the greatest joy of his life to think that he had been working for years making things that would help people to be happy, but in all that time he had never turned his hand to the construction of anything designed to kill men. I hope he hasn't forgotten that." Ford suggested that Edison, still vacationing in Fort Myers but permanently residing and working in New Jersey, was too influenced by New York papers and their "scare bombs. . . . I hope the Florida fishing is fine and the weather is good, so that the jingo fog may clear away from the finest brain in the world." The article was accompanied by a photo of Ford on a tractor. He never missed an opportunity to suggest it was wiser for nations to build such implements of peace rather than weapons of war.

Edison was soon in possession of a clipping. Had he so chosen, every newspaper in the nation would have printed his outraged response to Ford's criticism. Instead, he chose a lighter, private response. Edison sent the clipping to Ernest Liebold, Ford's secretary, along with a note scribbled in the margin:

Liebold — glad to see Ford on that Tractor, that's good commercial ammunition.

Ford's domination of headlines wasn't through. Nineteen sixteen was a presidential election year, and Democratic incumbent Woodrow Wilson was considered vulnerable. His first term had been possible in part because former president Theodore Roosevelt, running as a "Bull Moose" third-party candidate, challenged Republican president William Howard Taft, who at one time had been Republican Roosevelt's chosen successor in the White House. That split the conservative vote, and Wilson won. Much of Wilson's initial term had been occupied with keeping America neutral in the European war; that status remained shaky, and so did his presidency. Across America, Republicans believed Wilson was eminently beatable if only their party could rally around a consensus candidate. The prospective field included Supreme Court justice Charles Evans Hughes; Roosevelt, if he could be tempted back into the Republican fold; several senators and governors — and Henry Ford. Though he proclaimed himself uninterested and made no effort to campaign, he won the Republican presidential primary in Michigan and, as a write-in candidate, came close in other states. Ford credited this, accurately, to many voters sharing his antiwar views, and encouraged further Republican hope by saying that a president ought to be chosen by popular demand rather than active candidacy.

In June at its convention in Chicago, the Republicans took three ballots before choosing Hughes as their candidate for president. Delegates preferred an experienced campaigner over a self-described nonpolitician, though Ford received support on all three ballots. In the weeks following, Ford gradually found himself preferring Wilson over Hughes, especially when the president's campaign slogan became "He Kept Us Out of War."

That didn't mean Ford immediately endorsed, or even publicly praised, Wilson. He was against any Americans taking up arms and potentially fighting foreign foes, and about the same time he lost the Republican nomination, Ford spoke out again. A lengthy revolution was ongoing in Mexico; there had been incidences of rebels crossing the border into the U.S. to attack military camps and towns. In June, President Wilson called out the National Guard to form a bristling buffer. Ford decried potential fighting with Mexico just as much as U.S. entry into the war in Europe and compared Wilson's order to a summons for "organized murder."

The great newspapers of the Midwest had consistently praised Ford editorially, none more than the mighty *Chicago Tribune*. It hailed the $5 workday as a personal triumph of "an exceptionally able and successful businessman"; in 1915, Ford was described on the *Tribune* editorial page as a "present day genius." But the newspaper took a stern stance against Mexican border aggression, and instantly turned on Ford after his latest remarks.

First came a story whose "FLIVVER PATRIOTISM" headline echoed the insult to Ford by San Diego mayor Capps almost a year earlier at the Panama-California Exposition. It pointed out that although not required to by law, "most employers have guaranteed not only to give patriotic workmen their old places when they return from fighting their country's battles, [they] have promised to pay their salaries while they are in service. Henry Ford's workers will not have a job when they return, much less will they receive pay while fighting for their country. . . . No provision will be made by Ford for their wives and families." The reporter didn't base the story on comments from Ford, who was unavailable for an interview. Instead, one of Ford's secretaries apparently talked to the journalist and described a draconian company policy, which the article presented to readers as fact. It wasn't. A plan was in place not only to protect employee National Guardsmen's jobs, but to assist their families during their absence. The next day's *Tribune* took the issue further in an editorial. Its all-capitals headline read "HENRY FORD IS AN ANARCHIST," and went on for nine paragraphs and 502 biting words. Ford was variously described as "deluded," "an ignorant idealist," and "an anarchistic enemy of the nation which protects him in his wealth."

The validity of the first two descriptions could be legitimately argued, but "anarchist," defined in the dictionary as "a person who rebels against any authority, established order or ruling power" and "especially one who uses violent means to overthrow the established order," appeared to be a blatantly unfair exaggeration. Far from advocating violent resistance to the government, Ford was trying to prevent anyone from committing violent acts, specifically war. He could have ignored the *Tribune*'s printed slurs, but in August, Ford announced a $1 million libel suit against the *Tribune.* In legal question was the editorial, not the incorrect story that preceded it and on which the editorial was based. The carmaker was tired of being called names in print. Venue motions alone would delay a trial indefinitely, but Ford was willing to wait as long as necessary.

Even as Ford's lawyers were preparing to

file their first court documents, Harvey Firestone and Edison's and Ford's staffs laid groundwork for the Vagabonds' late-summer trip. On July 15, one of Ford's assistants wired Edison that "Mr. Ford can go any time after August Fifteenth will write you later regarding burroughs." Firestone followed with another telegram to Edison, confirming Ford's availability after August 15 and promising he would "make all arrangements will you invite Mr. Burroughs." In a rare handwritten letter dated July 24 — Edison almost always preferred dictating messages through secretaries — the inventor wrote Firestone that "It looks doubtful that Ford will go, I have written him urging it. I have all the Camping outfit we can go anyhow. Will try and get Burroughs." Ford would never have gone without Edison, but Edison was quite willing to go without Ford. Edison selected a route that headed due north from his home in Orange, and up through eastern New York state and the Adirondacks, turning back just short of the Canadian border and heading down the western boundaries of Vermont and Massachusetts before cutting across the northwest corner of Connecticut and back through New York to Orange. Since Edison fully expected Ford to beg off, his plan was especially convenient for himself and Burroughs, who could join the caravan on the second day when it reached his home outside Roxbury, in New York's Catskill Mountains.

It was a relatively unadventurous route, for the most part along reasonably passable roads. They could rough it without suffering too much discomfort. With two weeks allocated to drive about 1,100 miles, few if any days would require driving 100 miles, or about six hours given driving conditions. There were plenty of farms along the way where the travelers could camp and also purchase fresh milk, meat, vegetables, and fruit. Edison had tents and cots with mattresses. He cobbled together portable storage batteries so the tents could be lighted at night. Firestone would bring some staff, including a camp cook. Burroughs would just bring himself, but Edison felt that was more than enough — the creaky naturalist could identify and tell about all sorts of plants, flowers, and birds, which would make the jaunt educational as well as relaxing.

Edison had a little fun with Firestone. He gave the tire manufacturer only a general idea of the early route — the Adirondacks would be their initial destination. Beyond that, Firestone would just have to wait. Firestone was expected to put together a caravan of about four cars, plus a truck to haul the tents and other equipment. On Monday morning, August 28, Firestone would pick up Edison at the inventor's home in New Jersey. They'd drive to just outside Roxbury and meet Burroughs at Woodchuck Lodge, the property he often wrote about in his books and magazine articles. From there, they'd be happy wheeled wanderers. If Ford did come as promised, there would be room for him and one or two of his staff in the cars.

The first stories about the trip made print on the weekend before, most of them produced by wire services for national distribution. Edison chatted with a few journalists and articles in hundreds of papers resulted. Far more than Ford, who considered the press a necessary evil even when stories about him were glowing, Edison was sympathetic to reporters. Ford's publicity gift was an instinctive knack for catchphrases, reflected best in his company's marketing. Advertising copy for the early Model T submitted by the staff to Ford read, "Buy a Model T and save the difference," making the point that the Ford was much cheaper than competitors' cars. Ford insisted that the wording be changed to "Buy a Model T and spend the difference." He realized that middle-class Americans liked to think of themselves as carefree consumers; for their self-esteem, the act of buying a car was every bit as important as the money they saved on the Model T.

But Edison understood the press from an insider's perspective. At age twelve, his first job was as a railway newspaper boy, hawking wares to passengers on a Midwest rail line. But Edison soon realized he could make more money selling his own newspaper. The preteen began reporting and publishing the *Grand Trunk Herald,* a gossipy conglomeration of short articles about railroad employees, regular passengers, and bits of news about popular stops and amenities to be found there. In the process he learned that readers were especially entranced by small, colorful details that helped them identify with the people they were reading about.

Now, in his effort to publicize the Vagabonds' first quasi-official car trip, Edison harked back to his railroad reporting days and, in the vernacular of 1916, he laid it on thick. A ubiquitous wire story found Edison emphasizing how he and his friends intended to abandon civilization entirely: "We'll steer by sun and compass only, [and] not a razor in the party. . . . John Burroughs, the naturalist, is camp cook, but I can fry fish myself." These fish, Edison stressed, would be caught with "a bent pin hook and a birch limb rod." Firestone "will tell the stories," presumably at night beside a crackling campfire, and Edison, conveniently forgetting the portable storage batteries, swore he was "going as far away from anything electrical as I can. [I'll wear] an old suit and an old hat . . . and I'm going to chew tobacco."

The resulting headlines were exactly what Edison wanted, from the *Detroit Free Press*'s "Edison Will Fish with Bent Pin Hook" to "Three Kids to Rough It in Two Weeks" in the *Boston Post.* The article emphasized that these rough-and-tumble pioneers would drive toward the Adirondacks and essentially live off the land, camping at farms and buying food along the way just like ordinary Americans out for a holiday on the road. The only deviation between the stories was that some added Ford's name to the Vagabonds list, taking for granted that the auto manufacturer was also included.

Firestone still hoped that might happen. On Friday, August 25, he wired a last-minute appeal to Ford, pretending that Edison still thought Ford would come and playing off the carmaker's devotion to the inventor:

> Just leaving to join Mr. Edison understand he is looking forward with great interest to your joining party Hope you will not disappoint him if only for a day or two. Don't know his plans or itinerary Will wire you later.

When there was no immediate response, Firestone went ahead, putting together his caravan of four cars (two Packards and two Model Ts) and an equipment truck and driving from his home in Akron, Ohio, to meet Edison in New Jersey. At 10 a.m. on August 28, they departed, with the *New York Times* reporting that "the vacationists will meet Henry Ford and John Burroughs on the way, and, under the guidance of Mr. Burroughs, the party will explore the woods and study nature. . . . The inventor said he expected to have 'a rattling good time' and had left orders . . . he was not to be disturbed unless some emergency arose."

The drive up to Woodchuck Lodge was uneventful. The cars mostly followed a relatively smooth-surfaced turnpike. Burroughs's home was too far to reach in a day, so after some eighty miles the travelers decided to camp for the night by a creek near the road a few miles from Ellenville. Firestone's staff began setting up camp, and as they did so the farmer whose land they were on stormed up, called them "tramps and gypsies," and ordered them off his property. All across the country, this was not an unusual occurrence. By 1916, it was common for auto vacationists to seek evening campsites on farmland, since many farms abutted roads and often had access to creeks, which the campers used for drinking water and bathing. Hotels would have been far more comfortable, but for many automobile travelers, hotels were also inconvenient. The whole idea of driving trips was grounded on the concept of going where you wanted for as far as you liked. Particularly in rural parts of America, towns were infrequent, and the hotels in them, if any, varied greatly in cost and quality. If you found yourself driving between towns and it grew dark, continuing on the road was dangerous. Car headlights were still primitive, and even the best roads were poorly marked. Wildlife and livestock frequently ambled across — at night, a deer or cow might be practically on your fender before you realized it. Even if you did reach town safely, its hotels might not have rooms available. If there were rooms, and if the hotel was a nice one with a restaurant, guests were frequently required to "dress for dinner," coats and ties for gentlemen, nice dresses for ladies. Much of the appeal of car trips lay in wearing comfortable clothes. Then, too, many travelers were on tight budgets — auto travel meant buying gasoline at perhaps 25 cents a gallon, and paying for tire repair since blowouts were inevitable. If your car broke down, there was the expense of having it towed to a town offering a garage and mechanic, plus the cost of repairs themselves. For many, adding the cost of hotel rooms — at least another dollar a day — was profligate.

That left camping. Sleeping bags, or more likely blankets, could be rolled and stowed easily enough in cars. Tents, though desirable, took up much more space — often, they were strapped to the car's sides or to the roof if it had one. In early twentieth-century America, there were few national or state parks, and none of the ubiquitous roadside rest areas that would proliferate a few decades later. The best open spaces near roads were usually farmland, and at first, when there were still very few auto travelers, most farmers didn't mind autocampers. Farmers often made a dollar or two selling provisions to their overnight guests. But by about 1910, the number of car travelers — and also the number of overnight campers — began to multiply at a dizzying rate. In 1910, about 500,000 passenger cars were registered in America. A decade later, there were eight million, and most passenger car owners used their vehicles at least occasionally for travel.

Farmers whose acres included pleasant roadside areas found themselves hosting car campers on a regular basis, and many of these weren't thoughtful guests. Their meals often relied on canned foods, and the emptied cans were just as frequently left on the ground. Fruit was picked from orchards without permission. Carelessly attended campfires became brushfires. Paper of all kinds was crumpled and tossed. Even farmers who rented camp space for the night (usually for about a dollar, the same price as an average hotel room) grew sick of cleaning up garbage and began posting signs warning campers to pick up after themselves or stay away. Some spent weekends, the most popular camping days, guarding their property with shotguns.

There were some, though, who acted

initially inhospitable to raise the cost of camp space rental, and the Ellenville farmer insulting Edison and Firestone on their first night out was one of these. Firestone tried to interrupt the man's ranting by pointing out that one of the campers was Thomas Edison. The farmer didn't care. He was placated instead with $5.

The next day it rained, and for all of a damp morning and dreary afternoon the caravan kept heading north, to Roxbury and John Burroughs's hilly Woodchuck Lodge property. Edison and Firestone looked forward to reconnecting with the old man, and also to the presence of reporters who would be there to record the happy reunion that evening and departure north the next day. They surely assumed that this time when they set up camp, their host Burroughs would be much more welcoming than the ranting Ellenville farmer.

If anything, he was even less pleased to see them.

Hoping for a little extra color in his story, a *New York Times* reporter arrived at Woodchuck Lodge early that morning, where he found the eighty-year-old naturalist digging potatoes in a hillside garden. Burroughs was in a foul mood. Asked about Thomas Edison's various achievements as an inventor, the old man snapped that so far as he knew, Edison was currently working on refinements to the phonograph. He added, "I much prefer having him work at that to having him devote his attention to motion pictures."

Movies, Burroughs continued, would be the ruin of the American intellect: "The average person goes to the moving-picture theater and looks at senseless films for a couple of hours, and goes away without having really had to use his brain once. . . . In the old days, he might have been spending that time with a book before him, which would have given him more information and would have made him exercise his brain a little to get it."

If movies increased in popularity, Burroughs prophesied, people might stop reading altogether. Left unspoken by the naturalist was that he made most of his income from writing books and Burroughs's belief that infernal motion pictures, made possible in part by Thomas Edison, threatened to deprive him of his livelihood. He'd been anything but an overnight success; the son of a farmer who couldn't afford to pay for his ambitious boy's higher education, Burroughs worked his way through college and supported his fledgling writing career with jobs as a teacher, clerk, and eventually a federal bank examiner. A protégé of Walt Whitman, Burroughs emerged as an author of national note only in late middle age. He was naturally threatened by movies or any other modern entertainment innovation that might lure potential readers away from his books.

Burroughs spoke more kindly to the journalist about Henry Ford, whom he apparently expected to arrive along with Edison and Firestone. A while back, he said, Ford had helped him clear rocks from a Woodchuck Lodge field, the two of them in shirtsleeves working in the sun like real men should. It took two weeks, and afterward Ford took some of the rocks back home to Michigan, where he used them to build a birdhouse. In his friend's honor, the naturalist named the cleared area "Ford Field," and painstakingly chipped the words on a large nearby boulder. Burroughs clearly had no notion of naming anything on his property for Edison.

When Edison, Firestone, and the rest of the party arrived at Woodchuck Lodge around five that afternoon, Burroughs directed them to a spot in his orchard. As they began to set up tents and connect Edison's portable batteries, their crotchety host stood to the side, writing about them in his private journal:

They camp in my orchard — an unwonted sight — a camper's extemporized village under my old apple trees — four tents and large dining-tent and, [for] night, electric lights; and the man Edison, the center around which it all revolved.

When everything in camp was properly arranged and the *New York Times* reporter had left to write his story, Burroughs had a surprise for Edison and Firestone — he'd decided not to go. When they asked why, he told them that "he was too old, and . . . he was through with journeys."

This was very bad news. Many newspapers were still reporting that Ford was going to join the trip. When reporters found that not only was he begging off, but Burroughs as well, subsequent stories might very well focus on why half the vaunted Vagabonds chose to stay home instead of helpfully describing to Americans how their favorite heroes were out vacationing in cars. Edison left it to Firestone to make Burroughs change his mind, and though the tire maker tried, he concluded that "there was no convincing" him.

But they still were there, and there was nothing for it but to camp in a steady drizzle and invite their balky host at least to take supper with them in the spacious dining tent. Firestone didn't note what his cook served, only that he "did himself extremely well that night . . . when we were through, Mr. Burroughs suddenly announced that he would join us in the morning." Edison, who skipped the fancy meal in favor of hot milk and toast, said, "That suits me best," adding, in Ford's absence, that "I could live for days just on the news of Rumania joining the Allies." It was a chilly evening. Burroughs probably slept indoors in his comfortable bed, but Edison insisted that he and Firestone had to shiver in their tents.

It took so much time the next day to pack up and for Burroughs to get ready to go that they weren't on the road until early afternoon. Since they were heading to Albany, that meant driving until well after dark. Though it didn't fit in with Edison's plan to rough it entirely, it made sense to check into a hotel rather than bumble about looking for a camping spot on the outskirts of the city. Firestone took advantage of an available telephone to call Ford in Michigan, urging him to change his mind, and to his delighted surprise, Ford indicated that he might try to join them after all. A telegram from Ford's assistant Ernest Liebold followed: "Mr. Ford has definitely decided to leave tomorrow . . . for Buffalo and will motor with Edsel . . . direct to your camp. Where can they meet you?" After consulting with Edison, Firestone responded by wire that Ford and Edsel should drive to the Lake Champlain Hotel in Plattsburgh near the Canadian border. There was apparently further communication back and forth until it was tentatively decided that Ford might meet the other Vagabonds at Saratoga, a point somewhat further south. Edison and Firestone were quick to share the good news with reporters, who hurried to Saratoga so they could provide their readers with eyewitness details of this happy vacation reunion.

On Thursday night, journalists and locals who'd heard the news about Ford's imminent arrival jammed the lobby of a hotel in Saratoga. The rest of the Vagabonds had already arrived. A wire service story reported that Edison and Firestone "much against their wishes" had to stay at a hotel in town rather than camp because their equipment truck couldn't handle its heavy load, and a sturdier vehicle had to be acquired in its place. Edison lingered downstairs awhile with the journalists, warning them he'd refuse to talk about anything not pertaining "to woods, camps, fishing or atmospherical conditions. . . . I'm on vacation." Burroughs told the press that he was looking forward to "a hotel bed," and that with a good night's rest "I'll be enjoying camp as much as I ever did."

It was good copy for the reporters, and helped mitigate their disappointment when, despite a nightlong stakeout, Henry Ford never arrived at the hotel. There was one false alarm. About 9 p.m. "a spare man with grayish hair strolled in and walked about as though he was looking for someone. . . . One man finally gathered courage to ask if he was Mr. Ford. There was decided regret in the tone with which he replied that he had no claim to the name, as his . . . friends had always called him J. E. Ward."

In the morning, with their new equipment vehicle secured, the rest of the Vagabonds returned to the road. They avoided towns and the press for two days. Burroughs's mood was good enough to note in his journal how glad he was to see Edison relaxing and, with the exception of his battery-lighted tent, really roughing it with baths in creeks and tending campfires by feeding sticks into the flames. Edison even eschewed the tasty meals prepared by Firestone's cook, continuing to subsist on toast and milk.

It was probably on the second night that Edison, so genial in public, showed an edgier side to Firestone. After sunset the air turned especially cold, and Edison and Firestone decided that Burroughs should spend the night at a hotel in a nearby town. The naturalist was all in favor of that plan, so Firestone obligingly drove him there, leaving Edison and Firestone's son Harvey Jr., who had come on the trip with his father, back in camp. Firestone stayed at the hotel, too. A fastidious man, so far on the 1916 trip he had reluctantly stuck to Edison's camp rule that no one was to bathe anywhere except a creek, or to shave at all. In his memoir, Firestone admitted that "when I saw the hotel bedroom and bath I could stand the strain no longer and I struck. Not only did I have a shave and a bath, but also I spent the night comfortably in a bed." The next morning, Firestone roused Burroughs and they returned to the Vagabonds' camp. The tire maker perhaps expected some good-natured joshing from his inventor friend, but Edison was peeved.

He "saw at once that I had shaved," Firestone wrote. "He did not so much mind having me out all night, but he did not like that shave — the breaking of the rules."

Edison called Firestone "a tenderfoot," and predicted that, despite their agreement to wear old clothes for the duration of the trip, "Soon you'll be dressing up like a dude."

Always careful to preserve Edison's genial reputation, Firestone noted in his memoir that the inventor "laughed" as he said this, but felt obligated to add, "Mr. Edison is seldom in bad humor." This was one of those times.

Edison's irritability wasn't entirely due to Firestone's shave. The scheduled two-week trip was nearly half over and Ford still dithered about joining them. Newspapers such as the *Kingston* (New York) *Daily Freeman* continued speculating about the automaker, keeping their readers updated on "the Adirondack jaunt of Thomas Edison, John Burroughs, and the Messrs. Firestone and Ford, the last named of whom has not yet put in an appearance." There was also some disappointment on the part of the press and the travelers themselves about the route being taken, with its relatively drivable roads and easy access to town amenities like hotels. Before departure, Edison had promised rugged wilderness adventures, but the region he'd chosen was already well-traveled by previous and current auto vacationists. The *Freeman* pointed out, "Mr. Edison will have to attain even greater heights as a discoverer if he can locate any such trackless way as he propose[d] to follow through the Adirondacks, which are no longer the wilds they were before summer vacations became popular."

At the approximate halfway point — Plattsburgh near the Canadian border — on September 5 the Vagabonds made their way to the Lake Champlain hotel where they had originally proposed that Ford meet them. They hadn't heard from him or any of his secretaries for a few days — perhaps he would be there after all. But what awaited them instead was a telegram from Ford assistant Liebold to Edison:

Regret very much to inform you that Mr. Ford . . . will not have time to join you. . . . However he expects to arrange for a real camping vacation sometime during the coming winter when he hopes to make up for the disappointment occasioned through his inability to go this time.

According to the telegram, Ford's excuse was that he needed to take an immediate business trip to the West Coast. Later, his office suggested to the press that Ford didn't go because he was preoccupied with planning his son, Edsel's, upcoming wedding in November. Probably Ford, embroiled in his new lawsuit with the *Chicago Tribune* and still smarting from press coverage of the Peace Ship, simply didn't feel like participating in such a public outing and risking more hurtful stories.

Whatever his reason, Ford left his fellow Vagabonds with a dilemma. They'd come for fun, but also for publicity, and now there was the very real possibility that the press might dispense with further trip coverage. Ford wasn't coming and there were no real wilderness adventures to report. Firestone's name was associated mostly with his tires, not with the man himself, and though Burroughs was well-known to those interested in nature, his celebrity was also limited. In reporting the Vagabonds' arrival in Albany, a city newspaper mistakenly identified the octogenarian as "president of the Burroughs Adding Machine Company."

But that left Edison, and he knew how to keep the stories coming.

■ ■ ■ ■

Henry Ford first gained fame as an automobile racer rather than manufacturer when in 1904 he set a new land speed record for cars at just over 91 mph. Four years later the Model T furthered his reputation, and in 1914 the $5 workday made Ford's name a household word. Beginning in 1915, the Peace Ship and his antiwar statements kept him almost constantly in the headlines to the point where there was a legitimate groundswell of support for Henry Ford for president.

But he still wasn't as famous as Thomas Edison. No one in America was. If it was never suggested that Edison run for president, it was because he was considered above politics. In 1916, the inventor had been a celebrity for some thirty-eight years, ever since he introduced the phonograph in 1877 and 1878. That coup alone guaranteed Edison's reputation. When he was invited to the White House to demonstrate his wondrous contraption to President Rutherford B. Hayes, he had to extend the visit while the First Lady summoned her friends to see (and *hear*) this amazing discovery, too. On April 1, 1878, the *New York Graphic* tried to play an April Fool's joke on its readers by publishing a front-page story claiming Thomas Edison had just invented a machine that made food out of "Air, Water and Common Earth." Because it was Edison, many people believed it must be true, and so did some competing newspapers that subsequently published similar stories.

Then in 1879 came the incandescent light bulb. Bright, powerful, dangerous arc lights had been in use for some time, but it took Thomas Edison to design a bulb that would burn not only bright but long in American offices and, more important, homes. Thrilled by the promise of electric light to read by rather than smoky oil lamps or flickering candles, grateful Americans missed the point that Edison's equally great contribution was the invention of generators that powered the bulbs economically.

The kinetoscope followed, an important step in bringing films to a wide audience. Many assumed that Edison had actually invented the whole movie concept. But as biographer Randall Stross points out in *The Wizard of Menlo Park,* to a great extent Edison spent the years after 1882 trying to come up with an invention that would match the impact of the phonograph and incandescent light bulb. Always, his goal was to invent things that were of practical use. In his early years, Edison's first patent application (out of a record 1,093) was for a telegraph-like vote recorder that, in state and national congressional chambers, could drastically shorten time needed for tabulations. What Edison didn't realize was that politicians liked to use a lengthy balloting process to cut deals. As Stross notes, "The vote recorder was a bust, and the lesson Edison drew from the experience was that invention should not be pursued as an exercise in technical cleverness, but should be shaped by commercial needs." Luck was also a factor in some of Edison's eventual successes. Early on, his electric pen was intended to make duplicate messages and signatures easy. The device became a market staple — not for writing, but in slightly altered form as a needle for applying tattoos.

Edison loved his work. Much of it was done in all-night laboratory sessions with talented assistants. Edison hired only the best and demanded excellence from them. The boss set overall goals, and the employees experimented and tinkered while he mostly supervised. Edison rewarded them with royalties when they contributed to inventions that reached the market as commercial products, but reserved all public credit for himself. It was *Edison's* phonograph, *Edison's* incandescent bulb. This was more important than ever as the years passed and no additional astonishing, culture-changing discoveries emerged from his laboratory. Edison's companies manufactured a variety of products based on his discoveries, and their best advertisement was the man whose name appeared on the boxes.

Because he knew how to continually engage public interest — appearing occasionally, smiling and always exhibiting his quite genuine personal warmth, but only rarely saying more than a few bland words — when Edison did choose to speak out, he always commanded headlines. On the 1916 trip, he shrewdly chose the perfect topic to divert the press from Ford's absence and the lack of any real back-roads adventures. Americans following the Vagabonds' trip were also fixated on the looming presidential election. Would voters ultimately support or repudiate President Wilson's policies? Edison never spoke about politics, and knew that if he did it would be a sensation.

On the morning after Ford failed to appear in Saratoga, Edison came down to the lobby and requested that reporters join him there. The journalists may have expected him to either admit Ford wasn't coming or else inform them when and where the carmaker was now expected to join his friends. Instead, he offered a ringing political endorsement, but not of Ford. A year earlier in San Diego, Edison could apparently manage only "I'm solid for children" after youngsters tossed heaps of flowers at his feet. Now he waxed positively eloquent.

"Not since (the Civil War) has any campaign made such a direct call on simon-pure Americanism," Edison declared.

The times are too serious to talk or think in terms of Republicanism or Democracy. Americans must drop (political) parties and get down to big fundamental principles. More than any other president in my memory, Woodrow Wilson has been faced by a succession of tremendous problems, any one of which, decided the wrong way, would have had disastrous consequences. Wilson's decisions so far have not got us into any serious trouble, nor are they likely to. He has given us peace with honor. . . . Neutrality is a mighty trying policy, but back of it are international law, the rights of humanity and the future of civilization.

Edison was asked if Wilson had always been his preference for president in 1916. He replied, "Roosevelt was my choice. He has had experience, and is one of the best of Americans, but the machine-controlled Republican party would not have him. Therefore I am for Woodrow Wilson." This comment was likely intended as a subtle dig at Ford; in the past year, especially after the Peace Ship debacle, Roosevelt had frequently criticized Ford.

For the rest of the week, Edison, Burroughs, and Firestone enjoyed an actual vacation. They camped out as planned, avoiding hotels entirely. Various acquaintances joined them for campfire meals. There was a ferry ride, and a long morning at a county fair. Coverage of these last days of the Vagabonds' 1916 trip was almost entirely Edison-centric: "Edison Goes Back to Nature"; "Thomas A. Edison Takes to Mountains for Recreation"; and, finally in the September 11 *New York Times,* "Edison Back From Camp," above a story describing the inventor as "sunburned and convinced that a vacation in the open is far more attractive and beneficial than living in hotels." With Burroughs dropped off back in Roxbury, and Firestone on his way home to Akron, the newspaper reported that Edison briefly greeted his family, then "donned working clothes, went to his laboratory . . . [and] immediately started to work on several experiments which occurred to him on the trip." The inventor's only concession to road weariness was an afternoon nap.

The last line of the *Times* article briefly noted, "Henry Ford had planned to make the trip, but business made it impossible for him to do so."

Afterward, Burroughs wrote a long joint letter to Edison and Firestone, thanking them for the trip and indirectly apologizing for his initial reluctance to go on it:

My health had been so precarious during the summer that I feared I could not stand more than two or three days of the journey, but, as it turned out, the farther I went the farther I wanted to go. . . . The doctors think that, as we grow old, there is great remedial power in mechanical vibrations. I think the vibrations of a motor car over the good state roads on a trip to the Adirondacks with such a company in it as we had beats all other appliances. . . . I am only sure that I took the most delightful shaking up — such as I had not had for forty years."

Burroughs and Firestone even collaborated on *In Nature's Laboratory,* a privately printed memory book of the trip, including photographs and verse composed to commemorate various adventures and stopping places. Neither showed any potential as a poet, but the intended message was clear: They'd had a nice time.

The friendship between Edison and Ford was unaffected by the carmaker's decision not to go. A few weeks after Edison declared for President Wilson in Saratoga, Ford followed suit with a Wilson endorsement, and, in his usual all-in way, committed his money, too. Ford's key contribution was payment for pro-Wilson ads in newspapers all across California. Wilson won the state over Hughes by a razor-thin margin, and that gave the president a narrow national majority vote and electoral victory of 277–254 over his Republican opponent.

Ford partially fulfilled his promise to arrange a Vagabonds winter trip. Edison and Firestone were otherwise occupied, but in February 1917 the carmaker took Burroughs on a boat trip to Cuba, where Ford explored various business interests while Burroughs sunned himself on deck. During the trip, Burroughs learned that his wife,

Ursula, had died after a lingering illness. The two had been emotionally estranged for many years, and Burroughs did not leave Cuba and return to New York after hearing the news.

In March, America's entry into the world war became virtually certain. British intelligence intercepted a telegram from the Germans to the Mexican government, offering Mexico the return of lands lost to America in the U.S.-Mexican war in return for a victorious Germany-Mexico military alliance. Soon afterward, German subs sank several American merchant ships. In early April, America joined the war. Many Americans who previously advocated neutrality became supportive. Prohibition, formerly despised by many, became a patriotic rallying point — drinking beer was now linked to the Germans.

No one changed direction more than Henry Ford. He instantly announced that all his factories would focus on war-related manufacturing for the duration. This, to Ford, was not in any sense a contradiction. He opposed war, but he also considered himself a loyal American. At government request, the Ford Motor Company began assembling a variety of military products,

155

from ambulances to small boats designed to hunt down and destroy submarines. Ford announced that everything would be made at cost; he'd accept no personal profit for his company's contribution to the war effort.

Edison devoted his full attention to the Navy advisory board that he had agreed to chair. The committee was especially tasked with inventing some effective means of countering the Germans' strength on the seas. Edison mostly divided his time between southern Florida, where key naval installations were based, and Washington, D.C. He soon began submitting plans and inventions for the government's consideration. To thwart enemy spies, none was made public.

It took much of 1917 just for the American military to bolster its small, poorly trained and equipped ranks sufficiently to send forces overseas. But merely the knowledge that U.S. help was on the way boosted the Allies' morale and set enemy leaders to considering how much currently gained territory might be retained in a negotiated peace. Meanwhile, a muddy, bloody virtual stalemate in Europe dragged on.

Despite all the war-related responsibilities he and Edison assumed, Ford still wanted the Vagabonds to set out on another car trip. In August 1917, he began peppering Edison with requests for the inventor to pick some potential dates and routes. Edison put him off, citing various Navy-related experiments that were in progress and couldn't be interrupted. Edison really was busy, but it's also likely he wanted to remind Ford that he, too, could beg off a car trip. Ford wasn't deterred, and finally Edison decided to make his point clearly.

In early September, Ernest Liebold wrote on Ford's behalf to W. H. Meadowcroft, Edison's secretary, inquiring, "How does the matter of a camping trip stand with Mr. Edison at present? Has he completed the experiments which prevented him going on a trip two weeks ago?"

Meadowcroft passed the letter on to his boss. Edison scrawled a long response across half of the page:

Say I am at sea nearly all the time in a 200-ft. submarine chasing all around inland water . . . & have a large number of experiments still to finish — hope Ford gets a chance to come on yacht & help out, the experiments are very interesting. Edison

Rather than restate Edison's message in a typed letter, on September 14 Meadowcroft returned Liebold's original letter with the inventor's handwritten notation. Meadowcroft also added his own scribbled post-script:

Dear Mr. Liebold: I send this just as it is. Please show Mr. Edison's memo to Mr. Ford. If Mr. Ford will accept Mr. Edison's invitation to go on the boat, I will give you the address. Yours sincerely, W. H. Meadowcroft.

That ended the year's Vagabonds-related correspondence. The press was informed that there would be no trip in 1917, due to Edison's and Ford's involvement with their war-related work.

Chapter Four:
1918

In August 1918, Thomas Edison was ready for a vacation. The past twenty months had been among the most difficult of his life.

Edison approached his Naval Advisory Board responsibilities with the same enthusiasm that marked his previous efforts as an inventor. He committed his time and his heart to creating devices that would enable America and its Allies to overcome the enemy at sea. At one point, he and his wife, Mina, lived on a boat anchored at New London, Connecticut, so he could experiment and confer on a daily basis with naval officials there. Work on personal projects at his laboratory in New Jersey was virtually abandoned.

There sprang from his mind and floating workshop all sorts of potential equipment and weaponry, more than forty possibilities in all, each presented by Edison to the Navy with enthusiasm and the expectation that it would be accepted, manufactured, and put to effective use. The proposals ranged from a special anchor that would enable ships to turn quicker in efforts to dodge torpedoes to listening devices that would allow quicker detection of enemy submarines.

None were implemented by the Navy. No specific reasons were offered; apparently none of his projects was studied further, let alone tested. It was hard not to take it personally — he was Thomas Edison after all. The insult was compounded when the Navy accepted proposals by other advisory board members. Edison decided the problem lay with a naval bureaucracy incapable of understanding the work he did on its behalf. After the war he wrote to the Secretary of the Navy that "when you are no longer Secretary I want to tell you a lot of things about the Navy that you are unaware of." Under similar circumstances, Henry Ford would have gone public with his dissatisfaction, denouncing the Navy and probably suggesting that some element or other within the government actively plotted to block his eminently useful contributions. But that was not Edison's way. He kept his resentment to himself.

Still, as a patriot, Edison felt frustrated. Surely at least a few of his innovations could have been of use to the war effort. As a private citizen, his own business interests would have been bolstered by widespread publicity for any Edison invention that helped turn the tide against the Germans. He was seventy-one now, with limited creative years remaining, and he'd wasted almost two of them. So in midsummer, when Harvey Firestone wrote that he and Mr. Ford hoped Mr. Edison would consider a 1918 trip, Edison made it clear that he was eager to go and, for a change, could make room in his schedule for an excursion pretty much at their convenience.

In retrospect, the 1916 trip had fallen short of expectations both in terms of coverage and adventure. Ford's absence was a contributing factor — the newspaper articles had first been about that, then Edison's announcement of political support for President Wilson, plus some coverage of roadside picnics and a stop or two at local attractions. The route itself was nothing out of the ordinary. The roads involved were well-traveled by other vacationists. There were stories all the time about travelers in New York state and New England. More intriguing destinations were needed, places that would pique media interest and at the same time offer new sights and experiences to the Vagabonds themselves.

Even a few years earlier, a cross-country trip might have served that purpose. There were several possible routes, the best-known and most direct of which was the Lincoln Highway, some 3,400 miles of road starting in New York City, wending its way through thirteen states, and ending in San Francisco. The highway was the brainchild of Indiana businessman Carl Fisher, who made his fortune selling automobile headlights. In 1912 Fisher began touting an East Coast–to–West Coast highway that would be completed in time for the 1915 opening of the Panama-Pacific Exposition. Initial funding would come from car and tire manufacturers, and companies whose products — asphalt, gravel, machinery to level and dig ground — would be used in construction. Fisher received a gratifying response from those businessmen he approached, with a single prominent exception. Henry Ford refused to participate, saying that if the public got such an impressive road for free, they'd expect someone else to pay for all the other roads that the country needed instead of assuming financial responsibility themselves.

Even without Ford, work on the Lincoln

Highway commenced, and some early sections proved eminently drivable. But most of it was primitive, often nothing more than sand or packed earth, particularly in the middle states. In 1918 the highway remained a work in progress, but American car vacationists increasingly accepted the challenge of driving coast to coast. Within five years of the 1915 opening, an estimated twenty thousand drivers had traveled the entire route. For those willing to bring along lots of extra tires and drive twenty hours a day, it was occasionally possible to complete the trip in five or six days. It more likely took two or three weeks — even families packed into a Model T could manage that. There was enough newspaper coverage of these adventures that a Vagabonds jaunt on the highway from New York to California wouldn't in any way seem special, except for Edison and Ford being involved. But there was another direction, one that in terms of car travel and media coverage remained virtually uncharted.

The South.

Nineteen eighteen America was a nation dominated in most ways — politically, economically, in media attention and coverage — by the Northeast. In terms of formal education and personal wealth, its population far exceeded that of any other region. The Pacific coast — California especially — was on its way up. The burgeoning film industry was based there, and the Panama Canal presented fresh trade opportunity. The Midwest had its farmers and a good deal of manufacturing. The Southwest was ranching and oil; Texas, New Mexico, and Arizona still retained a sense of *frontier*. But much of the South was scorned, particularly in the Northeast, where Southerners were widely regarded as intellectually backward, almost subhuman. The South was considered good for certain crops — tobacco and cotton chief among them — and a potential workforce fit for basic tasks requiring minimal intellect. People from the South looked north for an opportunity for better lives, not vice versa. Resentment over the Civil War still lingered, in both the North and South. That conflict had concluded only fifty-three years earlier — Edison was a teenager when the first shots were fired, and Ford was born a few weeks after the Battle of Gettysburg.

Additional outsider disdain for the South was based on unfamiliarity caused by lack of access, especially in the new age of the automobile. There simply weren't many decent roads there. Car owners might drive from New York to San Francisco on an extended vacation, but few attempted New York to Atlanta or Biloxi. Those who did generally went by train, which provided a relatively smooth, quick trip but lacked the same opportunity to experience the passing land and its people in a way that was possible in a car. An automobile trip through Virginia, West Virginia, Tennessee, and the Carolinas would range far enough south to satisfy the Vagabonds' quest for a little adventure and intrigue the press at the same time. It would be almost the equivalent of travel to a foreign country populated by colorful, primitive natives.

Henry Ford understood the publicity potential and took steps to maximize it. Once the general area for the trip was decided, Ford took over most of the planning. Operators of Ford dealerships in that portion of the South were instructed not only to expect visits, but to galvanize area press for maximum local coverage. It wouldn't be enough for big-city papers and national wire services to write about the trip. Ford wanted every small-town daily and weekly to deliver front-page coverage, too. He demanded reports that included the complete transcripts of every story written about the campers — woe to dealership owners whose local newspapers' stories disappointed him. Ford also brought along cameramen to record Vagabonds escapades in photographs and on film, so that the public could see as well as read about their hijinks. The photos would, of course, be made available to the print press, and the film to movie theaters for inclusion in the newsreels that preceded featured motion pictures.

So far as his famous friends were concerned, Ford made it clear that on this and future trips he'd pay for everything. His staff would set up camp with equipment brought from Dearborn. Ford's personal chef would cook. Ford provided vehicles, too — comfy luxury cars for the Vagabonds themselves to ride in, Model Ts for staff and for tents and other camp gear like chairs and tables. Edison's storage batteries would once again provide power to light tents at night. Southern reporters in particular would surely be astounded by such a sight. As Ford biographer Charles E. Sorensen later wrote, the 1918 and subsequent Vagabonds outings "were as private and secluded as a Hollywood opening."

Edison decided to bring a friend along — R. J. H. DeLoach, a professor at the University of Georgia whose research in the cotton industry had caught the inventor's attention. Ford invited a guest, too — Edward N. Hurley, chairman of the Federal Trade Commission and chair of the wartime Shipping Board, on which Ford also served. A starting date of August 18 was agreed on. Everyone would meet in Pittsburgh, which had sufficient quality roads to ensure a good start south before the bad roads began.

Edison arrived early. After registering at the Fort Pitt Hotel, he granted an interview to the city press and had plenty of headline-worthy things to tell them. The inventor guaranteed that Henry Ford would come along this time — Edison pronounced his friend's nerves "all a-shake." In the days ahead, the Vagabonds would try "hunting snakes and queer birds to put Ford back into a serene way of life."

There was no need to waste vacation time thinking up ways to fight the Germans: "We don't have to think when we fight the Huns. Why? Know what they are? Boneheads! Boneheads!"

In war as in life itself, women were forcing their way to the forefront: "We have about 300 women working in our plant and are running a school to train others. [Thanks to the war] male labor is scarce, as

167

I have heard in Pittsburgh, but there is not going to be any trouble. Their places will be filled by women and the work will go on."

Edison explained that the first part of the trip would include "the Great Smoky Mountains in eastern Tennessee and Kentucky." In all, counting DeLoach, Hurley, and Ford's battery of servants, the entire party would number about twenty. He joked about the Secret Serviceman guarding him while he continued serving on the Naval Advisory Board: "[I'm] doping out a scheme to ditch him." A reporter mentioned hearing that one hundred agents were assigned to Edison, who scoffed. "That was all bosh. [At first], only four. Nobody killed me, so now they only make me take one."

The rest of the party also checked into the Fort Pitt. Burroughs stalked upstairs to his room. A few reporters followed, and noted in their subsequent stories that Burroughs switched his street shoes for comfortable slippers, left the shoes outside his door to be polished, and shut himself up inside.

Burroughs hadn't wanted to go in 1916, and two summers later felt even more strongly about avoiding the South, which, based on a few previous visits, he detested. "I can see nothing beautiful in the Southern landscape," he wrote in his journal a few months prior to the Vagabonds' 1918 trip. "The everlasting blood-red soil, and the dark pine woods, the disheveled fields, the houses upon legs, ready to run away, the mud-bespattered horses and vehicles and pedestrians, the absence of grass, etc. etc., all offend my eye." The drive from his home in Roxbury to Pennsylvania displeased Burroughs considerably. Edison and Firestone picked him up again, and he felt because of their "furious speed the car fairly kicked up its heels at times and we were unseated all too often. It was not easy to unseat Mr. Edison beside the chauffeur — there is a good deal of him to unseat, and he is cushiony and adjustable, and always carries his own shock absorbers with him. My own equipment of this sort disappeared long ago, I am very sensitive on the subject of hard driving."

When they arrived, Burroughs was equally unimpressed with Pittsburgh and all its industry: "I think I [get] nearer the infernal regions there than I ever [do] in any other city in this country. . . . It might as well be the devil's laboratory." Ford's presence on this trip was probably the factor that made Burroughs decide that he was obligated to go — it was hard to refuse the man whose largesse had saved the Burroughs family property from bank foreclosure. Complete respect for one of the richest businessmen in the country was also in keeping with Burroughs's personal philosophy of nature — all forms of life, plants to animals to humans, remained in constant states of competition. Only the strongest thrived, because they deserved to. To Burroughs, that meant the worthiest men could be recognized by outsized personal fortunes: "Millionaires add to the positive health and well-being of all." By that measure, Ford excelled.

The carmaker and the naturalist shared certain philosophies. Burroughs had a genuine love of nature and a firm belief in the simple virtues of hard work and unsentimental judgment, the same qualities held in highest esteem by Henry Ford. Like Ford, Burroughs never publicly qualified his personal beliefs to accommodate differing opinions. When other naturalists on the public speaking circuit enthralled audiences with heartwarming tales of sweet goings-on in nature, Burroughs made a point of calling them out. He insisted that there was nothing soft about survival on any level. Only those who accepted this reality could claim that they were truly in tune with nature. Fairy tales of any sort were only for the weak-minded. When his son Julian was a child, Burroughs informed him that "Christmas [is] a fraud based on a folk tale."

Ford adored the unapologetic old man and demonstrated his affection by insisting Burroughs be part of the Vagabonds' trips. The octogenarian may not have wanted to go, but Ford brought him along so that he would have a fellow ornithologist to bird-watch with, and an expert to identify any plants or flowers that caught the travelers' eyes. Burroughs was among the very best at these things and that trait earned him a place in camp alongside the nation's most successful inventor, carmaker, and tire manufacturer. In exchange for the privilege of sharing Burroughs's wisdom, the others overlooked his prickliness and constant complaining.

On Sunday, August 18, the Vagabonds left Pittsburgh for the open roads heading south, though not on Ford's anticipated early morning schedule. A truck bringing camp supplies in from Michigan was late, and even after it had arrived and its cargo transferred to a hardier vehicle, Edison wouldn't be rushed. He had a brother-in-law in town and insisted on meeting him for lunch. Ford tolerated the additional delay because it was Edison. Burroughs was in Ford's debt, and Firestone would never have dreamed of upsetting Ford's schedule. But Edison, temporarily free of his Naval Advisory Board obligations, ignored the clock.

Even though the road was good, they still made only about fifteen miles before dark, driving southeast from Pittsburgh. Along the way they passed what Burroughs described as "processions of army trucks . . . the doom of the Kaiser is writ large." The Vagabonds' caravan consisted of six cars, and when they stopped for the day, servants set up camp in a roadside grove of trees a few miles outside the town of Greensburg. After dinner — a "delicious supper," according to Firestone's journal about the trip — everyone gathered by the campfire for hours of uninhibited conversation. No reporters were present, and everyone there trusted in each other's discretion. Because Hurley had to leave the group and return to Washington the next day, he did much of the talking, answering questions from Ford, Edison, and Firestone about proposed Atlantic shipping routes for the duration of the war, and what new routes would come into play after the Allies' anticipated victory. Their curiosity was based both on patriotism and self-interest — all three men did considerable overseas business before the war and expected to do so again as soon as it concluded. Ford lamented the cost of the conflict: "We must win, and to do it we shall have to use up a lot of our resources. It is all waste, but it seems necessary, and we are ready to pay the price." It wasn't all business — Firestone noted that there were also "stories" — and they lingered around the flickering flames until midnight. It was a chilly night and Burroughs had trouble falling asleep. He gave up about 3 a.m. and spent the rest of the hours until daylight beside the campfire "indulg[ing] in the 'long, long thoughts' which belong to age much more than youth. Youth was soundly and audibly sleeping in the tents with no thought at all."

The rest of the camp was up around eight the next morning. After breakfast, the four Vagabonds, DeLoach, and Hurley amused themselves with some target shooting while the staff packed up the tents and equipment. Any hope for a relatively early departure was thwarted by the arrival of a delegation from Greensburg. Someone had spotted the Vagabonds' camp, so the mayor, a contingent of businessmen, and a reporter from the local newspaper hustled out to greet the great men and invite them into town. Firestone assumed the role of host. The dignitaries were shown the kitchen and refrigerator trucks, the tents and the batteries that lighted them, and given promises that the party would stop in Greensburg on their way south. They likely would have stopped anyway — the cars needed gas, and fuel was to be found only in towns, most of which had at least one garage and fuel pumps adjacent to even infrequently traveled roads.

Lack of easily accessed, durable power sources had plagued American car owners since 1805, when millwright Oliver Evans attempted to drive a clunky steam-powered vehicle through the streets of Philadelphia, the first such recorded attempt at "driving a car" in American history. Evans had received a patent for a "steam wagon" back in 1787 — it took him another eighteen years to come up with a working model. The vehicle went only a few blocks before the city's rock-chunked streets broke its wooden tires to bits. Almost a century later, those financially able to afford cars could choose between steam, electric, and gasoline models. All had considerable drawbacks. Steam-powered cars required fireboxes, and the fires required time to light and heat the water necessary for sufficient steam. That problem paled, compared to the fact that the boilers kept exploding. Electric cars needed batteries that constantly required recharging, and these batteries remained powered up for only a few dozen miles at best. Even Thomas Edison, with financing from Henry Ford, failed to come up with a car battery that could hold a charge for hundreds of miles. Gas-powered cars were most practical, since early era tanks could hold perhaps eight to ten gallons, but finding gasoline was a challenge. Initially it could be purchased mostly in small quantities at grocery and hardware stores — people mainly used it for "vapor stoves" and lights. Some believed gasoline had healing powers if rubbed on the chests of children with colds.

As combustion (gas-powered) cars began to dominate the auto market, garages popped up in many roadside towns, often as add-ons to car dealerships. New York, Pittsburgh, and St. Louis all claimed the first stand-alone "service station" during the early years of the twentieth century, but it was 1925 before the first national chain of gas stations appeared in American towns and alongside roads. Gas was initially sold to motorists by the bucket or can, and then, gradually, via outside pumps. While gasoline remained scarce, proprietors charged whatever they could get, as much as 60 cents a gallon in isolated roadside towns where drivers had a choice of refueling or running out of gas miles from anywhere. Most early gas-powered cars managed perhaps 15 miles per gallon, with the lighter Model Ts doing somewhat better. Still, a range of about 150 miles per fill-up left motorists at the financial mercy of gas sellers until 1901, when the massive Spindletop oil strike in Texas and other subsequent successful drillings around the country made gasoline much more available throughout America. Average prices per gallon dropped to around 20 cents, with some fluctuation of a cent or two in either direction, depending on region.

The Vagabonds party filled their gas tanks in Greensburg, and also bought a linen "duster" coat for Burroughs, who wasn't sparing in his complaints about being cold the night before. There followed a further delay caused by what would become a common irritant on the trip. Virtually everyone in Greensburg surrounded the cars, maneuvering for clear glimpses of their iconic visitors. The Vagabonds wanted to get back on the road again, and town officials wanted some sort of ceremony, including remarks by Edison or Ford. But Edison never made speeches in public, and after his bumbled attempt at a public address prior to the departure of the Peace Ship, Ford wasn't about to, either. They were willing to acknowledge the crowd with friendly smiles and waves — Edison, over the years, had also perfected a courtly public bow — and, to a limited extent, chat with local reporters (so there would be Vagabonds coverage in the next issue of their newspapers) and oblige autograph seekers. But in Greensburg and almost every other subsequent stop, everyone wanted more. Throughout the trip, Firestone was always willing to step in and offer brief remarks, but in Greensburg no one wanted to listen to him. Gracefully extricating themselves from town took some time. Firestone wrote that only "after considerable effort we finally got started on our way toward Connellsville," the next town along the day's anticipated route.

But the way south to Connellsville lay on an "unfinished road," meaning it was not paved or even sanded. Hard-packed dirt pocked with divots and freckled with sharp-edged rocks proved especially hard on one of the caravan's two heavy Packards. A bouncing rock punctured the car's radiator and broke the fan that cooled it. The procession ground to a halt, too far from Greensburg to go back and still a considerable distance from a garage in Connellsville. Most auto vacationists would have been stranded, but the Vagabonds traveled with Henry Ford, who raised the Packard's hood and tinkered with the radiator leak until it was temporarily plugged, hoping it was capable of lasting the dozen miles or so to Connellsville. It did — just. But mechanics at the Wells-Mills Motor Car garage in town pronounced the damage unrepairable — all four arms of the fan were broken off. A replacement fan would have to be sent for. Considerable delay was inevitable, certainly a day at least. A reporter for the town paper wrote that "hundreds of persons" gathered around, all eager for a good look at "Edison, Ford and Burroughs [who] were of chief interest . . . all [three] were easily recognized." Firestone apparently was not.

Ford listened to the mechanics, then asked if he could borrow some of their tools. Using his own penknife and their soldering iron, he poked holes in the broken bits of fan, stitched them together with thin wire, then soldered the wire in place. The punctured point on the radiator was also soldered tight. The ignition was switched on and the

Packard ran perfectly. Ford's repair work took two hours; as soon as it was finished, he was anxious to be going. Before the passengers could pile in and resume the trip, a delegation of Connellsville ladies approached. They requested that Ford and Edison pose for a photograph beside a pile of tires being donated to the Red Cross. Probably with Firestone doing most of the talking, the Vagabonds were able to demur without causing any offense. It was a relief to get back on the bumpy road.

But not for long. Soon someone noticed that the battery-cooled commissary truck had fallen far behind, in fact out of sight. One of the Ford staff was sent back in a Model T to investigate, while the rest of the cars went on to Uniontown near the Pennsylvania–West Virginia border. Everyone was frustrated by the delays and hungry because their lunch, packed in camp that morning and described by Firestone as "fried chicken and other good things," was back on the missing commissary truck. Either Firestone or Ford had an agent in Uniontown, and he reported a phone call from the staff member who'd gone back to look for the lost truck. His message was that the vehicle's drive shaft was broken. A replacement part was on the way, but there would be further delay

179

until it arrived and could be put in place.

Ford and Edison had begun the trip determined that there would be no hotel stays at all. This time it would be camping all the way. But without the commissary truck there was no food to cook on the kitchen truck, and on only their second day out the Vagabonds found themselves in need of a hotel that could provide rooms and feed them — Burroughs was especially touchy about missing any meals. Fortunately, Ford and Firestone knew of a splendid place only a half-dozen miles from Uniontown. The Summit Hotel was a wonder, situated partway up a mountain whose crest offered a panoramic view in all directions. Many important people had stayed there, often while they attended auto races on the outdoor wood track in Uniontown. The Vagabonds had no reservations, and it was summer and the height of vacationist season, but surely no hotel of any kind would turn away Thomas Edison and Henry Ford.

They were in luck. Several rooms were available — Burroughs and DeLoach shared, as did Firestone and Harvey Jr. Ford and Edison had private rooms. Hotel staff obligingly fed the party immediately after its arrival. Firestone noted that although "all were very much opposed to a hotel," he personally found it "a very delightful opportunity to get a bath and a shave." Any notion Firestone had of a comfy late afternoon and evening indoors was soon dashed. Immediately after eating, Ford announced that he intended to hike to the very top of the mountain and wanted Firestone to come along. The tire maker afterward recalled, "Of course I wanted to be congenial, and said, 'Certainly, I will join you in anything.'" That response typified Firestone's relationships with Ford and Edison — doing what was asked of him, helping out in whatever way the two great men required.

By 1918 Harvey Firestone was a businessman of considerable national stature. Like Burroughs, Edison, and Ford, he was very much self-made. Firestone left the family farm in Ohio to work as a bookkeeper for a coal company, a salesman for questionable health-related nostrums, and, finally, a dealer in horse-drawn carriages and accoutrements. In the mid-1890s, Firestone wrote in his memoir, "for the first time it struck me that my future was right on the wheels of my buggy." Using his meager savings as start-up money, Firestone eventually established a company manufacturing rubber tires for automobiles. He realized that the solid rubber wheels utilized on early-era cars would not hold up sufficiently on the country's rough roads. Besides virtually disintegrating at a rapid rate, the solid tires had to be wrestled off car axles and replaced with the same excessive physical effort. When rich men bought the earliest American cars, they almost universally hired an assistant who not only served as chauffeur — driving involved manipulation of a complex series of levers, far beyond the ken of the nonmechanically inclined — but provided the muscle necessary for frequent tire changing.

Within a decade or so, tire manufacturers began offering "pneumatics," automobile tires modeled after those on bicycles, with hand-pump-inflated inner tubes that helped cushion rides on bumpy roads. These were almost universally crafted as "clincher" tires, somewhat bloated and doughnut-shaped, held in place by "beads" that made them easier to remove and patch or replace. Clinchers still punctured at a fearsome rate.

Much like Ford, who manufactured practical, affordable cars for the multitudes, Firestone envisioned better, longer-lasting tires. Defying established companies that adhered to rigid compliance with "clincher" patents, Firestone started his own business, naming it after himself, and through extended trial and error developed a tire with straight rather than rounded sides and a deep, wide tread for better traction on roads of all kinds. Though Firestone now had a superior product, he lacked the means of making his tires widely known to potential customers. Firestone tires would fit only on Firestone rims, and it seemed to him that all the major car manufacturers were aligned with his competitors. "We were ready to go on the market," he wrote in his memoir, *Men and Rubber,* "But there was no market to go on."

But in 1905, Firestone heard that Henry Ford of Dearborn, Michigan, planned to manufacture a fleet of two thousand cars that would sell for an unheard-of $500 each. "If I could induce him to put out these cars with our rims, then we [would] have 2,000 customers who had to use our tires to the exclusion of all others." Firestone met with Ford, who agreed to test Firestone's tires. He found them preferable both for their road performance and their price — Firestone offered them to Ford at $55 a set, compared to the $70 charged by his competitors. Firestone borrowed frantically to finance production of the huge order. In

1908, when Ford began producing Model Ts by the tens, then hundreds of thousands, he remained loyal to the manufacturer who had earlier sold him quality tires at a reasonable price. Firestone tires became one of the best-selling brands on the market, and Firestone's fortune was made.

On a personal level, Ford found that he and the younger man — Firestone was five years Ford's junior — shared several business philosophies. They disdained planned obsolescence, believing customer loyalty was best retained by providing reasonably priced commodities that could be depended upon to last a long time. Ford and Firestone were mutually convinced that the most work-efficient employees were those who felt they had a true stake in their company's success, so they paid higher wages as well as offering various forms of profit sharing. In particular, both believed that companies could be efficiently run by only one man, whose orders must be carried out by efficient subordinates.

This carried over to their acknowledged roles as Vagabonds, where they were friends but not equals. Ford paid for everything and had the overall vision for the trips. Firestone, as a willing lieutenant rather than fellow general, took care of the details. Every summer that the Vagabonds went on the road, it was Firestone who served as go-between for Ford and Edison, helping the great men coordinate schedules and pick mutually agreeable dates. Ford, or sometimes Edison (whom Firestone also considered a commanding officer), chose a general region for each excursion. Firestone studied the area, suggested routes, and was expected to know where garages and hotels might be found should the need arise. When foodstuffs like fresh milk, fruit, vegetables, and meat were needed for roadside meals, Firestone visited farms to make the purchases while Edison napped, Ford explored, and Burroughs found things to grouse about. Firestone was, in effect, trip factotum, a fact that Burroughs memorably noted in his journal: "We might pass as a real gipsy troop. Mr. Edison could play the magician and Mr. Ford the watch and clock tinkerer. I do not know about Mr. Firestone, maybe he could pass as an umbrella mender." Firestone cheerfully accepted his secondary role. It was an honor to assist Mr. Ford and Mr. Edison, and, besides, every time Firestone's name was mentioned in an article about the Vagabonds, it was splendid free advertising for Firestone tires.

It was Firestone who procured rooms at

the Summit Hotel in Uniontown, and Firestone who had to smooth things over the next day when Ford had a temper tantrum in Oakland, Maryland. The carmaker had strong opinions about diet and nutrition, abhorring manufactured sweets in particular. At an early stop in Keysers Ridge, his hackles raised when Edison asked Harvey Jr. to fetch him a "pop" from the general store. Ford loathed sugary soft drinks but couldn't bring himself to criticize his idol's indulgence in one. He still seethed, and a few hours later in Oakland when Harvey Jr. obligingly bought Burroughs some caramels from another shop — the old man's favorite kind of candy — Ford couldn't restrain himself. Harvey Firestone Jr. was poisoning venerable John Burroughs. Ford stormed over, snatched the box of confections out of the young man's hand, and flung it into the street. This violent act was witnessed by a crowd of gawkers gathered in the Oakland street, and Firestone wrote that they reacted with "great surprise." This was hardly the sort of positive publicity the Vagabonds' trip was intended to attract. Firestone apparently calmed the crowd with a few genial remarks, then hustled the travelers out of town before Ford could rant any further.

They camped that night beside Horseshoe

Run River in West Virginia. Burroughs and Ford spotted a rare bird, identified by the naturalist in his journal as a "painted bunting." This lifted the carmaker's smoldering spirits, and just in time — when word spread about their camp's location, some logging crews working in the area decided to see the celebrities. Firestone described them as "a rough-looking crowd," and one of Ford's staff reached for a Smith & Wesson holstered on his belt. But Ford, once again in control of his temper, instructed him to put the gun away, saying that "kind treatment of these friends [will] ensure our perfect safety." Firestone was less certain, but on Ford's instruction "we went out and made peace with the enemy, offering them cigars." To the tire manufacturer's surprise, though not Ford's, "they proved to be the most congenial and hospitable people we had met." They told about their work, and offered to come back in the morning, when they'd show the travelers the engine and logging train they used to haul loads from the forest to the sawmill. Ford's contingent of hired photographers came in handy — newspapers around the country carried photos of the Vagabonds posing on the train, with Ford prominently stationed at the controls of the engine.

Afterward, the loggers helped Ford's staff pack up camp, and later when the caravan stopped for gas in Parsons, West Virginia, Edison pointedly got out of his car, walked into a drugstore, and purchased what Firestone described as "a supply of milk chocolate," wordlessly rebuking Ford for his actions the day before and satisfying his sweet tooth at the same time.

The next few days of the trip were mostly uneventful. In virtually every town they passed, Edison and Ford were begged to speak. Both politely declined, and sometimes Firestone said a few words in their place. But they all posed for photos, signed autographs, and enjoyed the stories appearing about them in local papers. There were some adventures, too — once Ford spotted a farmer "cradling" or harvesting oats in his field. He jumped out of his car, helped the farmer for a while, then insisted Firestone try his hand with the oats, laughing when the city boy fumbled at the task. Burroughs, not quite as caustic as usual, described Firestone as having "doubtful success . . . the [process] was not so easy as it looked." The cars kept breaking down on rough roads. Sometimes Ford was able to perform emergency repairs, but at others the vehicles had to be left with garage mechanics overnight and for a time the caravan had to proceed in sections. West Virginia, with its hills and narrow, rutted roads, proved especially challenging. But Ford had dealerships throughout — at the time, the state economy was flourishing — so press coverage was constant, and agreeable camping spots proved easy to find. There was a hiccup in Tazewell, Virginia, where a shop owner failed to recognize Ford and refused to cash his check. One night the temperature dropped just below freezing and Burroughs and some of the crew took refuge in an area club.

August 26 found the Vagabonds entering the next phase of their journey, crossing into Tennessee, from where they would proceed to North Carolina and then back through Virginia. Burroughs compared the sensation to time travel: "A plunge into the South for a Northern man is in many ways a plunge into the Past . . . things and people in the South are more local and provincial than in the North." Most initially annoying were the ubiquitous toll roads charging each car a dime or more to pass for a few relatively smooth miles. The first well-tended American roads were toll "turnpikes" in the late 1700s. State legislatures granted licenses to private individuals who constructed lengths of smooth road at their own expense, then charged for their use — perhaps one cent per mile for a horse and rider, a similar token fee for farmers herding sheep and cattle, three cents for those well-off enough to ride in horse-drawn carriages. Those who couldn't afford tolls, or else resented paying for the use of any road, stuck to the rough dirt paths that served as alternatives. These were popularly known as "shunpikes." By the early 1900s, when automobile use proliferated and gas prices fell, many states began adding a penny or two of tax on each gallon of gasoline, using the money for road construction, improvement, or repair, and closing down toll roads. But a considerable number still remained in the South, and the Vagabonds had to fumble in their pockets for the change required to pass. Burroughs noted a 1918 Southern toll of two cents a mile for cars and five cents for trucks.

The Vagabonds' main source of regional contempt, however, shared by many fellow Northerners, was the Southern people themselves. Burroughs wrote that "at a station in the mountains of North Carolina a youngish, well-clad countryman smoking his pipe stood within a few feet of my friend[s] and me and gazed at us with the simple, blank curiosity of a child . . . there was not the slightest gleam of intelligent interest or self-consciousness on his face. It was the frank state of a five-year-old boy. He belongs to the type one often sees in the mountain districts of the South — good human stuff, valiant as soldiers and industrious as farmers, but so unacquainted with the outside world that their innocence is shocking to see."

The first day in what the Vagabonds considered the true or deep South was a difficult one in both expected and unpleasantly surprising ways. By this ninth day of the trip, everyone had grown accustomed to Burroughs's carping. He found fault with the cool night temperatures, the meals — no hot food for lunch was his chief complaint — and most of the roads. A longish stretch on the way to Bristol, Tennessee, was especially rough, and there Burroughs raised his complaining to such heights that even genial Harvey Firestone, whose account of the 1918 trip is otherwise uniformly cheery, felt compelled to record the old naturalist's rantings. Burroughs declared the roads "the most damnable and despicable in the United States." He believed that they were built by Satan, or perhaps the Germans in "one of their most cruel acts." Respect him as they did, the others were becoming weary of Burroughs's negativity.

Still, the old man's grumblings had become part of the daily routine. What happened upon arrival in Bristol wasn't. So far on the trip, reporters had appeared on virtually every stop, all of them small-town journalists thrilled at the opportunity to meet Edison and Ford, and uniformly respectful with their questions — Were they enjoying themselves? Where did they think they might stop for the night? Any amusing anecdotes to share about life on the road?

But reporters for big-city newspapers and national wire services joined local newsmen in Bristol, drawn both by the chance to impress readers with bylines from the relatively unfamiliar South, and because August 26 was just one day before a significant political primary. Henry Ford was running for one of Michigan's seats in the U.S. Senate, and voters there would go to the polls on the 27th. The questions from the press in Bristol were pointed and, for a clumsy public speaker like Ford, fraught with opportunities for poorly thought-out responses. Why was he running? If Ford won a primary nomination and went on to the general election in November, on what issues would he base his campaign? If elected, what would his first act as a U.S. senator be?

Ford was caught off guard in Bristol, and it showed. His immediate instinct, and first response, was to make clear that it hadn't been his idea to run — he did so at President Wilson's request. That much was true. By mid-1918 it seemed clear that the Allies would eventually win the war — America's late entry tipped the scales in terms of military size and war matériel. It remained uncertain how long it would take for Germany to accept defeat and seek terms, and Woodrow Wilson's vision of a postwar world was controversial. In a January speech, the president announced what became known as his Fourteen Points, a list of principles he felt must be met to ensure lasting peace. Among them was the creation of an international body where the nations of the world joined together to mediate disputes, and, if necessary, come to the immediate defense of any member finding itself under attack by an aggressor nation. This concept drew vigorous opposition from senators who believed it would surrender American autonomy to choose its own negotiations and, if necessary, battles. Any such postwar treaty proposed by Wilson would have to be ratified by the Senate. Wilson recognized that the vote would be tight. One of Michigan's Senate seats was open leading into the 1918 election cycle, and the president knew that Henry Ford, whose support had been so crucial to his own reelection two years earlier, would surely vote in favor of America's membership in the international partnership that Wilson proposed. Ford quickly agreed to run — but only on his own terms.

In Bristol, he explained these terms to the press. First, he allowed his name to be placed on both the Republican and Democratic primary ballots. In 1916, when he emerged as a possible challenger to Democrat Wilson, Ford was a Republican. But now Senate Republicans were vociferous in their opposition to Wilson's proposed international ruling body, and Ford supported the plan. Declaring himself a converted Democrat went against Ford's personal grain. He considered himself independent of partisan politics — he said what he thought, beholden to no person or organization. There was also a more pragmatic reason to enter both party primaries — Democrats and Republicans alike bought cars.

Once he declared his joint party candidacy, Ford took further steps to separate himself from traditional politicians. In Bristol, he reminded reporters about them. Ford refused to solicit campaign funds — people gave candidates money only when they wanted something from them. He wouldn't spend a cent of his own money seeking the Washington job, either. Ford also refused to actively campaign. Everyone in Michigan already knew who he was and what he stood for. If they wanted him as their senator, they'd elect him without requiring that he crisscross the state making unnecessary speeches. If he won both party primaries — and Ford felt certain that he would — then in November he'd be the only candidate for senator on the Michigan ballot, and so there would be no need for a fall campaign.

In Bristol, Ford should have concluded his remarks there. He'd made his points, and the reporters had plenty to write about. But one generic weakness among poor public speakers is not knowing when to stop. When a reporter asked which party he'd choose if both selected him, Ford quipped, "I would pitch a penny to decide which nomination I would accept, or leave it to my secretary to decide." Then, unprompted, Ford added that he couldn't actually remember the date of the primary. Was it really tomorrow?

Coverage of the Vagabonds' arrival in Bristol and Ford's comments about the Senate race took two distinct forms. The small-town press led their stories with descriptions of the visitors' stay in town, how they ate lunch at a local hotel and obligingly signed autographs. Ford's political remarks were boiled down to a sentence or two in concluding paragraphs, almost universally limited to his insistence that he wasn't actively seeking the office but would serve if the people of Michigan wanted him.

It was different among major newspapers. A *New York Times* editorial was particularly critical, citing "the bottomless depths of [Ford's] political ignorance," reminding readers that "it has not been customary to reward such [men], however amiable their characters and fat their bank accounts, with high offices of State," and concluding that his supposed plan to flip a coin in choosing between the Republican and Democratic nominations "is a sufficient fatal argument against Mr. Ford." The *Times* editorial was widely reprinted in other big-city papers, or else quoted in their own anti-Ford editorials.

That night, in the Vagabonds' camp outside Jonesborough, Tennessee, fireside talk after dinner turned to Ford and his chances in the next day's Michigan primary. Away from reporters, Ford was more thoughtful. According to Burroughs, Ford repeated that he had "no ambition that way," and admitted that his one vote among ninety-six senators might not have sufficient influence. But if Edison would also run for the Senate from New Jersey, Ford speculated, they "might together do something." First, they'd work to repeal "all the patent laws" that restrained the work of innovators like himself and the inventor. Edison wanted no part of it. He expected that Michigan would elect Ford. Speaking as though his friend wasn't present, he told the others that "when Ford goes to the Senate, he will be mum. He won't say a damn word." As for himself, Edison said, he'd never be a Senate candidate — among other things, he was too deaf. Ford took issue with that: "It isn't what you hear that makes you useful, it's what you do or say — what you tell the people." Edison wasn't convinced.

Tuesday, August 27, dawned bright and clear, but everyone in camp was still weary. Prior to their campfire political talk and post-midnight bedtime, they'd been practically overrun by well-wishers from Jonesborough, many of whom wanted to regale the visitors with extended tales of local history. Ford, frazzled by his earlier media inquisition in Bristol, lacked the patience to listen attentively. Edison stepped up, escorting the ladies in the group around camp, giving special attention to the tents and his batteries, which, he told them, brought "electric current" all the way from Orange, New Jersey. It took some time for the Tennesseans to leave the travelers in peace, and then after they finally took to their cots, cattle and pigs wandered into camp and, as Firestone recalled, "upset all the kitchen utensils and paraphernalia that was around." It made for a poor night's sleep, and any hopes of a few extra hours of cot time in the morning were shattered when a delegation of local farmers announced themselves, bringing choice watermelons for their famous visitors' breakfast. The farmers wanted the Vagabonds to come back to Jonesborough for a while — there were sights they wanted to show off. Firestone tactfully explained that the Vagabonds had to break camp immediately — they planned to end the day in Asheville, North Carolina, which was at least eighty miles away over questionable roads. Firestone felt some trepidation for what waited in Asheville. Without consulting Edison, who they knew would object, he and Ford had decided they would spend the night at the Grove Park Inn, a popular stopping place for well-to-do travelers. Burroughs's complaints about camp life had them worn down, and everyone but Edison felt the need for a bath and a night in a real bed. After Asheville, there would be another four or five days to go. Until then, the Grove Park Inn was their best chance to clean up and get some uninterrupted rest. And, since Asheville was a city of some size and connection with the outside world, at some point on Tuesday night officials there could surely inform Ford of the results of the day's U.S. Senate primary in Michigan.

The day dragged. When they stopped for lunch in Newport, Tennessee, Edison kept Firestone waiting in the hot sun while the inventor leisurely perused a newspaper. Ford and Burroughs, in a separate car, chose to drive on ahead. In Hot Springs, just within the North Carolina border, Firestone convinced Edison to stop and visit a German prisoner of war camp. The facility struck the tire maker and Edison as overly pleasant. Firestone wrote later that the 2,200 interned Germans "all looked well-kept and well-fed and certainly were having a nice vacation."

The next twenty-five miles of the route involved steep mountain roads, which made Firestone so nervous that he kept shifting from one side of his car's back passenger seat to the other, always trying to stay opposite the precipice and annoying Edison, who was sitting in back with him. Around 5 p.m., still well outside Asheville, the inventor suggested it was time to find a campsite for the night. Firestone pointed out that Ford and Burroughs were still somewhere ahead of them "and a few minutes later casually remarked that they really had gone to Grove Park Inn and we were to meet them there." When Edison balked, Firestone offered to camp for the night wherever the inventor liked, although that meant missing his own chance for a bath and bed. Edison remained displeased, but agreed to go on to the hotel.

The inventor was still testy when, in one small town on the way, the president of the local college insisted that Edison speak to the crowd gathered around him. Ford and Burroughs had driven through earlier and Firestone whispered to Edison that Ford had made a speech there, so the inventor was obligated, too. The tire maker meant it as a joke, but Edison got even. He stood up as though to speak, then turned and said loudly, "Firestone, *you* make a speech." Firestone did, remembering afterward that it was "a short talk."

The entire group reunited at the Grove Park Inn. At some point Ford learned that the news from the Michigan primary was mixed — he'd won the Democrats' nomination by a wide margin, but lost the Republican primary to former secretary of the navy Truman H. Newberry. It was upsetting because now Ford would have to compete in the fall race. It was especially galling because Newberry had adamantly opposed the $5 workday. Local reporters and some national press wanted Ford's reaction, but he refused comment. Edison, stepping in to give the journalists something to write about besides his friend's surly nonresponse, offered an opinion on the cause of war: "It's man's foolishness. That's all you can make out of it. Man is a fool."

The next morning, Burroughs announced that he'd had enough. He and Professor De-Loach took the train back to New York. No one tried to talk him out of it. After a late breakfast, Ford and Firestone went on a long walk. When they got back to the Grove Park Inn they spoke with Edison, and the three men agreed that the trucks with camping and kitchen equipment would be sent back to Michigan. For the remainder of the trip, they'd spend nights in hotels. It would prevent inconvenient evening visits from town delegations and livestock, and not coincidentally give Ford a room to shut himself up in if the media badgered him too much about the Senate race. They couldn't call off the last four days of the trip — Ford dealers and Firestone representatives in the towns ahead had already alerted local media that the Vagabonds were on the way.

The party was now down to two Model Ts for staff and a Packard with Harvey Jr. at the wheel, Edison beside him, and Firestone and Ford in back. They didn't leave Asheville until midafternoon and had almost one hundred miles to drive before reaching Hickory, where they would spend the night. It rained hard during some of the drive. They stopped in a small town for supper in a café — no more campfire meals — and didn't check into a Hickory hotel until well after dark. Ford informed local reporters that he still had no comment about the Michigan primary. It was apparently a dismal day for everyone — all Firestone wrote about it was that the hotel was noisy and he had difficulty sleeping.

Thursday was better. The morning drive to Winston-Salem was interrupted when one of the cars broke down near the town of Statesville. Ford put political concerns aside and fixed the problem within an hour. Twenty miles outside Winston-Salem, a delegation of officials in a half-dozen cars intercepted the Vagabonds on the road and announced they would lead them into town. Edison and Ford agreed to attend a luncheon in their honor and then, for the only time in the trip, made ceremonial visits to local businesses. Trailed by local reporters, Ford went to a factory where Camel cigarettes were packaged and rolled. He set aside his personal disgust with smoking to ask many questions about how the products were made and shipped, then entertained the press by comparing the Camel process to the manufacture of "U-boat destroyers and small tanks" at his own company plants, which had been converted from building cars for the duration of the war. Just before leaving, Ford made a show of taking a sample of loose tobacco for his friend Edison, who he emphasized didn't smoke, but chewed. After that, Ford briefly stopped at the Slater Industrial School "for the colored race," where some of the black students were trained as farmers. Ford donated a tractor to the school.

Edison spent his early afternoon practicing direct marketing. At a furniture store where Edison phonographs were on display, he warned a sizable group of townspeople following him that they all needed to buy his company's models while they were still available. More and more, Edison warned, his businesses would have to concentrate on "government work" until war's end. That would mean a looming, possibly lengthy shortage of Edison phonographs, which, of course, were the only brand directly associated with the man who had invented the machine.

In late afternoon they set off for Martinsville, Virginia, making the turn north that would eventually take them to their final destination in Hagerstown, Maryland. The Packard, with its famous passengers, left a little before the Model Ts. They hadn't gone far on the hard dirt road when the Packard bogged down in mud left by the previous day's rains. Edison and Ford insisted that raising the vehicle up with jacks would extricate it in no time, but after some failed attempts Firestone decided on an old-fashioned method. It was likely a relief to Ford that no press was around to record how the Packard was hauled out of the muck by a team of mules Firestone rented either from a farmer or at a nearby rail yard. The mules were hitched to the car with a chain Firestone borrowed from an impoverished woman who lived close by. She watched along with her son, a small boy Firestone described as "sickly and crippled." The mother herself had no teeth.

When the Packard was yanked free, Firestone thrilled the woman with a payment of $25, asking her to please stand by the road and warn the drivers of the Model Ts to swing wide and avoid the treacherous mud. With that, Firestone assumed his companions would be ready to be on their way, but Ford thought otherwise. His reputation for personal thrift was well-known and deserved; Ford regularly denounced most forms of charity, which he believed encouraged the collective downtrodden to rely on others rather than taking responsibility for themselves. But he could be, and occasionally was, greatly moved by the plight of individuals. Since there was a little time to spare before the Model Ts were expected to arrive, Ford escorted the toothless mother and her crippled son back to their shabby home and told her that things would be taken care of — she would have the services of a dentist and a set of fine false teeth, and her child would be taken to a hospital and receive the best care available. Afterward Ford contacted his company agent in Winston-Salem, ordering him to see that this was done. The press was never informed about the generous gesture. Ford probably feared that any stories about it would result in a flood of requests from others in similar circumstances beseeching him for largesse.

Friday was mostly spent sightseeing. Ford and the two Firestones took a tour of "Natural Bridge . . . the Cave, the Lost River and other points of interest." Edison, worn down by two weeks of continuous travel, chose to stay in the car. The others returned to find him surrounded by admirers — it was well-known that the Vagabonds were in the area, and almost everyone in America could identify Thomas Edison on sight from newspaper photos and newsreels. Edison was extricated from the crowd, and the Vagabonds ended their day at the Castle Inn in Lexington, Virginia. A private party was being held there, and the hostess tried, but failed, to get Ford and Edison as guests of honor. Firestone and Harvey Jr. substituted for them. It was certainly a source of relief that no press was present — by this point, they'd had all the publicity they wanted and, thanks to Ford, some of it not as positive as they'd hoped.

On the trip's last day, they drove through pouring rain to Hagerstown, with the drive's duration irritatingly extended by numerous stops to pay tolls — Firestone counted nineteen of them. In Hagerstown, they decided the hotel where they'd booked rooms "did not look good," so they asked others, probably Ford or Firestone agents, to recommend a better one. They were informed that their original hotel was the best in town, so they stayed there after all. After checking in, Ford and Firestone went for a walk while Edison napped in his room. They enjoyed being relatively incognito that night, and in the morning when they were ready to depart — Edison to New Jersey, Ford and the Firestones to Pittsburgh — they discreetly drove together out of town before parting to go their separate ways. Firestone wrote that they "regretted" having to part.

A few weeks later, Firestone received a letter from Burroughs, who apologized for his cantankerousness and praised Harvey Jr.: "His patience and forebearance with me and my contrary moods, I shall never forget." And, although Ford and Edison apparently took Firestone's assistance in all things for granted, Burroughs complimented his "serenity and good nature and spirit of helpfulness towards us all."

Burroughs and Firestone both wrote lengthy essays about the 1918 trip. Burroughs's was included as one chapter in a collection of remembrances titled *Under the Maples* published three years later. Firestone's never saw print, though he suggested in a December letter to Edison that his and Burroughs's work might be combined "into quite a nice souvenir book." But once they were home, neither the inventor or Ford seemed much interested in fondly looking back on the excursion. They had more immediate matters on their minds.

The war would end with the Allies triumphant on November 11, freeing Edison from his infuriatingly impotent role on the Naval Advisory Board. Now he could return to his beloved laboratory in New Jersey and focus on whatever might become his next great discovery. His ongoing fame was assured — in all the press coverage of the Vagabonds' 1918 trip, Edison's name appeared first among them in every headline except those reporting Ford's political statements and the editorials lambasting the carmaker for some of his remarks. But Edison was a proud man, and uncomfortably aware that most of his celebrity was based on achievements several decades in the past.

Though he immediately immersed himself in laboratory work with his assistants, the winter of 1918–1919 was also a contemplative one for Thomas Edison. He'd already given so much, but he was determined to find some means of accomplishing more.

Henry Ford, in contrast, spent the rest of 1918 *doing.*

First came the race for the Senate. As he'd pledged, Ford refused to campaign. Newberry, his Republican rival, spent lavishly and papered the state with print ads and cardboard placards. By normal campaign standards, Newberry should have gained an insurmountable advantage, but no amount of traditional advertising could sway the support Ford enjoyed with working-class voters. The election was clearly going to be close, and two days before, Newberry and the Republican state committee resorted to dirty politics. Though the war would end just eight days later, the conflict was still in a shooting stage and anti-German sentiment was high. The Republicans placed a full-page ad in the Sunday, November 3, *Detroit Free Press* accusing Ford of employing German sympathizers, in particular a native German named Carl Emde. The charge was ludicrous. Emde's responsibility at Ford's Highland Park, Michigan, plant was to oversee work on the Liberty airplane engines that the company built for the government, and all during the war his work had been exemplary. But the accusation was public, and instead of forcefully repudiating it, Ford dithered. He'd promised, after all, not to campaign in any way. If he responded, that would not only dignify the unfair charge, it might make Ford seem to go back on his word. He finally allowed the release of a press statement supporting Emde, but by then many Monday newspapers had already repeated the unfair charge, and on Tuesday it still lingered in the minds of voters as they went to the polls. This charge undoubtedly made the difference on Newberry's narrow victory — he beat Ford by 217,088 votes to 212,751.

Under any circumstances, the carmaker was a sore loser, and this one especially infuriated him. He hired a small army of private detectives to investigate the Newberry campaign, especially potential shady financing aspects. That effort lasted several years, and yielded sufficient results to force Newberry to resign in 1922. Even then, Ford suffered an additional indignity when the Michigan governor appointed former Ford executive James Couzens to the vacated Senate seat.

Ford couldn't control political results, but he was determined to be the sole controlling voice of Ford Motor Company. Ford owned only 58.5 percent of the company. For many years, he'd resented the half-dozen or so fellow stockholders whose views sometimes conflicted with his own, especially when two, brothers John and Horace Dodge, successfully sued him for putting too large a share of profits back into the company rather than paying appropriate dividends to shareholders. Angered by his loss to Newberry, and still nursing a grudge against the Dodges for their lawsuit, on December 30 Ford shocked America by resigning as company president. His son, Edsel, would assume the job in his place, but no one need worry that Ford himself would still make the decisions. Instead, he was going to start an entirely new automobile manufacturing enterprise, one based out in California. Word soon reached the press that Ford had already designed a better, cheaper car than the Model T. His new company would build it and wrest control of the market. Ford Motor Company stockholders assumed the threat was real, and within weeks agreed to sell Ford their shares at a whopping $12,500 a share. (James

Couzens, who knew Ford best, held out and received $13,000 for each of his.) Though Ford had to borrow $60 million of the near $106 million total cost, he was still glad to do it. It had been an elaborate bluff, but he was now in complete control of Ford Motor Company.

A subsequent act typified the complex nature of Ford's personality, the sort of contradictory act that made him then and later so difficult to fathom. Ford had sworn at the outset of the war that he would not accept even a penny of personal profit for company war-related services. On November 11, 1918, the war ended, and Ford Motor Company had charged the American government in full for its work. Now was the time for Henry Ford to send a check to the U.S. Treasury, reimbursing the government for whatever percentage of its payments ended up in his personal bank account. Eventually that sum was calculated at $926,780.97 — and Ford never repaid it.

Ford ended 1918 with one more act that initially received little notice. Angry at what he considered unfair reporting, mostly by the powerful Eastern and Northeastern press, he decided to buy a newspaper of his own. The content would reflect Henry Ford's views in all things from politics to economics, just as the Model T reflected his firm belief in dependable no-frills automobiles. The American public embraced the Model T. Ford was certain they'd be equally enthusiastic about a newspaper he owned, which soon would rival even the major New York papers in circulation and influence. In December, even as he played his successful trick on Ford Motor Company shareholders, Henry Ford purchased his local newspaper, a tiny, undistinguished weekly called the *Dearborn Independent.*

CHAPTER FIVE:
1919

Americans had reason to stand united and proud immediately following World War I. U.S. entry into the conflict essentially won the war for the Allies. For the first time, America was recognized internationally as a global power. Domestically, the economy appeared healthy, even robust, and many citizens enjoyed better lifestyles — including higher wages and resulting access to forms of entertainment and travel — than would have been possible only a generation earlier. Even the 1918 flu pandemic, which killed nearly five times as many Americans as had the enemy during the war (approximately 500,000 sickbed deaths to 110,000 on the battlefield), apparently was over, though no one was entirely certain why. Yet between the Civil War and the turmoil of the late 1960s, 1919 was the most chaotic year in American history, as civil unrest shook the nation.

It began with widespread suspicion of insidious foreign designs on America's government and workforce. Following the war, isolationists vehemently opposed President Wilson's intention of committing the nation to any peace treaty mandating U.S. membership in an international ruling body. Why should America, apparently on the brink of a Golden Age of military, economic, and cultural superiority, be obligated to risk it all in foreign squabbles? America would prosper best on its own, free of outside demands for its blood and treasure. Yet between December 1918 and July 1919, President Wilson was almost entirely abroad in France, negotiating with foreign leaders, apparently paying no heed to the daily affairs of his own nation, where there was much that could — and to many minds, should — have commanded his undivided attention.

Beginning in Seattle in early February, America was plagued by prolonged, often violent labor strikes, more than two thousand of them by September, encompassing not only factory workers but telephone operators and policemen. (Massachusetts governor Calvin Coolidge gained national notoriety when he broke a Boston police strike, stating memorably, "There is no right to strike against the public safety by anybody, anywhere, any time.") Union organizers were determined to gain some level of management parity for their members, not only higher wages but improved conditions and fewer hours for the workers.

Race-related riots erupted from Longview, Texas, to Chicago. The Great Migration began before World War I, as black Americans mired in Southern poverty sought greater employment possibilities in the industrial North. Racial tensions flared in both regions. In the South, lynchings proliferated, and, for the first time, major Northern cities developed black slums. Many white-led labor unions refused membership to blacks. It was inevitable that violence should occur, and it frequently did.

American women determined to claim the universal right to vote abandoned genteel protest for more vocal demands. While Woodrow Wilson attempted to help form a new world order in France, sixty-five U.S. suffragists burned the president in effigy in front of the White House.

Many national leaders, and a burgeoning number of ordinary citizens, attributed the widespread turmoil to a single, malign source:

Bolshevism. Or, even more frequently,

216

Reds. Many Americans feared an influx of Red (or Bolshie, or commie) agents posing as immigrants pouring into the U.S. and initiating unrest. It was common knowledge that the Russian Revolution began with a series of labor strikes, and in many of those now occurring in the U.S., organizers were suspected of communist sympathies, if not outright Bolshevik ties. From there, it was easy for the suspicious-minded to link Red influence to American race riots — the commies were *encouraging* the blacks! — and the suffragist movement — egged on by the Bolshies, women no longer knew their place. Then on June 2, a coordinated terrorist attack set off bombs in eight cities across America, including on the front steps of Attorney General A. Mitchell Palmer's residence in Washington, D.C. Two people died, and it was widely accepted that these might prove to be only the first such attacks, which almost certainly were the work of Bolshevik agents, possibly in league with American sympathizers.

It was in this paranoid atmosphere that Woodrow Wilson returned to the U.S. in July, determined that the Senate should ratify the Treaty of Versailles, including American membership in a League of Nations to preside over international affairs.

Wilson was a Democrat. Republicans, sensing a convergence of moral responsibility and political opportunity, stood firm in opposition. With a two-thirds majority vote needed for ratification and Republicans holding just over half of the Senate's ninety-six seats, the treaty could be approved only if all Democratic senators voted in favor (itself a dubious possibility) and Wilson convinced more than a dozen Republicans to defy their party leadership. When too many senators balked, Wilson took his case directly to the American people — if he could persuade enough voters in both parties to support the treaty, senators back in Washington would get the message. The president embarked on a trip intended to last more than three weeks, crisscrossing the nation, attempting to sell the relatively new notion that America's responsibilities no longer ended at its shores. It was an exhausting task for a fit man, and Wilson had never been especially healthy. Worn down by headaches, asthma, digestive problems, and double vision, Wilson suffered a severe stroke that resulted in paralysis of his left side. White House doctors covered up the extent of the president's illness, describing it as "nervous exhaustion" that could be remedied by rest. In November, with Wilson still out of action, the Senate rejected the Treaty of Versailles and the League of Nations by a vote of 38 for and 53 against.

It seemed that almost every week in 1919, Americans found themselves confronted with more staggering news, awful events piling up one upon the other, reinforcing the spreading belief that it was dangerous to trust anyone. Even the country's beloved national pastime was tainted that year, when eight members of the losing Chicago White Sox were indicted for fixing baseball's World Series against the unfortunately named Cincinnati Reds. (In 1953, during the Cold War and a second Red Scare, the Cincinnati club changed its name from "Reds" to "Red-legs." It changed back to "Reds" five years later.)

America desperately needed some kind of wholesome distraction from its troubles, and reassurance that at least a few of its most famous citizens were above suspicion. A highly publicized, widely covered car trip by the Vagabonds perfectly fit the bill — but first there was an opening act. Three years after filing a million-dollar libel suit against the *Chicago Tribune,* Henry Ford was finally getting his day in court.

To everyone other than himself, Ford

219

seemed unlikely to prevail. Even if the *Tribune* story stating Ford Motor Company denied leave to employees called up for National Guard duty on the U.S.-Mexico border had key details wrong, the information was furnished to the reporter in an on-the-record interview by a company spokesman, though not Ford himself. The subsequent *Tribune* editorial was certainly insulting, and "anarchist" was a poor description of the automaker, who plainly favored dialogue over violent government overthrow. But florid editorial overstatement was an accepted part of a free press — editorials were, after all, expressions of opinion. Finally, and perhaps most critically, every other major newspaper in the country was certain to take the *Tribune*'s side — a successful suit by Ford might encourage other national figures to initiate their own lawsuits.

It was not in the nature of Thomas Edison and Henry Ford's friendship for one to directly offer personal advice to the other. Any counsel was communicated through messages between their secretaries, so on November 12, 1918, the day after World War I officially ended, Edison's secretary W. H. Meadowcroft sent a letter on Edison's behalf to Ernest Liebold at the Ford

Motor Company, warning that in the libel trial "the lawyers on the other side will lay a great deal of stress on Mr. Ford's statements in the early part of the war, and the newspapers will magnify it and make the most of it. . . . Mr. Edison hopes that Mr. Ford will think the matter over carefully and inasmuch as the war is all over that Mr. Ford will call off his suit against the *Chicago Tribune* and let the matter drop. Will you please give this message of Mr. Edison to Mr. Ford?"

If Liebold did, Ford ignored it. He fully expected to win. It wasn't simply hubris — Ford beat the odds in a previous, highly publicized court case, and emerged not only vindicated but as a hero to much of the public. The risk to Ford had been far greater then.

In 1879, well before more than a handful of automobiles lurched along American roads, a Rochester, New York, attorney named George B. Selden made a patent application for a gas-powered car that existed only in his imagination. Over the next decade and a half Selden made periodic adjustments to the application, and when the patent was eventually issued in 1895 (there were finally enough cars in America to make it worth

221

Selden's while) it meant that all manufacturers attempting to build and sell gas-powered vehicles for the next seventeen years, or through 1912, legally required Selden's permission to do so. And that would be expensive.

Selden sold the patent rights to the curiously named Electric Vehicle Company, which in turn created the Association of Licensed Automobile Manufacturers. Carmakers who didn't want to face legal wrath had to join the ALAM, paying a $2,500 entry fee and a 1.25 percent royalty of the total price of each gas-powered car they sold. Selden and the Electric Vehicle Company split the proceeds. Auto manufacturers grudgingly complied — it seemed they had no other option. ALAM membership was granted only to those applicants whose companies seemed likely to succeed at a level making them lucrative. When Henry Ford applied in 1903 on behalf of the newly formed Ford Motor Company, he was rejected. He'd failed with his two previous companies so ALAM had no confidence in his chances with a third.

Faced with giving up and folding his company or fighting, Ford fought. He built and sold his cars anyway. Ford's publicists pointed out in numerous newspaper ads that one reason his cars were cheaper was that no "patent royalty" was included in the price. Ford proclaimed himself an underdog in the ongoing squabble, a small-business owner brave enough to defy a corporate giant. It played well with consumers, especially after an ALAM ad in Detroit papers warned that anyone even "using [non-licensed cars] . . . will be liable to prosecution for infringement." Ford's response ad promised that his company would "protect" its customers "against any prosecution for alleged infringements of patents," adding that "no court in the United States" would rule in favor of ALAM. It was an obvious dare for the Electric Vehicle Company and ALAM to bring suit against Ford.

Soon afterward, they did. The case dragged on for years. ALAM had Selden's 1895 patent, good through 1912, and Ford had public opinion, plus his argument that he'd been building experimental gas-driven vehicles before Selden's patent went into effect. The machine Selden finally patented was barely functional. It could hardly be called the model on which superior gas-powered cars were based. But in 1909, a federal court found in Selden and ALAM's favor. Ford refused to accept the verdict and filed an appeal. In the interim, most of the other car manufacturers who'd sided with Ford gave up and joined ALAM. That was fine with Ford — it only embellished his role as the brave, lonely businessman who had the courage to take on a conglomerate. But now the stakes had changed for Ford. In 1903, he was trying to get his company started. In 1909, Ford's Model T was the rage among American motorists, and if his appeal was lost, millions of dollars would be awarded by the court to ALAM, possibly bankrupting Ford Motor Company.

Ford's gamble paid off in January 1911, when an appellate court reversed the federal court's verdict, essentially ruling that Selden's patent was insufficient and no carmakers were required to pay licensing fees because of it. Every auto manufacturer in America benefited, but none as much as Ford, particularly when ALAM decided not to appeal and eventually disbanded. Just as he had with the utilitarian, inexpensive Model T, Ford had defied the odds and prevailed. Once again, his instincts were right and everyone else's wrong. In 1916, cautioned from all sides that continuing his libel suit against the *Chicago Tribune* was sheer folly, Ford relished the opportunity to prove his doubters wrong again. Even before May 12, when the judge gaveled the first day of testimony into order, Ford worked to ensure that every possible aspect would be in his favor.

It began with the trial's venue. The *Tribune* wanted the case tried in a major city's court, where the majority of the juror pool would, presumably, be sophisticated enough to recognize the right of the media to express editorial opinion. Ford and his legal team wanted a rural venue, where Ford's man-of-the-people appeal would seem in stark contrast to a big-city newspaper's elitist name-calling. Ford's team of lawyers prevailed here — after much debate, the trial was set in Mount Clemens, Michigan, a modest town not far from Detroit, and where the jury was comprised mostly of farmers.

By now Ford mistrusted big-city media as much as he did Wall Street bankers, and he realized that the only daily coverage likely to emanate from Mount Clemens would be generated by major newspapers like the *Tribune* and the increasingly ubiquitous national wire services, mostly based out of New York City and Washington, D.C. All across the nation, small-town dailies whose readers wanted news of the trial could rely only on what Ford expected to be biased coverage by news outlets intent on supporting their fellow print heavyweight. But for the past six months, Ford had his own newspaper, and now he put the *Dearborn Independent* to work on his behalf. From the outset, Ford and the experienced editors he'd hired, mostly from Detroit newspapers, realized that they must completely refurbish the *Independent*'s editorial and art content if it was to attain the kind of circulation necessary to equal (and eventually surpass — Ford never aimed low) that of nationally influential papers like the *New York Times*. Ford even broke unspoken protocol to directly request that Edison look over the *Independent* and make suggestions for improvement. Edison, for once feeling free to tell Ford exactly what he thought, responded bluntly. He described the *Independent* as "a dreary proposition" for most readers, with "very poorly executed illustrations" — readers wanted to look at pictures as well as read — and with potential subscriber appeal limited by too many editorials espousing Ford's personal beliefs and otherwise "not a lot of interesting things." Edison stressed that his intention wasn't to offend Ford — "I am anxious that [you] shall make the paper one that everybody wants." If his friend would "get on to the style of the stuff the public wants, [you] will gradually bring [the] paper around to a point where its power for good will be immense."

In May, just before the *Tribune* trial began, on Ford's instructions the *Dearborn Independent* established a news bureau in offices across the street from the Mount Clemens courthouse. A map of the United States was hung on one wall, and in *The Public Image of Henry Ford* historian David L. Lewis notes that it "was bristling" with colored pins, about 12,500 blue ones representing small papers believed sympathetic to Ford and 397 yellow pins for larger, anticipated anti-Ford publications. Each day of the trial — and it turned out that there were many of them — the *Independent*'s newly minted "Mount Clemens News Bureau" made available to the sympathetic papers news stories of the day's proceedings written by bureau reporters. Recipients were assured that these were objective reports, "not propaganda," though they routinely excluded details that presented Ford poorly. The mostly small-town daily and weekly papers gladly reprinted whatever the Mount Clemens News Bureau offered, since these were free and the other national wire services charged for their stories. Ford also granted pretrial interviews to selected reporters, telling one that "history is more or less bunk. . . . We want to live in the present, and the only history that is worth a tinker's dam is the history we make today." It was a comment that would come back to haunt him.

During the trial, both sides contributed to a circuslike atmosphere. The *Tribune* flooded Mount Clemens with Texans who took turns describing to the jury and pro-*Tribune* reporters how Mexican desperados had and continued to commit all sorts of depraved acts along the U.S.-Mexico border, the implication being that Ford didn't care if fellow Americans were beaten, robbed, and raped. The Texans ostentatiously wore outsized Stetson hats and jangling spurs. Ford, in turn, imported Mexican nationals, who wore sombreros and gave every appearance of being unthreatening. But the highlight of the trial's fourteen weeks, the only testimony that really mattered, came in July when Henry Ford took the stand.

Ford was questioned by Elliott K. Stevenson, the *Tribune*'s attorney. Stevenson was from Detroit, and already familiar with the carmaker's laconic way of expressing himself. Wearing a dark suit, Ford slouched in a wooden chair, appearing relaxed and even a little bored as Stevenson approached the witness stand. Stevenson's first question — "What do you know about history?" — revealed the heart of the *Tribune*'s trial strategy, which was to expose Henry Ford to the jury, and the world, as the ignorant man it described him as being, someone deserving editorial scorn even if one canard ("anarchist") had perhaps been misapplied.

After some verbal sparring, Ford said he didn't know much about history "because I live in the present." He similarly admitted not understanding the fundamentals of American government: "It's a long subject." Asked to give the date of the American Revolution, Ford guessed, "Eighteen-twelve." Stevenson followed with more questions, including who was Benedict Arnold, and what did the word "ballyhoo" mean? Ford's responses were, respectively, "A writer," and "A blackguard or something of that nature." He'd never heard of chili con carne. When Stevenson theatrically wondered how anyone could remain so uninformed about so much, Ford responded that he didn't need to personally know such things: "I could [hire] a man in five minutes who could tell me all about [them]."

Stevenson asked Ford several times to read portions of documents out loud. Ford repeatedly declined, saying he'd forgotten his spectacles. Sensing an opening, Stevenson pounced.

"I think the impression has been created by your failure to read some of these things that have been presented to you that you could not read. Do you want to leave it that way?"

"Yes, you can leave it that way," Ford replied. "I am not a fast reader and I have the hay fever and I would make a botch of it."

Stevenson persisted. "Can you read at all?"

"I can read."

"Do you want to try it?"

"No, sir."

Ford's responses were just as clipped in response to friendly questions from his own attorney, Alfred Lucking. Was Ford an anarchist? "No, sir." Ever personally broken the law? "Speeding, yes." Had he ever associated with anarchists? "No." Were, in fact, his associates Thomas Edison and John Burroughs, the naturalist? "Yes."

Lucking saved a key question for the end. He and Ford acknowledged that prior to America's entry into the European war, the automaker vigorously opposed U.S. participation.

"When the government got into the war,

you cooperated?"

"Yes."

Stevenson objected to the question — anything Ford had done after the *Tribune* editorial ran on June 18, 1916, ten months prior to the U.S. entering the war, was immaterial to the trial.

Lucking shot back, "The leopard does not change his spots, Mr. Stevenson."

On August 14, the case went to the jury. Ten hours later, their verdict was announced in Ford's favor — the *Tribune* had libeled him. But instead of the $1 million requested by the carmaker in damages, the jurors awarded Ford six cents. Both sides claimed vindication. It was the unanimous conclusion of most major publications on both coasts and in big cities throughout the U.S. that Ford had been humiliated and might never recover in public opinion. The *New York Times* compared Ford's witness stand quizzing to a history test in school, and "he has not received a pass degree." *The Nation* concluded that "the unveiling of Mr. Ford has much of the pitiful about it, if not the tragic. We would rather have had the curtain drawn, the popular ideal unshattered." The *San Jose Mercury Herald,* previously gung ho for Ford during his 1915 visit to the

Panama-Pacific Exposition, predicted that future mention of Ford "will be to the accompaniment of laughter and ridicule . . . the great problems affecting mankind are not to be understood by the ignoramus."

But rank-and-file Americans, particularly in Midwestern and Southern states, thought quite the opposite. Ford received thousands of letters with the general message that if he were an anarchist, then America needed more of them. Ford was the son of a Michigan farmer, and like most rural Americans of the time his formal education was limited to a few years in local schools and teachers who themselves had often not graduated high school. Then he had to leave school to make a living. Like Ford, many of his countrymen read only with difficulty, if at all. Their understanding of American history was limited, but like him they knew they loved their country, though they had suspicions about its leaders similar to Ford's. They, too, might not remember the exact date of the American Revolution, but they knew that Henry Ford introduced the $5 workday and a car that ordinary people could afford. They identified with Ford so strongly that newspaper attacks on him were taken as insults directed at them. More than ever after the trial, wrote historian Reynold M. Wik, "Reality became confused with legend [and common] people . . . visualized Ford as they thought him to be, not as he was."

One way or the other, all America was fascinated by Henry Ford, and this put many major newspapers in a contradictory position. Having done their best during and immediately after the *Tribune* trial to convince readers that Ford wasn't worthy of attention, they still were obligated to continue covering his every public statement and act — people wanted stories about Ford. That these stories continued giving Ford a platform for his frequently outrageous pronouncements, and free publicity for his cars, mattered less to his critics in the press than selling newspapers. Even before the *Tribune* trial was over, the same papers blasting Ford editorially also printed upbeat stories about the Vagabonds' latest trip, which commenced immediately after Ford stepped down from the witness stand, and almost two weeks before the jury returned its verdict.

On July 1, Edison received a telegram from Ernest Liebold informing him that Mr. Ford hoped for an "Adirondack motor trip . . . July twenty-fifth or shortly thereafter. Please advise." Edison replied that the plan was satisfactory — "We can look in Adirondacks and part of Vermont." On the night of August 4, with the Mount Clemens trial still ten days away from jury resolution, all four Vagabonds camped just outside Troy, New York, at Green Island, where Ford planned to build a tractor plant. The carmaker completely reoutfitted the group's camping gear with new tents, a lazy Susan table, and two specially crafted vehicles. Firestone described these as Car A — "As fully furnished a kitchen and pantry as could be devised. On the running board was a large gasoline stove fed from the motor tank, and inside the car was a built-in ice box and compartments for every kind of food that we needed" — and Car B — "compartments for each tent and bed and everything needed to make camp. It was mounted on a truck chassis."

The *New York Times* published a straight-forward story describing the planned-for "vacation camping trip through the Adirondack Mountains." The *Kansas City Times* preferred a snarkier approach: "Henry Ford will probably enjoy the vacation he is spending with Mr. Edison and Mr. Burroughs, there being hardly any occasion when either of those gentlemen will be likely to ask him for information on any subject." But major newspapers assigned reporters to write about the Vagabonds setting off, while smaller publications relied on wire services. Here the travelers broke from their previous tradition of speaking to the press only during stops in towns. For the first time, a wire service reporter was allowed to spend a night in camp with them and describe in detail what was supposedly a typical Vagabonds evening around the campfire. The reporter was George R. Holmes, staff correspondent for the Hearst International News Service (INS). During the *Tribune* trial, Hearst newspapers had been supportive of Ford — a Hearst columnist suggested that the automaker's supporters write him letters declaring America needed more anarchists like him. The four famous campers anticipated that the INS wire reports, reprinted in hundreds of daily and weekly papers throughout the country, would be glowing. Holmes's initial story, published on August 9, was exactly what they wanted:

Out of the inky blackness that hangs like a shroud over the Adirondacks these nights, there blooms nightly along some quiet mountain stream a ghost-like tented village. . . . Eight tents, almost transparent with the incandescent lamps inside them, stood out last night like so many jewels against the velvet blackness of the forest on all sides. In the center of the tiny village a campfire burned, for it is nippy in the mountains these nights.

After setting the scene, Holmes portrayed the campers as sitting up late, discussing weighty subjects. Ford, "holding up a two-day old newspaper which he had picked up in some forgotten village," noted that "there's a big rumpus over the cost of living down in Washington." As Holmes described it, Burroughs "nodded affirmatively." Edison, dozing in a camp chair, "said nothing." Ford declared that the real problem was national leaders who overthought such problems: "Like all things, the solution will be easy when it comes. What the world needs is men who know how to do things." Burroughs speculated that prices rose because "nowadays everything comes wrapped up in fancy packages. That's one reason why the cost of living is so high."

Ford lamented "middle men" who charged outrageously to take farmers' products and convey them to market, as well as the excess time and trouble required of farmers to harvest their crops at all: "I know one thing that I can do to bring [prices] down. If for the next four or five years I would devote all my time to developing [a more efficient] farm tractor and put it on every farm in the United States, it will bring down the cost of living. And I'm going to do it."

The Vagabonds certainly staged the conversation for Holmes on the evening he was allowed to visit their camp. But they also talked around the campfire on the other nights when no press was present — it was part of the trips' appeal that, away from outsiders, they could express themselves on whatever topics and however bluntly they chose. Sometimes an evening's main topic had nothing to do with business or politics. One night on the 1919 summer trip there was lengthy debate over the quality of acclaimed literary classics. Edison dominated, insisting that the greatest works ever were Longfellow's epic poem *Evangeline* and Victor Hugo's novel *Les Misérables.* He dismissed Shakespeare's plays, insisting they would "read better" if translated into "common everyday speech."

Another evening, a campfire conversation between Firestone and Edison firmly set the seventy-two-year-old inventor on the research path that consumed him for the rest of his life. Firestone recalled it in his memoir:

I started to talk to Mr. Edison about rubber and its properties, and I was astounded at the knowledge of rubber that he had on hand. I had been working with rubber for many years, but he told me more than I knew and more than I think [my] chemists knew — although, to the best of my knowledge, Mr. Edison had never given any attention to rubber. . . . But it is that way with any subject one brings up with Mr. Edison.

In fact, rubber had been at least occasionally on Edison's mind since his 1915 visit to Luther Burbank's laboratory in Santa Rosa, California. He and Burbank chatted briefly then about the latter's efforts to breed latex-bearing plants that would flourish sufficiently in the U.S. America used the majority of rubber available throughout the world but produced virtually none of it. In his World War I tenure on the Naval Advisory Board, Edison became aware of a critical reason for America to supply its own rubber — it was always possible for rubber-producing nations to deny the product to

Americans, and during wars enemy submarines could prey on rubber shipments to the U.S., in particular crippling military motor vehicles through tire shortages.

Though he'd certainly considered rubber-related research before, Edison's 1919 campfire interaction with Firestone apparently made his mind up — the means of producing American rubber would be his next great focus. It would require not only extensive study of how to get the necessary plants to grow in some part of the country, but also the development of new methods of extracting latex in the most efficient, economical way. Besides the national benefit — tires and other rubber products had become increasingly necessary — inventing the means of mastering rubber production, and establishing companies that did it, would also boost Edison's personal finances. He was far from a poor man, but his wealth was considerably less than might have been expected of a man whose imagination and hard work had brought countless popular products to consumers. Press speculation pegged the overall value of Edison-related goods and the industrial firms manufacturing them at an astronomical $15 billion, but not much of that accrued to the inventor himself. Time and again, he'd invented things with long-term market appeal only to lose interest or miscalculate what form of his inventions consumers wanted to buy. Examples were plentiful.

Edison invented the phonograph and his company was first to bring it into stores, but for nearly a decade after that he focused on other projects while competitors built and marketed their own phonographs, over time depriving the originator of what could have been an Edison-dominated business. Edison not only invented the incandescent bulb, he created the most efficient generator systems to light them. Edison's company was poised to power every major city, and by 1919 almost half the households in America had electricity. But Edison didn't financially benefit. Years earlier, he sold his power interests to competitors. They eventually formed General Electric, and GE rather than Edison raked in substantial profits.

Edison Company films were huge hits during the early years of motion pictures. Popular Edison titles included *The Great Train Robbery* and *Uncle Tom's Cabin*. All were two-reelers; the longest was twenty-five minutes. But moviegoers soon wanted longer films, and four-reelers became the norm. Edison, though, liked two-reelers better, and wouldn't produce anything longer.

Ticket sales for Edison films declined precipitously, and by 1918 he'd sold off all of his film interests. The same was substantially true for recorded music. For years, Edison recordings dominated. But Americans began enjoying jazz, and wanted those records. Edison hated jazz. He insisted that his company release only recordings of more traditional music, especially the symphonies and operas that he personally preferred. Predictably, competitors' recordings soon outsold Edison's, and by 1929 Edison's companies no longer produced "entertainment" records.

Edison's Vagabond friends lamented his business judgment. Ford said, "Edison is easily the world's greatest scientist. I am not sure that he is also not the world's worst businessman. He knows nothing of business." Firestone agreed: "Mr. Edison thinks almost wholly creatively and does not give the same thought to commerce that he gives to creation." When Edison evinced interest in exploring means of growing latex-bearing plants and manufacturing rubber in America, which would provide him with new opportunities not only to invent, but to make money, both Ford and Firestone enthusiastically encouraged him to do so, and promised to invest in his efforts.

While Edison pondered the possibilities of rubber, Ford spent much of the 1919 trip frolicking. He was certain that he'd emerge triumphant in the Mount Clemens trial, and he expressed his high spirits in a Firestone-related prank. Ford ordered the camp cooks to slice thin strips off wooden tent stakes, then boil them into soup served to Firestone, who gagged on them. Firestone responded by bedecking Ford's shiny new kitchen and equipment trucks with signs reading "Buy Firestone Tires."

Burroughs, as usual, was the grumpiest among the group. Though the naturalist found some things to like about Vermont — "The view of the White Mountains . . . very impressive. These great rocky peaks shouldering the sky. . . . Simply stupendous!" — Burroughs wasn't impressed with upper New York state, especially since their route north was almost exactly the same as the Fordless Vagabonds had followed in 1916. He noted in his journal, "Coming from New England . . . into New York is stepping down to a lower level."

Each trip, Burroughs had specific complaints. On this one, it was the meals. Ford had along his personal chef, and the new kitchen/refrigerator truck ensured that fine ingredients were always on hand. But Burroughs found fault with food temperature and serving times. "It is the same old story — dinner at 8 or 9 p.m.," he wrote. "I have just told Mr. Ford I must have a warm dinner in the middle of the day or I quit. . . . Mr. Ford says I shall have the warm dinner. I will not live on cold snacks." The inventor came in for criticism, too: "Edison is a dictator. He shuns all the good state roads and hunts up rough, hilly dirt roads."

Even so, in his public and private writings Burroughs generally praised Edison and Ford. To some extent, self-interest was involved. As with Firestone's tires, Burroughs's books increased in public appeal through his presence on the Vagabonds' trips. But Burroughs's admiration for the pair seems genuine. He wrote of Edison, "He is a great character, and we are all devoted to him." The old man's praise of Ford was even more lavish: "Not withstanding his practical turn of mind and his mastery of the mechanic arts . . . he is through and through an idealist. This combination of power and qualities makes him a very interesting and, I may say, lovable personality."

■ ■ ■ ■

But one night's 1919 campfire conversation, probably early on the trip and without INS correspondent Holmes on hand to eavesdrop, partially convinced Burroughs that Ford was less than lovable and Edison unworthy of absolute devotion. As they digested their dinners, the two famous men took turns regaling each other, Firestone, and Burroughs with reasons that Jews were the scourge of mankind. Their joint diatribe apparently began after Edison complained about the rampant problems he'd perceived during the war while dealing with the Navy. That set Ford off. According to Burroughs, the carmaker "attribute[d] all evil to the Jews or Jewish capitalists — the Jews caused the war, the Jews caused the outbreak of thieving and robbery all over the country, the Jews caused the inefficiency of the navy which Edison talked about." Ford even had a specific culprit in mind, railroad speculator Jay Gould, whom he scornfully described as a Jewish "shylock." Here Burroughs interrupted, explaining that, as it happened, he and Jay Gould had been childhood friends, and the Gould family was Presbyterian. After that, Burroughs retired to his tent, leaving Ford and Edison to continue the conversation on their own, and troubled that Edison seemed in complete agreement with Ford. Burroughs failed to describe Firestone's reaction, and neither the tire manufacturer or the naturalist ever mentioned the incident in their public writings about the Vagabonds. They apparently accepted that antisemitism was an unfortunate flaw among the many positive attributes of their two famous friends.

Despite Burroughs's and Firestone's efforts to conceal it, Ford's antisemitism would soon become common knowledge. In the century since, historians have tried to determine its root cause. Some point to Ford's childhood, where his limited formal education was based in part on the McGuffey readers, popular tomes for children setting out moral guidelines and relegating Jews to the role of swarthy villains opposed to white, moral Christians. Others point to Ford's reflexive belief in plots and cabals, particularly involving international banking and finance, which many (Ford included) believed were controlled by Jews. Possibly through Ernest Liebold, his secretary and primary Ford Motor Company confidant, Ford was familiar with *The Protocols of the Elders of Zion,* a malicious manifesto of Jews conspiring to gain control of the world through infiltration of business and government. *Protocols* had long been revealed as a clumsy forgery, but Liebold and Ford persisted in believing every word because it reinforced their own prejudice. The carmaker himself sometimes said that he truly learned to mistrust Jews during the Peace Ship effort — Rosika Schwimmer was the obvious culprit.

All these factors certainly had some effect on Ford, but identifying any as the single key factor in his antisemitism ignores a simpler, more common influence. In the early twentieth century (and, it can be argued, ever since), America was the domain of white Protestant males who automatically considered anyone else inferior, and, if in any position of even potential influence, a threat to the *right* way of doing things. Ford in some ways was more enlightened than most of his white male peers. He hired blacks at his companies, where some attained management positions. There were a few individual Jews whom Ford considered friends. He didn't openly oppose the suffragist movement, and he held his wife, Clara, in high regard, valuing her advice in both business and his private life. But in his mistrust and loathing of the Jews as a race, he was typical of his times.

Although Edison's prejudices remained less public, they were racist as well as anti-semitic. Prejudice was part of some Edison recordings' market appeal, including "The Whistling Coon" and "Row at a Negro Ball," which simulated sounds of (supposedly) black men brawling before police arrived.

In the draft of a 1911 letter, Edison attempted to qualify his mistrust of Jews, explaining that current prejudice against them was really the responsibility of earlier generations of bigots:

The Jews are certainly a remarkable people, as strange to me in their isolation from the rest of mankind as those mysterious people called Gypsies. . . . [While] the moment they get into art, music, science & literature the Jew is fine — the trouble with the Jew [is] that he has been persecuted for centuries by ignorant malignant bigots & forced into his present characteristics and he has acquired a 6th sense which gives him an almost unerring judgment in [financial] affairs. . . . He has taken too great an advantage of it & got himself disliked by many.

No mention of disturbing campfire conversations marred press coverage of the 1919 trip. Local papers enthusiastically described even brief Vagabonds stops in their towns. On August 11, the St. Johnsbury, Vermont, *Caledonian-Record* noted that the town had "the honor Sunday afternoon of entertaining for half an hour four of the country's most famous men . . . the party got out [and] enjoyed a cool bottle of ginger ale. . . . They all looked like they were having the time of their 'young lives.' " A few days after his initial report, INS correspondent George Holmes was allowed another exclusive visit to a Vagabonds camp, this time for breakfast in a field near Plattsburgh, New York. The celebrated travelers spoke in favor of the proposed League of Nations and deplored ongoing labor strikes around the country. Burroughs pointed out that nature never went on strike, and Ford declared that "strikes are all put-up jobs, anyway . . . the [strikers] themselves suffer. Strikes are senseless things." Ford then directly addressed Holmes about the proper role of the media: "You are in the greatest business in the world. The press in this country can do more good than anything in the world if it will only print what's right and drive home essential things." Holmes dutifully repeated the comment in his story.

With access to the travelers limited to a few moments during their stops in towns, other wire services and major newspapers had little option but to entertain their readers with innocuous Vagabonds minutiae. The *Kansas City Star* described what they ate for lunch on August 13 in a Hartford, Connecticut, restaurant: "Mr. Ford had clam broth, spinach, apple pie and tea. Mr. Edison had apple pie, Rocquefort cheese, hard crackers and iced coffee." When the bill of $14.25 arrived at the table, Ford deftly turned paying for the meal into an opportunity to display his appreciation of the working man. As one journalist described it, "Mr. Ford extracted a $50 bill from his pocket and handed it to the head waiter. 'Split up the change among you,' he remarked as he pushed back his chair and lighted his cigar." The cigar-lighting was an obvious embellishment by the writer, since Ford didn't smoke. Even the *New York Times* published a flattering photo of the Vagabonds lined up in front of their "kitchenette" car.

Burroughs left the group that afternoon, claiming "an engagement he had made many weeks previously," but just as likely determined to sleep in a real bed at home and have warm dinners at whatever hour he liked. The joke was on the naturalist — soon after his departure it started raining heavily, and the remaining Vagabonds chose to spend the night in a comfortable Danbury, Connecticut, hotel.

On Thursday, August 14, they abruptly decided to drive the rest of the way back to New York City and end the trip there. In *There to Breathe the Beauty,* Norman Brauer speculates that bad weather was the cause, but that same day the jury rendered its verdict in the *Tribune* trial. Ford was kept apprised of news from Mount Clemens throughout the trip, and on August 13 when word that the jury had retired to make its decision reached him in Connecticut he undoubtedly wanted to have immediate access to any updates. Ford was gratified by the verdict in his favor, if not the six cents in token damages awarded to him. But the coverage of the trial, both hostile and positive, brought Ford an additional bonus.

From the first stories of their 1914 trip to the Everglades together, Edison's name always came before Ford's in newspaper headlines, except in some Detroit newspapers. But beginning with coverage of the

1919 trip, that order began to change. From the mighty *New York Times* ("FORD ON A VACATION: To Go Camping with Edison and John Burroughs") to the newswire-dependent *Oregon Daily Journal* ("Ford, Edison and Burroughs Enjoy Living the Simple Life"), the controversial automaker gradually assumed top-of-the-bill status over the beloved inventor. The 1919 Vagabonds trip through New York state and New England was essentially a victory lap for Henry Ford.

CHAPTER SIX:
1920

A main purpose of the Vagabonds' summer trips was to demonstrate how much they had in common with other Americans. Though their vacation trappings were fancier, Edison, Ford, Firestone, and Burroughs embraced the national enthusiasm for outdoor exploration and adventure made newly possible by the proliferation of cars. The resulting publicity kept not only their names but their products prominently in public consciousness, and in the process the four famous friends had fun, too.

It seemed fitting in 1920 that the Vagabonds shared something else with their fellow citizens — financial scrambling and setbacks caused by an economic downturn that caught them and the rest of America by surprise.

In the years immediately prior to U.S. entry into World War I, foreign demand for U.S.

goods ramped up as never before. European nations enmeshed in the conflict needed raw materials and foodstuffs that their own war-weakened economies could no longer provide. American farmers stepped up and were rewarded with stunning profits. Before hostilities commenced in Europe, cotton sold internationally for an average of 12 cents a pound. During the war, that rose to 40 cents a pound, and as Europe struggled to recover economic equilibrium following the armistice, a pound of U.S. cotton fetched 50 cents in overseas markets, with 60 cents anticipated. All across America, farmers naturally wanted to expand their landholdings so they could raise even more crops, and banks were eager to provide the loans making it possible. Wartime manufacturing in America contributed to the economic boom — every factory in the land worked frantic shifts, so company owners raked in profits and well-compensated jobs were widely available. Americans had never enjoyed such a time before. Virtually everyone in the middle class had more money to spend on leisurely pursuits, from movies to car trips, and they happily indulged. If prices went up, too, it was not considered a problem, since that gave distributors and store owners their own opportunity to make more money — there was plenty to go around. Nineteen nineteen and its internal chaos caused deserved national concern, but amid the uproar there was still a comforting sense that the economy, at least, continued expanding in new, thrilling ways with no apparent end in sight.

But across the Atlantic, recovery was under way. European nations that had seen much of their territory reduced to blood-soaked mud regained equilibrium — farmers in France and Belgium and Germany once again tilled their fields. Early in 1920, revitalized U.S. competitors overseas started taking advantage of international shipping lanes regained with peace and undercut American prices in global markets. Suddenly, farmers in the States could get only 10 cents a pound for cotton, then 8 cents. Meanwhile, notes at banks on loans for purchases of additional farmland came due, and throughout the nation farmers defaulted on those payments and the banks began foreclosing.

There was a ripple effect. It took some months for the rest of America to realize what was happening, but the farmers' troubles led to struggles for the banks, and from there the blossoming U.S. economy went into steady wilt. When enough jobs were lost to cause national concern, even the most reckless middle-class spenders began cutting back, beginning with leisure-related purchases — phonographs, books, cars, tires.

Among the four Vagabonds, Burroughs was least affected. He didn't have much money to begin with, and at age eighty-three he no longer made appearances along the Eastern Seaboard lecture circuit. Burroughs's books always sold reasonably well, but he never rivaled authors like Mark Twain, whose royalties ensured them considerable steady income. The naturalist mostly stayed home in New York, where his journal notes for much of 1920 concerned the death of similarly aged friends ("April 28: The octogenarian has no alternative but to live in the past. He lives with the dead, and they pull him down") and the ongoing minor travails of living close to nature ("July 22: Had a skunk in a trap that I set for a woodchuck, and in trying to liberate him got some of his essence. . . . What marksmen [they] are! I held his tail down with a stick, but he managed to uncork his bottle all the same").

In late 1919, Firestone Tires in Akron operated at absolute peak efficiency. In that single year, its factories produced four million tires and sold them all, resulting in $9 million in corporate profits. Firestone recalled, "We could not keep up with demand." Ford remained his best customer, and Model Ts still dominated the automobile market, but other car manufacturers did brisk postwar business, too. Firestone's tires rolled along every mile of American roads. Nineteen twenty was expected to be a banner year; Firestone borrowed heavily from banks to finance the rubber and fabric necessary — the loans totaled $35 million. Then in May, raw materials in hand and an endless bull market apparently assured, he rented an estate in England and crossed the Atlantic to live there with his family on a vacation expected to extend through much of the summer.

But back in America, early summer brought a hiccup in car sales — the problems of farmers and banks began spooking consumers. July was always a strong sales month for Firestone Tires, but not in 1920. Before the month was over, inventory backup overflowed company storage and factory shutdowns seemed imminent. Firestone hurried back to Akron and chose aggressive marketing over retreat. He told an emergency meeting of branch and district managers that "the public has not stopped using tires, but they are not going to buy at present prices," which he ordered reduced by 25 percent. "It was a fire sale," he admitted later. "We thrust aside all our dignity and customs." Firestone's competitors, caught off guard, closed their factories and charged full price for inventory tires. Within a month, they changed course and cut prices, too, but by then Firestone, who "plastered the country" with ads touting his discount, had a solid head start. He reduced his workforce by 25 percent, too, and remained ready to slash prices and employment further.

For years, Thomas Edison endeavored to remove himself from day-to-day company supervision, preferring to spend work hours experimenting in his laboratory. By 1918, his son Charles had assumed a leading role in management, enjoying considerable autonomy. Edison's decision on the 1919 Vagabonds trip to focus on rubber-related research seemed to ensure Charles's permanent position as overall head of company business. But the economic troubles of 1920 diverted his father from the laboratory. People weren't buying phonographs or electric fans or even as many light bulbs. Edison always took a basic rather than nuanced approach to business. If not enough money was coming in, that simply meant too much in salaries was going out — "Too much supervision of supervision, from too many executives, in short, from too many non-productive additions to both manufacturing and selling." Charles Edison prided himself in the modern, multilayered corporate workforce he'd put in place. Now, without consulting Charles, Edison embarked on a series of what longtime employee A. E. Johnson termed "firing campaigns . . . he'd stop you and say, 'Who are you? What do you do?' You'd tell him, he'd ask a couple of questions . . . say, 'you're fired.' " While most Americans still loved the genial inventor whom they felt they knew, Johnson recalled that "around here in West Orange [there are] people who say, 'Oh, he was rotten, he was an S.O.B.' " Charles Edison was just as unhappy with his father, who by year's end reduced the company's manufacturing workforce from ten thousand to three thousand, eliminating his son's prized personnel department in the process.

Among the Vagabonds, the 1920s economic slump may have surprised Henry Ford most. The late spring/early summer gradual decline in Model T purchases should have been a harbinger, but during those months Ford was distracted by sagging sales of another pet product.

Since he had acquired the weekly *Dearborn Independent* in December 1918, Ford's intention was that the newspaper would quickly become one of the nation's most popular periodicals, just as Ford himself had established himself as a preeminent national presence. He hired seasoned journalists as editors and writers and reserved prominent space for "Mr. Ford's Own Page," which, while ghostwritten, was assumed by many readers to be Ford's personal beliefs expressed in print by the man himself. As with the Model T, Ford expected that he would hire the best professionals, provide them with product direction, and preside over matchless sales success, all the while maintaining complete control. To work for Ford was to submit to him. He had little patience with disagreement and less for results that didn't meet his expectations. In January 1919 the first new-era *Dearborn Independent*s rolled off the presses, sixteen pages long and a nickel per copy, with yearlong subscriptions available for $1. Ford did not offset production and editorial costs by selling ads — advertisers might expect editorial quid pro quo, which Ford suspected was the norm at competing papers. Just the fact Ford was associated with the *Independent* impressed the public. New customers boosted the initial subscription total to forty thousand, then more than fifty thousand, many times higher than what the weekly had reached prior to being acquired by the carmaker. But the *Independent*'s sterile copy and primitive illustrations — Ford biographer David L. Lewis describes it perfectly as "colorless" — combined with the economic troubles of 1920 dropped circulation by more than half. The *Independent* was hemorrhaging Ford's money, which was bad, but also, in his opinion, tarnishing his hard-earned reputation as a winner in every endeavor, which was worse.

Ford turned to his automobile dealerships for help. Besides unwavering devotion to selling cars, they were now instructed to peddle the *Dearborn Independent,* too, installing racks in their showrooms and, when possible, folding annual subscriptions into the purchase price of a Model T. That helped over the next several years, but not quickly enough to satisfy Ford. At one point, determined to gain immediate subscriber traction, Ford turned to Edison. Though his inventor friend was laying off workers in droves, Ford still asked that Edison allow G. C. Smith, "an Independent sales representative," to set up shop in Edison Company plants "for the purpose of enrolling [those] who may desire to subscribe." Already unhappy with their own boss, Edison's remaining employees were in no mood to accommodate his friend. Only two weeks after Smith set up in New Jersey, Edison's secretary W. H. Meadowcroft sent an apologetic note to Ernest Liebold, now Ford's right-hand man both for cars and the *Independent*:

Mr. Edison wishes me to write to you in regard to Mr. Ford's representative Mr. G. C. Smith who has been here several days for the purpose of obtaining subscriptions from our employees for the Dearborn Independent. We have given him every facility for getting in contact with our people. . . . Mr. Smith worked hard and faithfully, but has only been able to secure about fourteen subscriptions in spite of all his hard work and faithful endeavor.

By fall 1919 Ford made clear to the experienced journalists staffing the *Independent* that his patience was running out. He was prepared to spend whatever was necessary for the weekly to succeed, but he needed some strategy to bring that success about. The vision was his; implementation was theirs. Recent hire Joseph J. O'Neill, though, poached from the *New York World,* submitted a memo laden with capital letters and spelling out a solution instantly dear to the conspiracy-obsessed Ford's heart:

> Find an evil to attack, go after it and stay after it . . . PUSSYFOOTING and being afraid to hurt people will keep us just where we are if not send us further down the ladder . . . FEARLESS, TRUTHFUL, INTERESTING, PLAIN-SPOKEN articles . . . LET'S HAVE SOME SENSATION-ALISM.

Ernest Liebold probably made a strong suggestion about the evil to be attacked, but Ford needed little encouragement. Beginning in 1920, the *Dearborn Independent* began a series of antisemitic editorials and articles that continued for ninety-one consecutive weeks. These were largely presented as part of a theme whose headline was emblazoned in every issue — "The International Jew." Much of the material was dredged from *Protocols of the Elders of Zion.* The first few issues described the rise of Jews to power and presented as fact secret

Jewish control in America of various industries, including "the liquor business . . . the loan business . . . the motion picture industry . . . news distribution." According to the *Independent,* Jews had even insidiously seized control of Major League Baseball.

Some of the weekly paper's staffers refused to participate and quit before they could be fired. A few brave members of Ford Motor Company management suggested to Ford that antagonizing a significant section of the public might very well result in a Jewish boycott of Ford cars. Ford professed indifference. If the product was good and the price was right, Jews and everyone else would buy it. In Ford's view, the majority of hardworking Americans agreed with the *Independent*'s stand, or at least welcomed attention-grabbing plainspokenness. Circulation picked up considerably during the ninety-one weeks of antisemitic editorializing, peaking at about 650,000 by 1925 — Ford chose to believe it was the ongoing attack on Jews that spurred sales. He failed to realize that almost the entire increase was based on subscriptions sold by Ford dealers to Model T buyers as part of the car's overall price. Only an infinitesimal percentage of *Independent* sales came from street racks and non–Ford Motor Company customers.

To Ford, the *Independent* was doing America and the world a service. All right-thinking men of any faith would surely be supportive. Jews ought to feel relieved that their secrets were out and they no longer needed resorting to subterfuge. Any Jews who somehow weren't aware of their "race's" schemes would not only learn about them thanks to the *Independent,* they'd probably be won over by the editorial arguments, Ford believed. He was shocked and hurt when Jews he considered friends took offense at the articles. His regard for Rabbi Leo Franklin of Detroit was such that he'd recently presented him with a Model T as a gift. Soon after the *Independent* began its antisemitic campaign, Rabbi Franklin returned the car. He received a personal phone call from the baffled Ford, who asked plaintively, "What's wrong, Dr. Franklin? Has something come between us?"

But Ford's attention was eventually wrenched away from the *Independent* and its campaign. It was one thing to have difficulty selling a five-cent weekly newspaper, and very much another to suddenly be faced with a precipitous decline in sales of

Model Ts.

The economic slump of 1920 could not have come at a worse time for Ford. Payments on the bank loans he'd taken to buy out his Ford Motor Company partners in 1919 were coming due in 1921. There had been considerable additional outlay for plant expansion and/or construction. Total obligations were $58 million. Ford Motor Company had $20 million in cash on hand. Had Model T sales continued as expected, ramping up year after year (now about half the cars sold in America were Fords), the bills would have been no problem. Suddenly, they were.

Ford's immediate response was similar to Firestone's — he cut prices on the Model T, from 14 to about 30 percent depending on car style. Ford did it with considerable flair, announcing at the same time as the price cuts that he would continue paying the generous wages that gained him so much positive coverage in 1914. Most media coverage was gratifying. Some editorials speculated that Ford's largesse toward his workers and consumers compensated for his witness stand bumbling during the *Tribune* trial. Others, like the *Denver Post,* simply lauded him: "Your life, your character, and your achievements should be an inspiration to every laboring man, to every good American citizen, and to every rich man and capitalist in the country — plain, simple, good-hearted, just, generous Henry Ford!"

The price cuts moved some cars, but not enough. Financial pundits began speculating that Ford might have to swallow his pride and go crawling to the banks that he traditionally enjoyed disparaging. There was every expectation that, at the least, they would make him grovel. But Ford had a different plan.

Ford dealers had a strict financial arrangement with the parent company. When they ordered cars, they paid for them in advance rather than as they sold. The premise was that with their money at stake rather than the company's, they'd work even harder to sell the cars. Since the Model T was constantly in high demand, this was no hardship for the dealers. They considered themselves lucky to be affiliated with Ford, even when the boss wanted them to sell newspaper subscriptions as well as cars. But the 1920 economic slump left Ford dealers anxious to move the cars they had on hand and reluctant to order more. No one knew how long the crisis would last — the dealers wisely wanted to play it safe.

They were shocked, in the fall, to receive shipments of Model Ts that they hadn't ordered. The edict on these cars was the same — Ford Motor Company must be paid for them. Refusal would terminate the dealer-company relationship. Dealers already had considerable personal stakes in their car showrooms and lots, often in attached garages, and car inventory already on hand. If they refused to accept these additional Model Ts and were fired by Ford, they could be ruined. Or, as the parent company suggested, they could accept the cars, if necessary get loans from their own banks to pay Ford for them, and then aggressively keep trying to sell Model Ts and hang on until the national economic crisis was over. The dealers had little choice but to accept. That provided Ford with enough money to meet his immediate corporate debts — the dealers had to risk wrath from their banks instead.

The car shipments to dealers eased current corporate overstock, but Ford plants couldn't remain open and turn out even more Model Ts. Ford kept production going longer than most competitors, who completely shut down operations by summer or early fall 1920, but in December car sales remained stagnant and Ford closed his plants through early February 1921. He also laid off about one-fourth of his employees, fifteen thousand in all. Since Ford, like Edison, insisted on nonunion shops, he risked no strike or other worker retaliation. When the economic crisis finally eased and the Ford plants reopened, the pared-down workforce operated at maximum efficiency, turning out Model Ts at a furious rate (about 900,000 in 1921, contrasted with 420,000 in 1920 before production shut down that December). Relieved dealers were happily hard-pressed to keep enough cars on hand to satisfy consumer demand. Once again, Henry Ford acted creatively. Once again, he won.

All the economic news wasn't bad. During the bleak summer of 1920 and immediately afterward, there was an unexpected but unmistakable indication that Americans hadn't entirely given up on automobiles and leisure expenditures. Very few were buying cars, but many who already owned one still used it for travel — "autocamping" was the popular new term. A *New York Times* survey indicated that fully half the nation's estimated ten million cars were being used at least partially for that purpose. Another study divided autocampers into four general categories — farmers on trips to buy supplies and sell crops, travelers crossing the country in search of new homes, migrant workers following anticipated harvests, and, largest of all, "middle-class tourists" out for sightseeing and adventure, half of them or more likely squeezed into Model Ts crammed with folded tents and camping gear. This continued even during hard economic times, proving that car travel could no longer be considered a fad. In less than two decades, it had become ingrained in American culture. In 1920, with communities across the land desperate to attract every available dollar, middle-class autocampers in particular offered a rare, thriving target market.

As the number of car trips increased, so did autocampers' need of safe places to stop overnight. Hotels cost money, often $2–$3 or more per night (with more Americans on the road, hotels raised prices to meet increased demand), and many travelers were on limited budgets. Farmers were increasingly unwilling to allow campers on their land. Campers in turn grew less eager to risk random stops; it was hard to count on potable water, and there was always danger of attack by thugs seeking easy prey.

Across the country, town officials stepped into the breach, particularly in rural communities along roads and between larger cities. They established "autocamps," often in parks right in the center of town, where travelers were welcome to stop for an hour or an afternoon or a night. They parked free of charge and were encouraged to set up tents and stay awhile. Their hosts calculated that the visitors would reciprocate by purchasing gas and getting repairs at local garages or buying supplies or meals from town merchants. It worked — by 1922, autocamps proliferated throughout the country; estimates range from three thousand to six thousand. Some were primitive, roughly marked lots with minimal shade and space for only a dozen cars. Most offered pleasant settings, room for fifty or more cars (Denver's massive Overland Park accommodated two thousand) and enticing amenities: In *Americans on the Road,* Warren James Belasco writes that "the average 10–15-acre camp offered, as basic necessities, good water, maintained privies, electric lights, wood- or gas-burning stoves in a central kitchen building, a lounge area, cold showers, a caretaker, and a laundry room with tubs and washboards."

Entrepreneurs sensed opportunity. Restaurants began springing up on long stretches of roads between towns, often advertising free water and gambling that enough travelers who stopped for a drink or to refill radiators would also decide to spring for a sandwich or a heartier meal. Often, these roadside eateries also had small campgrounds — early 1920s American travelers found themselves presented with any number of camping and dining options, most free (camping) or at least affordable (food) to even the most budget-minded. They responded — the *New York Times* estimated that now at least "10–15 percent" of the entire population in all corners of America took car trips at some point each year.

Since 1914 in the Everglades, the Vagabonds were among them, excepting only 1917 when the public was informed that war-related responsibilities kept Edison, Ford, and Firestone off the road. In July of 1920, amid launching the antisemitic campaign of the *Dearborn Independent* and staving off corporate financial disaster, Henry Ford took the first steps to gather the gang and autocamp again. Firestone was still in England, but Ford assumed the tire maker would agree to any trip at any time. Burroughs's summer in New York was being split between Roxbury and Riverby, where the naturalist had a second country place. Probably the old man would balk, but he'd always come before and Ford would insist he do so again. All that really had to be determined was if and when Edison could go. Ford had Liebold write and inquire of Meadowcroft whether the inventor, immersed in his own efforts to keep his company financially afloat, "will be in position to make the camping trip this year." On Ford's behalf, Liebold suggested northern Michigan as a likely destination: "Last year a number of us motored through the Upper Peninsula [inspecting Ford properties there] and it was equal to August weather. It is too bad of course to make [this year's trip] as late as this, but as Mr. Firestone is not expected to return until September, Mr. Ford dislikes to abandon the trip on this account." Even in 1920, when his own celebrity matched and sometimes eclipsed that of the inventor, Ford continued deferring to Edison: "It will depend on Mr. Edison's reply whether the trip will be made." Still, Ford clearly wanted to go — Liebold closed the letter by noting that "all the equipment is being put in shape so that if a trip is made there will be no other delay."

Edison promptly sent word back via Meadowcroft: Mr. Edison "wants me to say he is so loaded up with work, and has promised Mrs. Edison to skip one year of camping in order to take her on an auto trip of ten days, that he will have to give up the idea of this year's trip with Mr. Ford and his other friends."

Liebold replied that they "regret very much that Mr. Edison is unable to join in the camping trip this year. It is quite likely therefore that Mr. Ford's plans will be abandoned." In 1916, Edison went when Ford would not, but four years later, the reverse wasn't true.

That seemed to be the end of it for 1920. Firestone hurried home from Europe to save his company. Edison and Ford were equally occupied with theirs. But sometime in October, the possibility of a late-year Vagabonds trip resurfaced. The timing made sense. America remained in economic distress. There was widespread concern that the good times might be over forever. If the country's most famous businessmen took their annual trip together — see, *they* must think everything will be all right! — it might provide a much needed boost to national morale. Not coincidentally, it would also result in valuable publicity for them and their struggling companies.

A second element was the other Vagabonds' growing concern for John Burroughs, who increasingly showed signs of mental deterioration. Burroughs recognized this himself: "[My] memory [is] full of holes, like a net with many of the meshes broken." He took fewer rambles around his beloved properties, and rarely ventured beyond their boundaries. Burroughs made an exception in April 1920, when he spent his birthday at Yama Farms, an exclusive resort in the Catskill Mountains a few hours' drive from New York City. Though the surroundings were rustic, accommodations were luxurious. By day guests could romp in the woods. There was fishing, a well-stocked library for anyone who wanted to read, and screenings of the latest popular movies. At night, everyone gathered to hear lectures by visiting scholars and explorers.

Though the others tried to think of ways Burroughs could still participate in a typical Vagabonds camping trip — Edison proposed bringing along a full-sized bed and mattress for him — they finally accepted that the old man's autocamping days were done. Yet they didn't want to go somewhere without him, not only because they were so personally fond of Burroughs, but because to the public the naturalist with the long white beard was such an established part of the Vagabonds' image. By 1920, a joke about the group was in print or told on vaudeville stages throughout the country. There were variations, but the gist was generally the same:

A farmer is working in his field by a road when this car comes along and breaks down right across from him. There are four people in the car, and they get out and raise the hood to see what's wrong. After they scratch their heads for a while, the farmer comes over and says, "I'm pretty good with machines. Let me take a look." He does, and after a while he says, "Something's wrong with the engine." One of the four men standing there with him says, "I'm Henry Ford and I built this car. There's nothing wrong with the engine." The farmer says, "All right, then the problem is with the battery." The second man says, "I'm Thomas Edison. My company made that battery and there's nothing wrong with it, either." The farmer says, "Then it has to be the tires. Something's wrong with the tires." The third man says, "I'm Harvey Firestone, those are my tires, and they're just fine." The farmer throws up his hands and says, "You say you're Ford, Edison and Firestone! I suppose that this old guy with the white beard's going to tell me that he's Santa Claus!"

If Burroughs remained spry enough to travel, the other three were determined that he should come along. But that limited their choices of destination and route. It wouldn't do for Burroughs to become ill on some lonely country road miles from doctors and a hospital.

Weather was a factor, too. Wherever they went, they couldn't risk being stranded in a snowstorm or skidding for miles on iced-over roads — for good reason, autocamping was a seasonal endeavor. And there was another potential complication.

In July, Edison's reason for begging off a summer Vagabonds trip was that he'd promised his wife, Mina, "an auto trip of ten days." There is no record that he kept that promise, and, if so, Mina Edison was not a woman who forgot such things. Before her untimely death at age twenty-nine, Edison's first wife, Mary, had been miserable because she felt — and was — excluded from almost all of her husband's life. Mary came from a working-class family, and she was a low-level Edison Company employee before catching the boss's eye. Mary didn't understand the work her husband did in his laboratory and felt socially uncomfortable with the rich, often brilliant people who comprised Edison's limited social circle. Mina, the daughter of a wealthy Ohio industrialist, approached marriage to Edison much differently. Though only nineteen when they married (Edison was thirty-eight), she made certain to stay abreast of her husband's work, mingled perfectly with his distinguished friends, and made it her business to shield Edison from most of the demands of daily life. In return, she expected him to pay attention to her and their three children in those few hours each day when Edison tore himself away from his laboratory. Mina required, and got, Edison's respect for her as a full partner in their marriage, not an occasional accoutrement. She could understand missing the promised summer 1920 car trip because her husband's time had to be spent instead on saving his company, but not Edison's running off just a few months later on a men-only Vagabonds jaunt, when he could have kept his earlier word to her.

The Vagabonds themselves were a touchy subject with Mina Edison because she disliked Ford. Edison might have accepted the Vagabonds headlines and stories gradually featuring Ford rather than himself. From Mina's perspective, they proved something that she'd suspected all along — rather than provide her husband with much-needed chances to relax, these Vagabonds trips were mainly intended by Ford as platforms for his own shameless self-promotion. Despite her misgivings, Mina never forbade her husband to go. But she took advantage of opportunities to torment Ford. The best example was a car that Mina swore wouldn't stop rattling. Ford not only frequently gave Edison cars, he sometimes sent one to Mina Edison, too, with every available add-on to ensure her riding comfort — as a lady of standing, she never drove herself, but sat in the back seat while a chauffeur took the wheel. One year, Mina notified Ford that she couldn't abide the latest car. While on any road, even the smoothest, it rattled so loudly that it made her head hurt. Her chauffeur, who doubled as the Edison family mechanic, couldn't fix the problem. Ford, who undoubtedly realized Mina disliked him, didn't know why, and wanted badly to win her over, offered to replace the car. Mina said that wouldn't do. She wanted Ford to fix the one she had. Ford dispatched his best mechanics from

Dearborn to New Jersey. They tore the car apart, said that they couldn't find anything wrong, and put it back together. Mina went on a drive and said the rattling remained. Ford had the car shipped to Dearborn and examined there. His engineers swore to him that every car rattled at least a little. It was impossible to drive in complete silence. Ford sent the car back to New Jersey with the promise that if Mrs. Edison really couldn't stand the noise it made, he'd send another one, any car she wanted, whatever made her happy. Mina didn't respond. She'd made Ford squirm, so it was mission accomplished. Another year, she used a different tack. As Mina requested, Ford made sure that year's car for Mrs. Edison was painted blue. For months after receiving the car, Mina badgered Ford and his paint experts, who mixed and remixed trying to get the exact shade of blue that she insisted she wanted but couldn't precisely describe.

It had been 1915 and the trip to California when wives were last invited along, but Edison wasn't about to risk Mina's wrath and exclude her from the November 1920 Vagabonds trip. If Mina went, Clara Ford would have to be invited, and Idabelle Firestone, too. Mina's reservations about Henry Ford didn't affect her friendship with Clara. The

Edisons and Fords were winter next-door neighbors in Florida, and the women socialized there daily.

So it would be four Vagabonds and three wives, plus a small entourage. The remaining question was where they would gather. It was Edison who apparently came up with the perfect location — Yama Farms, where Burroughs had spent his eighty-third birthday in April. Burroughs clearly liked it there, the women would enjoy the fine accommodations, and potential cold or snowy weather wouldn't be a factor. It would be a brief vacation, perfect for Ford, Edison, and Firestone since they'd need to get back to their businesses. Yama Farms' proximity to New York meant that the reporters and photographers for the newspapers and wire services based there would have easy access — even if only a few days' worth of stories resulted, national coverage should be assured. Ford had Liebold check dates with Firestone and Burroughs, then confirm through Meadowcroft that Edison was on board. On October 29, Meadowcroft wrote that "this is very agreeable to Mr. Edison," and a few weeks later everyone met at Yama Farms.

THREE GREAT AMERICANS AT PLAY

Americans couldn't read enough about the Vagabonds and their car adventures. Edison (left) and Ford dominated press coverage, and until his death in March, 1921, white-bearded naturalist John Burroughs was almost as popular.

The Vagabonds' route from Fort Myers to the Everglades in 1914 included long stretches of splashing through deep pools of water on the road.

On their outing in the Everglades, the Vagabonds eventually left even rudimentary roads behind and ventured into the primitive heart of the swampy expanse.

Though a guide rather than Henry Ford shot this turkey on the Vagabonds' adventure in the Florida Everglades, the publicity-conscious carmaker posed with the trophy.

Battered by a sudden, violent rainstorm on the first night of their Everglades adventure, the Vagabonds and their guests tried to dry themselves by a small flickering fire.

OCTOBER 29, 1915. FRIDAY PRICE 2½ CENTS

Edison Is Given High-Voltage Welcome
Throngs Cheer, Children Scatter Flowers

Thomas A. Edison Greeting a Group of School Children in Los Angeles Yesterday

Edison received a rapturous greeting at the 1915 Panama-California Exposition in San Diego. Organizers were determined to make his reception far more colorful and overwhelming than the one the inventor had received earlier at San Francisco's rival Panama-Pacific Exposition.

Though they were the best of friends, Ford and Edison most often communicated through messages sent between Edison's secretary, William H. Meadowcroft, and Ernest G. Liebold, executive secretary to Ford. Liebold's message to Meadowcroft concerns Ford's purchase of an estate adjacent to Edison's.

Henry Ford
Detroit

June 2nd 1916

Mr Thomas A Edison
Orange
N J

My dear Mr Edison: Attention Mr W H Meadowcroft

Mr Ford has requested me to advise that we have just completed negotiations for the purchase of "The Mangoes" property adjoining your property in Florida.

He is already busy building a steamboat for fishing purposes which will most likely be completed in time to use during the next vacation.

He also expects Mr Burroughs in Detroit during the coming week and intends to have him lay the cornerstone of a permanent bird fountain and would like very much to have you write a letter of some kind, that can be handed down to posterity, to be enclosed in the cornerstone.

Mr Ford will appreciate very much if he may have the opportunity of hearing from you early sometime next week.

Very truly yours

E G LIEBOLD,
Secretary to HENRY FORD

EGL:Z

Despite Ford's entreaties, Edison refused to join his friend on the ill-fated "Peace Ship" mission to Europe that Ford organized in late 1915.

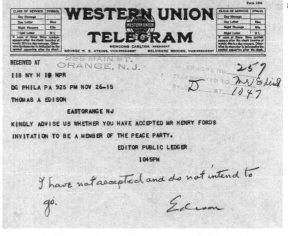

EDISON ON A VACATION IN THE ADIRONDACKS

When Ford declined to join Edison, tire maker Harvey Firestone, and Burroughs for their 1916 Vagabonds trip, Edison (left, with Firestone) retained media interest in the outing with a surprise endorsement of Woodrow Wilson's bid for reelection.

All over America, locals hoped to glimpse the Vagabonds' car caravan cresting hills or crossing bridges into their towns. The group's arrival anywhere was always cause for celebration.

Ford greatly admired naturalist John Burroughs. On Vagabonds trips, their car caravans would frequently stop so Burroughs could point out interesting plant, bird, and animal life to his companions.

The Vagabonds enjoyed elaborate camp dinners prepared by chefs who were part of the traveling company.

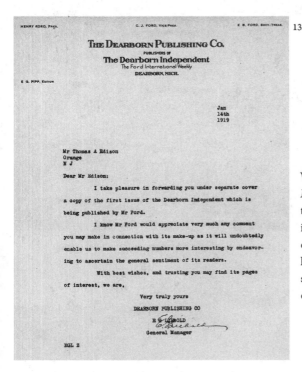

When he acquired the *Dearborn Independent* in late 1918 with the intent to turn the newspaper into a showcase for his personal opinions, Ford asked Edison, who had written, printed, and sold a small newsletter in his youth, to critique the *Independent*.

Edison, Burroughs, Ford, and Firestone pose alongside and atop a water wheel during their 1918 excursion.

The Vagabonds' fleet often jounced along "Wish to God" roads that had ruts, rocks, and ditches alongside the road that were subject to flooding and overflowing.

16

In 1920, Ford and Burroughs staged a tree-chopping contest for the press with Firestone as timekeeper and Edison as referee. Burroughs was declared the winner, and Edison congratulated him.

Though he publicly denounced cigarettes as poisonous (because of burning paper, not tobacco), Edison regularly enjoyed puffing on cigars when the Vagabonds stopped to camp.

Despite traveling with a retinue to set up expansive tents and prepare elaborate meals, the Vagabonds tried to give the impression of roughing it, even when their camp guest was President Warren G. Harding (far right).

Harvey S. Firestone checks one of his namesake tires during the Vagabonds' 1923 trip in Michigan's Upper Peninsula. On every Vagabonds excursion Firestone sublimated his own ego to those of the others.

Idabelle Firestone, Clara Ford, and Mina Edison accompanied their husbands on the Vagabonds' last few trips.

As two of the most famous Americans, Edison and Ford shared a unique bond that was strengthened by their mutual drive to excel. Throughout the Vagabonds' adventures they remained warm friends, as here on the 1923 trip.

Thomas Edison famously claimed to sleep only a few hours a night during most of the year, but on Vagabonds' trips he could often be seen napping under a tree or beside a creek.

In 1923, Ford purchased the Wayside Inn in Sudbury, Massachusetts, and set out to restore it. The Vagabonds used the inn as a base during the first portion of their 1924 trip.

The highlight of the Vagabonds' visit with Calvin Coolidge at his summer home in New Hampshire came when Coolidge (second from left) presented Ford with an antique bucket that was a family heirloom. The president, Ford, Edison, and Firestone all autographed the artifact.

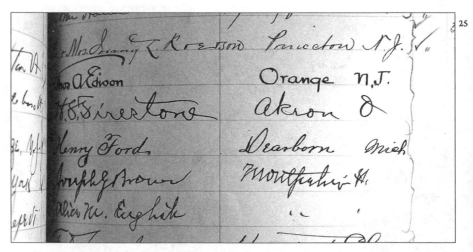

Stung by Coolidge's dismissal of them after an hour's visit at the president's summer retreat, the Vagabonds ate an impromptu lunch at the luxurious Woodstock Inn in Vermont. They signed the inn's guest book with their usual flourishes.

Ford

The Touring Car

$295

Runabout $265
Demountable Rims
and Starter $85 extra

Coupe $525
Tudor Sedan - - 590
Fordor Sedan - - 685
All prices f. o. b. Detroit

Utmost Driving Confidence

Driving a Ford is so simple, and requires
so little effort that you are free to devote all your attention to the problems
of traffic. There is a sense of confidence in driving a Ford, impossible
with any more complicated motor car.

Ford Motor Company

Detroit, Michigan

SEE THE NEAREST AUTHORIZED FORD DEALER

For many years, Ford Motor Company's print advertisements for the Model T spoke
directly to consumer demands for dependability and affordability. But by 1924, the
public had tired of lookalike Model Ts.

Ford dismantled his friend Edison's laboratory in Fort Myers, Florida, and pains-takingly reassembled it in Dearborn, Michigan. Mina Edison never forgave Ford for what she considered an imposition on her husband's generous nature.

Their challenge was to receive press coverage emphasizing the Vagabonds' commonalities with normal Americans without drawing undue attention to the fact that they were vacationing at a luxury resort instead of autocamping like people of modest means. The trip announcement on November 13 in the *New York Times* wasn't helpful. Though it didn't describe the lavish comforts of Yama Farms, the article noted that the Vagabonds' fellow guests there would include "Lady Eaton; Dr. Carl Ackeley, sculptor and naturalist . . . Dr. Carl Lumholtz, explorer; Miss Ethel Newcomb, pianist; Mr. and Mrs. Roy Andrews, heads of the coming expedition to Asia to investigate prehistoric man; Dr. F. B. Turck, biologist; and Jan Sickesz, Dutch pianist." These were not the sort of people to be found in adjoining tents at an autocamp.

The Vagabonds party was to stay at Yama Farms for only two days, beginning on Monday, November 15. Part of that first day, after everyone arrived during the afternoon, was spent posing for group pictures. These showed all the men but Ford swaddled in heavy winter coats. The automaker defied the November chill in a business suit and vest. The ladies wore furs, and Mina Edison and Idabelle Firestone sported jaunty hats with feathers. Clara Ford, daughter of a farmer, wore her sensible warm hat pulled so low that her eyes were barely visible. Edison draped his arm protectively around Burroughs's shoulders. Then the ladies repaired inside, while photographers followed the men on a tramp about the grounds. Media photos were taken of Ford using his own camera to snap pictures of Edison and Burroughs. Later, the press was allowed to briefly witness and photograph some of the group reading in front of a massive fireplace. It was all very nice, but as the publicity-savvy Ford, Edison, and Firestone were aware, there wasn't enough going on to give reporters material for the right kind of stories. They had an idea for the second day, though, a simple yet *visual* one that would surely please the journalists and entertain and impress the rest of America.

On Tuesday, reporters and photographers received word that a Vagabonds event of considerable interest would soon take place in the woods just outside the Yama Farms hotel complex. They arrived to find a small crowd comprised of Clara Ford, Mina Edison, Idabelle Firestone, members of the Vagabonds' retinue, and some other Yama guests gathered in a loose circle. At the circle's center were Firestone, Edison, Ford, and Burroughs, the latter two holding long-handled axes. Edison brandished a stopwatch. Someone, probably Firestone, explained to the press that Mr. Ford had challenged Mr. Burroughs to a tree-chopping contest. Mr. Edison was to be timekeeper while Firestone served as referee. Whoever brought down his tree first would be declared champion.

It seemed likely to be an uneven match. Burroughs appeared hardly able to heft his axe at all. Ford, at fifty-seven more than a quarter-century Burroughs's junior, remained lean and strong. But as Firestone explained to the press afterward, Mr. Burroughs had the advantage of knowing trees far better than did the automaker. The naturalist took his stance before a relatively slender birch, while Ford prepared to chop a thicker scrub oak. Edison clicked the stopwatch, Firestone shouted a command, and wood chips commenced flying. By most press accounts, it was four minutes later by Edison's watch when Burroughs's birch crashed to the ground while Ford's oak remained standing. A few reporters described an extended contest, with at least four trees falling before Ford admitted defeat, but that was lily-gilding. Only two trees died in service of Vagabonds publicity.

Edison clapped Burroughs on the back and exclaimed, "These youngsters aren't in our class at all." Firestone confided to the press that prior to the tree-chopping, Burroughs had challenged Ford to a tree-climbing contest. The automaker felt his chances were better at chopping. Some press accounts nicknamed the naturalist "Battling Burroughs." Virtually every article was accompanied by one or more eye-catching photographs of Burroughs and Ford in mid-swing. On Tuesday evening, the Vagabonds and their wives attended a lecture by Carl Lumholtz, who "informed them of the flora and fauna of the South Pacific." This much more static activity was mentioned briefly in a few of the next day's newspapers, and only after long, colorful accounts of the tree-chopping contest.

That was the extent of the Vagabonds' public excursion in 1920, and it was enough. For days afterward, small-town newspapers lauded them in editorials (the *Adams County Free Press* in Iowa: "Four

Great Americans Frolic for a Day"; in Arizona, the *Bisbee Daily Review:* "Famous Pals Play They're Boys Again"). The *Asheville Citizen-Times* noted, "The four camp comrades seem to be having the time of their lives, as they always do when they take a vacation together. There is no guarantee of long years' health and zest for living, but these things would come to more of us if the example set by Edison, Burroughs, Ford, and Firestone were more often followed." Almost every story emphasized that the four men were on their annual vacation, but failed to mention that it lasted only two days.

Though they left Yama Farms and the press behind on November 17, the Vagabonds didn't end their time together yet. Instead, they drove a short distance to Burroughs's property Riverby, and stayed overnight with the old man there. There was a comfortable house on the grounds as well as Slabsides, a rough-hewn cottage well-known to Burroughs's readers since the naturalist often wrote of staying there. He described it as an isolated place that provided him the privacy he needed to study nature, but in reality he'd built Slabsides as a retreat from his late, unbeloved wife, Ursula. It was there that he, Edison, Ford, and Firestone gathered for the late afternoon and early evening, just the four of them without wives or retainers, who probably remained back in the main house. They sensed, but almost surely didn't say out loud, that this might be their last gathering that included the naturalist. In contrast to some earlier years, Burroughs was a genial host. Despite what Firestone described as "driving snow," he insisted on preparing a meal for them himself, "brigand steak" cooked over an open fire, presumably one in a fireplace inside the cabin. It was a simple dish, essentially the most basic of shish kebabs — chunks of steak and bacon were alternately impaled on a thin, pointed stick, then placed over the flames. Afterward, the quartet rejoined the rest of the party in the main house. The next day found the Fords, Edisons, and Firestones on their way home.

Ford saw Burroughs again. As in several previous years, the naturalist spent the winter in California. On his way there in early December, Burroughs and Clara Barrus, an author-physician who'd become his close friend and occasional travel companion, stopped briefly in Dearborn to visit the Fords. Burroughs looked reasonably well. A day later, Burroughs told reporter Flora Ward Henline that "I feel better today than a year ago." Henline described Burroughs as "walk[ing] with a springy step, usually in advance of his escorts." But during his months in California, Burroughs faded. He was hospitalized for weeks with an irregular heartbeat, and by mid-March Barrus and his physicians there concluded that nothing more could be done for him. Barrus tried taking Burroughs home to Riverby by train so that he could pass his final hours in his favorite surroundings, but he died on the way. Ford, Edison, and Firestone attended his burial in Roxbury on April 3, 1921, which would have been Burroughs's eighty-fourth birthday. Ford provided the cars for the funeral procession. Another mourner described Edison as "look[ing] very old and white-[haired] and sad."

On November 2, 1920, voters went to the polls to elect America's next president. President Wilson had some hopes of securing the Democratic nomination and seeking a third term, but his party preferred a new leader. No candidate emerged as the obvious choice. It took forty-four ballots at their convention before Democrats finally chose Ohio governor James M. Cox. Party enthusiasm for him was lackluster. No prominent Democrat was interested in running as Cox's vice president. Thirty-seven-year-old assistant secretary of the navy Franklin D. Roosevelt was selected, mostly because of his famous last name — he was a fifth cousin to former Republican president Theodore Roosevelt. The Republicans took ten ballots before selecting Senator Warren G. Harding of Ohio as their standard-bearer. Harding was chosen because he got along well with his fellow senators and was a handsome man whom Republican colleagues believed looked presidential. He was joined on the ticket by Massachusetts governor Calvin Coolidge, who had gained national prominence for breaking Boston's police strike in 1919.

Cox and Roosevelt campaigned on a promise of continuing Wilson's domestic policies, with special attention to unemployment and labor relations. They supported continued U.S. involvement overseas. Harding and Coolidge opposed the League of Nations or any similar concept. The Republican ticket advocated tax cuts, mostly for business, which they believed would create more jobs, and restrictive immigration policies, promising to make it harder for certain groups to enter the country. Most major newspapers savaged Harding editorially, noting his complete lack of legislative accomplishment as a senator and describing him as one of the most unqualified presidential candidates in the nation's history. But Americans wanted a change, and there was strong sentiment. Harding and Coolidge won in a landslide.

The economic slump extended into 1921, but the national sense of panic gradually receded. The worst seemed over by spring. The only lingering damage was to farmers, who continued struggling. The country was now led by a president who advocated "a return to normalcy," and exhorted voters during the 1920 campaign "to safeguard America first, to stabilize America first, to prosper America first, to think of America first, to exalt America first." This, rather than unnecessary foreign commitments, Harding declared, defined "patriotic devotion." The election results made it clear: After the trauma of world war and the blight of economic recession, Americans were ready to have fun again.

CHAPTER SEVEN:
1921

In January 1921, Thomas Edison received an unwelcome letter from Harry A. Harrison, a director of Young Israel — the group's stationery described it as "An Organization of Young Men Devoted to the Furtherance of Traditional Jewish Ideals." Harrison began the January 14 missive with praise for Edison, declaring that "you are considered by the whole world at large as one who has brought comfort and relief to all of mankind." A pointed question followed: "And since all your labor is directed towards making the world a better place to live in, and since it is every man's duty to think and act in like manner, we would like to know your opinion as to whether Henry Ford is helping towards the progress of the world by attacking the Jews and by attempting to stir up ill-feeling where heretofore all has been peaceful and is in a state of friendship." The letter concluded, "We hope to be enlightened by your answer, and would appreciate the courtesy of an early reply."

Edison's response was disingenuous: "I know very little about Mr. Ford's efforts, & do not want to get into any controversy about the English, Irish, Germans or Jews — or even Yankees." In fact, Edison knew quite a lot. Just two weeks later, he sent a warm note of thanks to Ford for "the leather bound copy of . . . *The International Jew,*" the first of four collections of the *Dearborn Independent*'s series of antisemitic articles published by Ford in book form. Edison never gave any public indication that he entirely bought into the articles' theme that Jews were engaged in a comprehensive plot to gain control of American finance, politics, and culture. But he did share Ford's reservations about Jews in general and did nothing to discourage his friend's printed assault on them.

The Ford-Edison friendship was at its very warmest in early 1921. With the previous year's financial panic finally slackening, they were sufficiently encouraged to discuss a new professional collaboration. Edison still believed in the potential of electric cars and continued researching the development of a battery that would hold its charge longer than a few dozen miles. Now, at Edison's request, Ford assigned some engineers to design a compatible chassis — together he and Edison planned to create an electric truck. Ford's previous attempt to partner with Edison — 1912–1913's effort by the inventor to develop an efficient electric car storage battery — had failed, costing the automaker three-quarters of a million dollars or more. But Ford was still willing to gamble on Edison, and in spring 1921 he was again in the financial position to do so. When Ford Motor Company reopened its plants in February, it immediately began manufacturing — and selling — Model Ts at a record rate. Financial pundits predicted in 1920 that Ford might never regain his financial footing, if he was able to keep his company going at all. He delighted in proving them wrong, and Edison gloated along with him. On February 22, just after the Ford assembly lines were back in immediate, full operation, Edison fired off a congratulatory telegram to his friend: "How disappointed some people will be . . . over the news you send me. It will be an awful shock to them."

The next line of the telegram referenced their recent aggravation with a fellow Vagabond: "Firestone will now quit playing with rainbows and get down to earth."

When Ford shut down his factories in December 1920, the last automaker to do so, Firestone was in financial peril. At that point he apparently considered radical business options that his two friends disdained as fanciful, leading to Edison's "playing with rainbows" observation. Ford had his secretary forward the telegram to Firestone.

Ford's announcement of his plants reopening was accompanied by a massive order for Firestone tires, which in turn allowed the tire maker to recommence his own manufacturing operations. Firestone wrote "Mr. Ford" that "I am sure you cannot fully appreciate what a help and inspiration you gave us when you instructed your factory to give us such a volume of business. It put new life into our entire organization, to say nothing of the necessary financial help it will give us."

Firestone couldn't resist mentioning Edison's comment: "Since I received your fine order for March shipments my mind has quit wandering or 'chasing rainbows' as Mr. Edison says, and I have settled down in the factory." Of Edison himself Firestone wrote, "He has a keen comprehension of the psychology of things."

About ten weeks later, Edison's comprehension of psychology was called into public question. For years Ford was the Vagabond widely mocked in print, but in May 1921 it became Edison's turn. The inventor was constantly critical of higher education, complaining that colleges failed to teach students anything practical to life and business. To ensure that his companies hired only the best-informed applicants, Edison developed a 146-question test for prospective employees. The test required very specific answers. The *New York Times* obtained a copy. On May 11 it published a story about the Edison quiz, including sample questions, and reader response was so intense that the paper printed the full test two days later. Some of the questions were standard, especially those focusing on American history ("Who was Paul Revere?" "Where did we get Louisiana from?"). A few could be expected from any business seeking employees with sufficient backgrounds in science and physics ("Name three principal acids." "Of what is glass made?"). A few hinted at Edison's growing interest in rubber-related research ("Where do we import rubber from?" "What is vulcanite and how is it made?"). But many could only be categorized as bizarre: "What country consumed the most tea before the war?" "Where do we get prunes from?" "What is the price of 12 grains of gold?" "What city in the United States leads in making laundry machines?" "What cereal is used in all parts of the world?" The latter was a trick question. The correct answer, according to the Edison test, was "No cereal is used in all parts of the world."

The *Times* articles were reprinted in many other papers. Some decided to administer the test themselves. The *Chicago Tribune* tried twenty of the questions on college students and reported that male students averaged 35 percent correct responses, and female students averaged 28 percent. A reporter tracked down Theodore Edison, currently an MIT sophomore, and convinced him to give his father's test a try. Theodore's score was not revealed, but the honest young man admitted that he'd failed, since, among other things, he didn't know which states bounded Idaho. Edison, pressed by a reporter, admitted that after Theodore graduated, he'd give his son a job anyway.

Fortunately for Edison, in July the press

began writing stories that reflected better on him. The Vagabonds had announced another summer trip, and for at least part of the time a very special guest would join them.

For a while after the March death of John Burroughs, more Vagabonds trips seemed in doubt. Asked about it by a reporter at Burroughs's memorial service, all Edison would say was, "Maybe." But messages were already being exchanged between Ford and Firestone. The carmaker wanted a summer trip with his two surviving Vagabonds friends, and Firestone, as usual, was supposed to suggest a plan for one. Previously, one of the purposes of the trips was to gain attention for the possibilities of car travel, and that goal had been achieved. By 1921, autocamping had taken America by storm. But the proliferation of Americans out touring in cars and the thousands of autocamps springing up to accommodate them in towns across America complicated the Vagabonds' own trip logistics.

Only a few years earlier, they could choose almost any country road and count on having it virtually to themselves. They could stop for the night at whatever likely spot caught their collective eye, and relish the comfort of staff-cooked meals and leisurely campfire conversations in relative privacy. But now many roads were routinely busy; in a few areas in and around major cities there was even traffic congestion. Daytime stops in towns for meals or to purchase sundries had become problematic, because urban parking was suddenly a near-universal problem. Most town residences in 1921 did not include garages, so homeowners with cars had to park along curbs, and often there wasn't enough curb to meet demand. There were no downtown parking lots for those who drove in to buy groceries or enjoy coffee and doughnuts in local cafés. In many American communities, downtown streets were attractively lined with trees. In one town after another, these were torn out to create additional parking for residents and visitors, and still there weren't sufficient spaces. A multicar caravan like the Vagabonds' might circle a block for hours, unless the town included a Ford dealership, in which case the cars could be parked in that lot.

At night, the famous friends could no longer count on pitching their tents where they pleased. Farmers were far less likely to welcome campers, and it would never do for the famous Vagabonds to set up their tents in a town autocamp, where they would have to sleep and eat surrounded by hundreds or even thousands of strangers endlessly eager for autographs or handshakes. Ford, Edison, and Firestone wanted to appear *of* the people, but not cheek-to-jowl overnight *with* them. This was even more the case with their wives, who after the 1919 Yama Farms trip expected to be included on all future group excursions.

That meant Firestone's initial chore was to suggest a route that either avoided the most popular autocamping regions or at least allowed him and his friends some control over outsider access. His proposal in 1921, agreed upon by Ford and then Edison, was a trip through Michigan's Upper Peninsula. Though there might be some auto traffic to contend with, there were still plenty of back roads and spectacular scenery. Best of all, Ford owned properties in the region — he'd purchased several lumber interests. At least some of the time, they would set up camp on Ford acreage, and guards could keep away everyone but those members of the press or public that the group was willing to briefly entertain. While ordinary autocampers had to depend on ferries to cross portions of Lake Michigan, the Vagabonds could sail in style aboard the

Sialia, Ford's luxurious three-hundred-foot yacht. All that remained to be determined was the camping dates, but before Ford and Edison could coordinate their schedules for the Upper Peninsula, Firestone presented them with a new option.

Nineteen twenty-one would mark the Vagabonds' fifth publicly announced trip — the first came in 1916, when Ford failed to join the others in New York and New England. The Everglades in 1914 was a private excursion, and California in 1915 was mostly traveled by train, with cars in use for only one day between Los Angeles and San Diego. The first few auto trips attracted national coverage not only because of the participants' celebrity, but because they were vacationing by car. It was that rare. In 1921, Ford and Edison still ranked among the most famous Americans, but beyond that fame and the fancy trappings (staffs to set up and clean up campsites, chefs, tents with battery-powered lights), taking automobile vacations had become something that hundreds of thousands of other Americans did. It was possible that in the summers to come, interest in Vagabonds trips might begin dwindling until they were no longer considered particularly newsworthy at all. A fresh angle for press coverage — a "news peg," in journalism terms — was needed, and in a May 26, 1921, letter to Edison, Harvey Firestone described a sure-fire one.

Rt. Rev. William F. Anderson, Bishop of the Methodist Episcopal Church of Ohio is a close friend of President Harding and is also a good friend of mine. He is a real man's man — our kind of a man.

He had arranged with the President, Mrs. Harding, Mrs. Anderson and Himself, and Mrs. Firestone and myself, to spend a weekend at [Rev. Anderson's] old home on the Cheat River in West Virginia. He was at my home a few days ago and I showed him one of our camping books and told him that if it was agreeable to you and Mr. Ford possibly we could take our camping outfit and have our camping trip this year down in the mountains of West Virginia.

He wrote the President regarding such a trip and had a reply indicating that he would like to make a short trip with us in the middle of July. I am to call on [the president] June 8 or 9 with Bishop Anderson to complete the arrangements if he and Mrs. Harding can go. I wish that you would write me if it would be agreeable to you and Mrs. Edison to transfer our Michigan [trip] to the mountains of West Virginia so that we could have the President and his wife with us. . . . My thought would be that we would plan a three to five day trip for the President . . . and then we would finish up our camping trip in another five or ten days without [him].

I will be in New York before going to Washington and if you prefer I will try to call on you.

Edison scribbled to Meadowcroft in the letter's margin, "Say I will talk it over when he comes to lab — I have 1 or 2 suggestions." It turned out that Edison had quite a few suggestions, starting with how Firestone should find the perfect location for a presidential campsite. Secret Service agents' requirements for Harding's protection paled beside the inventor's insistence on a spot isolated enough to keep away everyone but the campers and their combined entourages. The agents wanted to ensure the president's safety; Edison hoped for Harding's undivided attention. During the day, the president could gambol all he liked, but at night by the campfire, he and Edison would discuss at length and uninterrupted America's rubber crisis, and the inability of the Navy (or, by logical extension, all branches of the U.S. military) to innovate by actually making use of input from outside experts, instead of soliciting, then ignoring it completely — subjects, in Edison's view, of vital national interest.

Harding had specified to Firestone and Rev. Anderson that he would need to be no more than a few hours' drive from Washington, so Firestone, certainly in tandem with the Secret Service, prepared a four-page typed report listing several potential campsites well within a day's drive from the capital. Firestone sent a copy of the report to Edison, admitting that "the main roads are well populated with tourists most of the hours of the day," but assuring the inventor that the proposed sites themselves were "well off the beaten track." All the suggested spots were "either along the course of [rivers] or high in the mountains and in spots well shaded thus giving the coolest temperature possible."

Edison found them all unacceptable and fired off a telegram: "If Mr. H. is to be a week with us the route proposed is very poor proposition nothing wild or secluded about it & only hills not mountains."

The eventual choice was a pleasant grove

on private land west of Hagerstown, Maryland, and a few miles from the town of
Pecktonville. A relatively busy road ran close
by, but access to the property — informally
known as the Island, framed by the waters
of Licking Creek and near the mighty Poto-
mac River — was by a bridge that could be
easily controlled by Secret Service agents.
The camp was sufficiently isolated to suit
Edison, who immediately embarked on
another task.

The inventor realized that presidents are
never entirely on vacation. During his camp
time with the Vagabonds, three to five days,
maybe more if he really enjoyed himself,
Harding would surely need at least occasionally to communicate with his staff in
Washington. The nearest phone to the Licking Creek campsite was a mile down the
road at a general store — Edison didn't
want the president frequently whisked away
to take or make White House calls. On June
21, the same day that Harding confirmed
that he and the First Lady could join the
Vagabonds on the weekend of July 23,
Meadowcroft made a written request of the
U.S. Signal Corps: "In order that Mr.
Harding may be in constant communication with Washington, Mr. Edison thinks
that the Signal Corps could probably pro-

vide a radio outfit in a good automobile, possibly equipped with a pole by which signals might be transmitted while in motion. . . . Mr. Edison thinks that the Officers of the Signal Corps might be greatly pleased to have the opportunity of doing a stunt like this."

They were. But as soon as the Signal Corps began building the special radio, the military expressed concern that vital government secrets might be discussed in an open transmission potentially monitored by foreign spies. Edison had a solution, which Meadowcroft explained in a letter to the Department of the Navy: "If they could provide a Code book of which Mr. Harding's Secretary had a duplicate, a code operator could be sent with the Outfit so that he could code any confidential dispatch and keep it away from the amateur wireless people."

That was agreeable, so long as Edison was able to procure the required order from the president. Edison now felt everything necessary was in place for Harding's convenient radio contact with his advisors from camp. The inventor wanted to personally break the happy news to him. He and Harding had never met, but Edison indicated his anticipation of a warm relationship by the salutation in a July 15 letter he had Firestone hand carry to the White House. Though in correspondence Edison invariably hewed to formality, this time he used a chummy, informal greeting he'd previously reserved for Henry Ford: "Friend Harding." The inventor took pains to make sure the president understood the trouble he'd gone to on Harding's behalf:

As you should be in hourly touch with Washington, I have arranged with the Radio Branch of the Government that an automobile with radio outfit can accompany the party. All that is required is authority from the Secretary of War to the Department to send the outfit with the necessary personnel. This will be quite a good experiment and I am sure it will work. . . . This may be a new way to mix recreation with business but it is perfectly practical, and I hope you will take the opportunity to revert to the barbaric state, for a little while at least.

A day later, Firestone gave Edison the president's typed, tone-deaf reply.

My dear Mr. Edison . . . I am writing to say that so far as I am concerned I have no desire for radio service in the camp. One of the attractive features of the camping party is freedom from all such things.

Harding said that if Edison wanted the radio setup as a personal experiment, he'd arrange it. Otherwise, "I am anticipating a pleasant session in company with you and your very attractive associates."

Edison was deeply offended. This was reflected in his formally worded letter of July 18. "My dear Mr. Harding" was advised that

so far as the radio service is concerned my first thought was for your convenience, and secondly as an interesting and instructive experiment from a government standpoint to see if radio service can be properly and quickly handled in a mountainous country under challenging conditions. . . . However, as my chief wish is that you shall have an enjoyable outing, please decide the matter according to your personal inclination and kindly advise me, as I have made some preliminary arrangements.

There's no record of Harding replying further, but he was not accompanied by a "radio service" car in the Vagabonds' camp.

■ ■ ■ ■

Ford, like Edison, had hopes of long, private discussions with the president. They had some obvious areas of philosophic disagreement. Ford enthusiastically supported the League of Nations. Harding opposed it. Harding embraced tougher immigration policies. Ford employed many immigrants — U.S. manufacturers found them willing to perform dull, rudimentary assembly tasks disdained by American workers. The president was a Republican. Political parties meant little to Ford, but he'd run for the Senate in 1918 as a Democrat.

Still, both men firmly believed that the obligation of government was to support business, not overregulate it. Mainstream newspapers had recently been editorially unfavorable to Ford and Harding, but both had their own connection with journalism — prior to entering politics Harding owned and operated *The Star,* an Ohio newspaper in his hometown of Marion, and Ford currently had the *Dearborn Independent.* Now, with their first meeting imminent, Ford was determined that he and Harding would agree on another issue.

■ ■ ■ ■

On July 8, two weeks before Harding joined the Vagabonds in camp but several weeks after it was confirmed that the president was coming, Ford made a formal purchase offer to the U.S. government for a ninety-nine-year lease on a dam complex and some nitrate plants in Muscle Shoals, Alabama. The projects were originally funded in 1916 by the Wilson administration at a cost of about $85 million. Harnessing water power along the Tennessee River was one objective, but a more crucial one was developing nitrate plants as a source of explosives for use in the war. Construction was completed in 1918, but only a few months later the war was over — and so was any sense of federal urgency at Muscle Shoals. President Wilson suggested that the government continue operating the plants and dam to make nitrogen fertilizers for farmers. This innovative concept would have been a tremendous boon to farmers, but to many it smacked of socialism and Congress rejected the proposed legislation. When Harding succeeded Wilson in the White House, the new administration put the Alabama project up for sale to private business, and

Ford wanted it. His offer of $5 million was trifling compared to the original cost to taxpayers, but Ford promised that in return he'd invest whatever was necessary to harness the vast hydroelectric power from the dams and manufacture cheap fertilizers at the nitrate plant, boosting both the regional economy and crop production. Muscle Shoals would, Ford believed, match or even exceed the benefits he bestowed on America by introducing an affordable car for the great multitudes.

Ford expected a quick, positive response — surely legislators would realize that he was doing this for public benefit, not personal profit. But established power companies and fertilizer manufacturers didn't relish a new rival who'd already crushed his competitors in the automobile industry. They immediately lobbied against Ford with Washington lawmakers, and the carmaker's bid was shunted off into a tangle of congressional committee hearings and staff studies rather than brought up for immediate decision. Harding's enthusiastic support could remedy that, and Ford was about to entertain the president as his guest at an isolated camp.

Firestone found himself far more preoccupied with logistics than in previous years. Keeping Ford, Edison, and, until his demise, the fussy Burroughs comfortable on the road without sacrificing their sense of adventure was challenging enough. Pleasing the president, First Lady, and the Vagabond wives (if Mrs. Harding was coming, so were they) and extended families added considerably to the difficulty. Ford, as usual, paid for everything, but Firestone had to oversee the purchases. Besides the usual Ford staffers needed to set up and strike camp, cook, and serve as general factotums, Harding would be accompanied by several male secretaries, teams of Secret Service agents on rotating guard duty, and at least one or two body servants charged with assisting the president in dressing and other tasks. All needed to be accommodated, as well as the retinue of hairdressers, wardrobe mistresses, and personal maids required by the First Lady and Vagabonds wives — it was impossible to know for certain the exact number of people staying in the camp. Estimates ranged from thirty-five to fifty. There had to be tents, cots, and bedding for them all, as well as chairs and mirrors (men's for shaving, ladies' for application of cosmetics), towels and soap, and vast quantities of potable water as well as discreet privies. The magnificent cooking truck that served the normal camping party so well needed to be supplemented for such a crowd, perhaps with full firepits to be dug in advance of the president's arrival. Menus had to be determined, and access to fresh meats and ingredients arranged. Here, Firestone proved ingenious. He prevailed on a church women's group in Ohio to pluck and dress one hundred chickens, bake dozens of cakes and innumerable cookies, and send the load on to Maryland in the Vagabonds' refrigerated truck. Other foodstuffs would be obtained from farms near the camp. Firestone's responsibilities didn't extend to providing for the media. So far as meals — and shelter and sanitation — were concerned, the press, held by the Secret Service beyond the bridge over the river that provided access to the campsite except at such times as the campers granted them access, had to fend for themselves.

No effort was spared to make the president and First Lady feel welcome and comfortable in the Vagabonds' camp — and then, just days before their scheduled arrival, the guests of honor balked.

Barely four months into his first White House term, Warren G. Harding was popular with the public and with the Republican majorities in the Senate and House of Representatives. To rank-and-file Americans, even those who voted against Harding, the new incumbent at least looked and acted healthy, a radical change from enfeebled Woodrow Wilson. He seemed comfortingly normal in other ways — Harding was an avid golfer (the sport was sweeping America almost as swiftly as autocamping), and like so many of his fellow countrymen, the president was known to enjoy a hand or two of poker. The senators and congressmen of his party appreciated his hands-off approach to legislation. Harding enjoyed espousing general themes — protect business, lower taxes, keep immigrants out and foreign entanglements minimal — but left designing and implementing specific policies to others. The press, so critical of Harding before his election, mostly demonstrated respect for him after his victory. Harding's failings as a president and husband were yet to be revealed, the former to a limited extent during his last months in office and the latter only after his death. The sole national "scandal" involving Harding so far was a persistent rumor during the 1920 presidential campaign that he was partly black, and the margin of his victory quashed that.

As a former newspaper publisher, Harding understood the value of publicity and the fleeting aspects of positive coverage just as much as Edison and Ford. As a newly inaugurated president, Harding currently enjoyed a honeymoon with most of the public and press, but at some point he had to do something to sustain their interest and support. It wasn't going to be groundbreaking legislation; Harding had no aptitude for that. The president's strongest support came from Middle America, so it made sense to associate himself with heartland heroes Ford and Edison. The United Press wire service story announcing Harding's plan to camp with the Vagabonds speculated that Harding would permanently replace Burroughs among them, and that their "selection of Harding to take the vacant place in this camping club of distinguished men [would be] considered one of the most unique honors conferred since he became president." The implication was that Harding was in some sense a supplicant. But the president made certain that impression didn't last long.

The articles announcing that the Hardings would join the Vagabonds sometime on

Saturday, July 23, appeared in papers only on the day before, with the secret kept until then for fear that earlier publicity would result in mobs thronging toward the Licking Creek site, hoping for glimpses of the famous campers. The ink was hardly dry on the newsprint when the White House notified Harding's hosts that the president and First Lady wouldn't be able to stay three or four days after all. Important matters required Harding to return to the White House by Sunday afternoon. Left unsaid was that the president didn't need to stay any longer than that to get the coverage he wanted. Photo-worthy activities already promised to the press such as horseback riding (Firestone trucked in a half-dozen of his personal mounts), fishing, tramping in the woods, a concert/singalong, and a lengthy prayer service now had to be shoehorned into Saturday afternoon and Sunday morning, leaving little if any time for Ford and Edison to proselytize the president on behalf of the Muscle Shoals bid and American-produced rubber. They had to accept it. They'd have at least some private time with the president and, besides, their wives would still hobnob with the First Lady, with photos in every newspaper to prove it.

But Florence Kling Harding came down with a cold or hay fever or the flu. White House bulletins weren't specific. Sometime late Friday or early Saturday the Vagabonds were informed that, due to her sudden and regrettable illness, and on advice from the White House physician, the First Lady would not join her husband at the camp. Clara Ford, Mina Edison, and Idabelle Firestone may have strongly suspected that Mrs. Harding simply didn't want to leave the luxury of the White House for a tent, but they had no recourse other than sending a gracious note to Washington expressing their disappointment and hope that the First Lady recovered soon.

Friday found almost everyone, Vagabonds and wives included, working to get the Licking Creek camp in order before the president and the press arrived the next day. Firestone told reporters later that "everything went like clockwork," but if the journalists had been there on Friday they would have known better. Firestone had arranged for forty cots, but neglected to bring any bedding beyond the usual rough blankets that were sufficient on previous trips. Clara Ford was appalled. The president and the ladies, at least, deserved decent covers, and pillows, too. She dispatched staffers to Hagerstown to make the necessary purchases. An extra-large dining tent was set up — it was impossible to know how many people would be on hand for meals, so additional tables had to be procured for those who'd have to dine alfresco. As expected, the weather was fine, but no one anticipated the swarming clouds of mosquitoes. Smudge pots needed to be set up all around the camp. Ford took charge of that. Scouting parties searched out the best routes for presidential hikes and horseback rides. Nothing was left to chance.

President Harding and his entourage drove out of Washington about 9:30 on Saturday morning, with cars jammed with journalists trailing behind. They made relatively good time on their ninety-mile trip — at one point the presidential car was reported to reach 50 mph. The plan was to meet Ford, Edison, and Firestone in Funkstown, roughly halfway to Licking Creek; the Vagabonds would then escort Harding the rest of the way to camp. The president got there a little later than expected — his car had blown a tire on the way. As soon as Harding arrived in Funkstown, he was initially greeted not by his camping hosts but a contingent of local leaders. They informed the president that the town was holding a special program that day and wanted Harding to stay awhile and make a speech. He declined, citing his previous commitment. Then Harding, his staff, and the press drove on a few more blocks to where the Vagabonds awaited them in several cars. After introductions by Firestone and Rev. Anderson, Harding was placed in a car with Firestone and Edison for the rest of the drive. Edison remained aggravated with Harding for the dismissal of his camp radio plan, and sulked as the car drove off. There were some moments of awkward silence. Harding reached into his coat pocket, extracted two cigars, and offered one to Edison. The inventor snapped, "No, thank you. I don't smoke. I chew." Firestone was mortified. He wrote later, "Mr. Edison does not take to everyone at once and does not pretend to. He [did] not set up as a hail fellow [with the President]." But Harding was equal to the occasion. He smiled, said, "I think I can accommodate you," and pulled what Firestone recalled as "a big plug of chewing tobacco out of his hip pocket." Edison took some and mumbled, "Any man who chews tobacco is all right."

They arrived at Licking Creek about 1 p.m. Reporters, photographers, and ten cinematographers surrounded Harding as he genially shook hands all around. Then Harding, declaring he was hungry rather than worn-out after the morning's drive, thrilled the press with the further announcement that he wanted to earn his lunch. One wire service report informed readers that the president approached some logs and "peeling off his coat, rolling up his sleeves and seizing an axe . . . started to make the chips fly. With deft swings that would have done justice to a north woodsman, he assailed the woodpile with a vim. Five minutes later he had chopped enough wood for fires to cook luncheon, with some left over as a starter for the evening meal." That chore accomplished, Harding further gratified photographers by drinking water from a metal dipper. He asked if they preferred having him pose standing or sitting on a tree stump. Lunch followed, and much was made by the press about the massive lazy Susan table inside the main dining tent. A few reporters who'd never seen such a table before wrote that it was undoubtedly invented by Edison.

For postprandial entertainment, the ladies, Harding, Ford, and Edison gathered on chairs underneath some shade trees while Rev. Anderson read aloud from "The Martial Adventures of Henry and Me," a not-so-short story by Kansas author William Allen White. The women knitted and gave every appearance of remaining engrossed for the hour or more that the minister droned on. Ford lasted only a few minutes before getting up to roam the camp area. Edison didn't pretend to be interested. He rolled up his coat as a pillow, lay down nearby, and fell asleep. Harding struggled — reporters noted that he blinked repeatedly, and his cigar "drooped" in his mouth — but stayed conscious until the end, at which point the president congratulated Rev. Anderson on a splendid performance, then took the photographers to his tent, where they circled the army cot with its fine new covers and clicked away. After a few minutes Harding firmly shooed them out, saying that he wanted to nap.

While the president snoozed and Edison still snored beneath his tree, the press asked Ford if there was anything else for them to write about and photograph. The carmaker suggested a friendly woodchopping contest between himself and Firestone, who initially declined but finally agreed. After cautioning that he had little experience with axes, the tire manufacturer cut gamely at a log, missing with most of his swings while the press prudently backed away, believing themselves in more danger than the wood. Firestone wore out quickly. Ford took up the axe and reduced the log to kindling.

After an hour Harding emerged from his tent, saying that he was well-rested and ready for more adventure. Firestone suggested horseback riding. The president agreed, telling reporters that the White House physician recommended riding as good exercise, and adding that he personally hadn't been on a horse in thirty years so the press shouldn't expect much. Then he, Firestone, and a few others trotted off. A few photographers were allowed to snap photos at a distance, and one or two hearty reporters sprinted to places along the anticipated route. Their accounts described Harding as solid in the saddle. While the president was gone, the press remaining at Licking Creek found something else to write about. One of the camp party had complained that his Model T, parked near the tents, wouldn't start, so reporters asked Ford to go over and crank it. He obliged, windmilling his arm dramatically.

When the riders returned, it was time for music. A local pianist played a variety of tunes, then asked for requests — the president wanted "Somewhere a Voice Is Calling" and "Underneath Hawaiian Skies." One of Firestone's daughters-in-law tried teaching Ford some popular current dance steps, and gamely assured the automaker that he showed great potential even as he repeatedly stepped on her toes. The concert concluded with a rousing rendition of "The Star-Spangled Banner." Everyone stood and sang.

Edison was awake in time for the music, and afterward Harding made a point of chatting with the inventor as reporters hung on every word. The president asked Edison what he did for recreation. Edison shrugged. Harding inquired, "Do you play golf?" Edison, either drowsy or still resentful of Harding's rejection of his radio service, grunted, "No." Harding grinned for the cameras as he delivered a punch line: "Not old enough?" Edison, seventy-four, had to laugh. Later, the inventor offered a jest of his own. Edison disappeared from camp for a while, eventually emerging with a handful of greenery. With the media within earshot, Edison called out, "I've got the mint. Who's got the julep?" It wasn't a summons for pre-prandial cocktails, but an inside joke for one of his fellow Vagabonds. Besides eschewing liquor out of health concerns, Ford loathed alcohol for what he discerned as its universally ruinous effect on drinkers' judgment. Only a few years earlier, he cited alcohol as a contributing cause to the Great War, with beer-drinking Germans "taking after" wine-swilling Frenchmen.

Harding crossed the bridge in late afternoon, leading the press on a leisurely mile-long walk to the general store. The president waved to children who lined the road along the way, and subsequent stories disagreed about whether Harding treated several kids to candy from the store, or else just one "blue-eyed, five-year-old girl." (Some accounts estimated her age as ten.) The president's announced purpose for the trip was using the store's phone to call the White House and check on the First Lady's condition. Reporters weren't allowed to listen in, but after a few minutes Harding emerged to report that his wife was feeling better, though still not well enough to come out to Licking Creek the next morning for a few hours.

When Harding got back to camp, he and the Vagabonds made a brief attempt to catch some fish in Licking Creek, but the fish didn't cooperate. Dinner followed, with Irish stew as the main course, and then the press was sent packing across the bridge and the Vagabonds and their honored guest finally enjoyed some privacy. Night fell, leaving the camp illuminated by a flickering campfire. The ladies retired, servants and Secret Service withdrew a discreet distance, and Harding, Edison, Ford, Firestone, and Rev. Anderson were left to stare into the flames and talk confidentially among themselves. This was certainly the moment when the carmaker and the inventor anticipated they would make their respective cases for Muscle Shoals and rubber research directly to the president. But Harding never gave them the opportunity. Though the fireside chat extended well past midnight, it was the president who chose the subjects and did most of the talking. There was some discussion of a "Limitation of Arms" conference with European powers, which Ford in particular found fascinating. Otherwise, it was a presidential monologue — Firestone wrote that Harding spoke "about the trials of being president and the vast amount of unnecessary detail imposed upon the office. . . . He also spoke of the nuisance of a President being forced to seek a second term, and thought that a single term of six years would be far better and leave the President with more time to attend to his duties." Harding declared "that it was time to stop attacking business because it was business, and legitimate business ought to be protected and not interfered with." Ford, Edison, and Firestone couldn't disagree with that.

While Harding filibustered, the reporters and wire service correspondents wrote and filed their stories, probably driving back to towns with available telephones and telegraph offices, then returning to their own camp area afterward. The headlines were almost uniformly glowing — "Harding Earns Dinner by Sweat of His Brow"; "Harding Rides Horseback in Shirtsleeves"; "President Takes Different Holiday." The lazy Susan table received considerable coverage — "Harding Eats on Gyrating Camp Table"; "And Now We Have Double-Deck Dining Table." The Licking Creek site was identified as "Camp Harding." The Vagabonds were secondary in those rare headlines mentioning them at all: "Harding, Edison, Ford and Company Campers De Luxe." The stories themselves lauded Harding's woodchopping and horseback riding skills, his splendid appetite, and his jovial

324

attitude. The Vagabonds were described as congenial hosts who enjoyed rugged back-country adventures with their president. These were the reports that appeared in most papers around the country, like the Mattoon, Illinois, *Journal-Gazette* and the *Des Moines Register* and the *Wilmington Press.*

The big-city *Baltimore Sun* and *New York Times,* relying on their own reporters rather than the wire services, told it differently. In their accounts, Harding only swung his chopping axe a few times before becoming so winded that Ford had to take over. The distinguishing feature of the horseback ride was Harding's inability to keep the presidential seat even somewhat settled in the saddle. The president's main exercise came from slapping mosquitoes. As for the Vagabonds, all Edison did was nap — this from the man who famously claimed to need only four or five hours of sleep during any given day and night. Henry Ford's cranking of the Model T was a complete fraud. The new car in question had an electric starter — the carmaker twirled an imaginary crank to please the photographers, and afterward quipped to them, "Well, what have you got to say about that?" But beyond their own newspaper's pages, these accounts weren't widely disseminated. On Sunday morning, most Americans read heartwarming stories extolling the chief executive and the friends who were honored by his presence.

Sunday morning at the Licking Creek camp found the media around early and everyone in camp but Edison and Harding up by 6:30. They finally emerged about eight, and along with Ford and Firestone obliged photographers by shaving from bowls of water, guiding their razors in the reflection of mirrors propped against handy trees. Breakfast was hearty ("eggs, bacon and flapjacks," according to the United News Wire), and afterward the president and the inventor talked at some length about tarpon fishing. A truck parked too near a gasoline range caught fire, and staff and Secret Service agents rushed to extinguish it. Then Firestone and Harding set off on a second ride, this one very short. To the delight of the photographers, they splashed through a narrow bit of creek. Several reporters wrote that the president seemed more comfortable in the saddle than he had been the day before, though they stopped short of writing that this time he seemed in no danger of being pitched off.

The plan had been for lunch after the ride,

then a Sunday worship service conducted by Rev. Anderson. But the order was reversed — Firestone explained to the press that the minister preferred not to officiate on a full stomach. Harding asked that about two hundred people held back beyond the bridge be allowed to come and worship, too — he wanted to be among his fellow citizens. The crowd filed in and acted appropriately respectful, taking seats on some scattered chairs or else on the ground. Harding, Ford, Firestone, and their families were given seats directly in front of Anderson. Edison never sat, and soon after the Reverend began the service, the inventor went off to the side of the temporary stage, curled up on the grass, and read a newspaper.

Edison missed a fire-and-brimstone performance. The Methodist bishop took full advantage of his own turn in the national media spotlight. He blasted the League of Nations concept ("which does not even recognize God"), gave thanks to the Lord that America, led by its current president, had spurned that sinful invitation, praised Harding for pursuing universal disarmament, lectured that the United States must be the Christian leader among all nations (only "principles of Christianity" could save the world), and concluded by promising that everything happened for divine purpose, since God had a plan for America. Harding may have had trouble staying awake the previous day while Anderson read aloud, but he was fully alert now. The Associated Press account of the service noted that the president "joined lustily in singing 'Rock of Ages,' 'Nearer My God to Thee' and other old-fashioned hymns."

When the lengthy service concluded, Harding insisted on shaking hands and sharing a few friendly words with everyone in the impromptu congregation. That took more time, so lunch was late and hurried. About 4 p.m. the president assured his hosts that it had been "a most wonderful experience" and departed for the White House, with his staff, Secret Service agents, and the press trailing in his wake.

Though Harding left on Sunday afternoon, the Vagabonds and the rest of their party stayed where they were through Wednesday morning. They'd planned the rest of their trip based on the assumption that the president and First Lady would be with them at Licking Creek for several days. Then after the Hardings finally took their leave, the Vagabonds' party would take a fairly short jaunt further west in Maryland, then across the state line to West Virginia and finally north to Pittsburgh. Ford and Firestone representatives in towns along the route had made arrangements with local dignitaries and press to expect the Vagabonds later in the week so they couldn't show up several days ahead of time. An alternative was to cancel the rest of the trip altogether. There's no record that this was considered. Ford and Edison weren't quitters.

They remained camped by Licking Creek for two more days, filling time by exploring the surrounding valley and hills. The reporters, photographers, and wire service correspondents who'd come to cover Harding on vacation left when he did. Stories about the president's Sunday in camp filled Monday's front pages around the nation. Harding evidently paused when he reached the White House and confided to reporters that while he'd had a pleasant time, the experience was still somewhat disappointing. A widely reprinted wire story stated "it is understood that [the President] was unable to rough it as much as he expected owing to the highly scientific manner in which the genius of Edison and Ford have contrived to eliminate the arduous tasks of camp life."

Edison came in for direct criticism in articles describing how the inventor ignored Anderson's Sunday sermon. Other stories intimated that Edison's frequent naps, including times when Harding was speaking, offended not only the president but everyone else at Licking Creek ("SLEEPS WHILE HARDING TALKS: Edison Astonishes Others in Camp by His Indifference" according to the *Brooklyn Citizen*).

There were also editorials. Most waxed eloquent about the amazing egalitarianism demonstrated by Harding — the *Oakland Tribune* enthused that "the President chumming with Thomas Edison and Henry Ford in a mountain camp is . . . characteristically American, illuminating a phase of life peculiar to this country. It would be impossible to think of a president of any other land chopping the wood to cook his meal." A few big-city papers quibbled, but even there the Vagabonds rather than Harding came in for derision. The *Atlanta Constitution* disdained the camp's many amenities — "No doubt President Harding would have more enjoyed [a] simpler outing" — and the *Philadelphia Inquirer* mocked the Vagabonds' thirst for publicity, though not the president's, in a biting bit of doggerel:

330

Firestone, Edison, Ford
Know what to do when they're bored.
In the woods they cut capers
And pose for the papers,
Firestone, Edison, Ford.

Monday also found the White House reporting that Mrs. Harding was completely recovered from her recent debilitating illness. Clara Ford, Mina Edison, and Idabelle Firestone received a typed, polite message from the First Lady, addressed to the site that the press named for her husband, not theirs.

To the Ladies of Camp Harding:
Your kindly note telling me that I was missed at Camp Harding last [weekend] compensates me in a measure for the disappointment I felt when I found I must forego the pleasure of accompanying the President. I am sure I should have enjoyed every moment of the time, and join with you in the hope that another season I may be more fortunate.
With warmest thanks for your message of sympathy, and kindest regards to you all,

Sincerely yours,
Florence Kling Harding.

On Wednesday Firestone had his horses shipped back to Ohio. Some of the party went home, too — the three Vagabonds and their wives remained, plus two Firestone sons, a Firestone daughter-in-law, and Rev. Anderson and his wife, Jennie. After all the camp gear was packed, they drove ninety miles through green valleys and tree-lined mountains to Garrett County in western Maryland. They'd been invited to camp in a particularly charming spot there by state forester Fred Beasley, who described a waterfall and surrounding hills of great beauty. The drive went well, and Beasley hadn't exaggerated the charms of their prospective stop, but some boys were already camped there. The youngsters moved to another part of what locals called "Swallow Falls" only when someone, probably Firestone, paid them $10 to leave. It was nearly dark by the time the Vagabonds' camp was set up. Their heavy camp kitchen, following their passenger cars, caved in the narrow wooden bridge on the only road leading in to the falls, and while its driver and some other staff worked to extricate it everyone had to eat their dinners out of cans. Afterward the travelers turned in. Before she slept, Mina Edison wrote a letter to her son.

My darling Theodore — This is nothing like [an enjoyable] camp experience. It is a Ford-Firestone crowd and I am absolutely homesick. Everything is . . . so elaborate and so fussy that there is no charm in it. The day we face homeward I shall be a happy woman. We are apparently remaining in camp a long time rather than moving on every day. I am in doubt as to which would be more desirable.

Despite Mina's moping, for the next two days the Vagabonds had a good time. The ladies wandered the woods. Ford and Edison studied Swallow Falls, calculating the hydropower that might be harnessed from it. Firestone, having just sent his own horses home, rented others from a local man and went out on rides with his sons. Everyone was entertained by the tales of local woodsmen Link and Hank Sines, whom state forester Beasley had asked to come out and visit with the campers. Ford bought an old steam engine that he found by a sawmill and had it shipped back to Dearborn. The automaker also spoke to a few reporters who turned up at the campsite. Ford was characteristically blunt when asked about the workers' strike currently plaguing some railroads, but not the Detroit, Toledo &

Ironton line he'd recently bought. Immediately after the purchase he gave raises to his new employees. This drew the wrath of other railroad owners, who claimed that Ford's unnecessary generosity to the Detroit, Toledo & Ironton workers caused dissension among his competitors' employees. Ford told the reporters that the problem wasn't with him, but with railroad ownership more concerned with lining the pockets of shareholders than properly compensating employees.

Ford was just as direct when asked about the *Dearborn Independent*'s antisemitic articles, saying he'd read and approved them all — "I have checked up on the facts and have come to the conclusion that everything contained in the articles is true." Future articles would reveal the full extent of Jewish scheming, which included the instigation of the Civil War. Ford explained that everyone "thought that the Civil War was fought to free the slaves. . . . We shall prove that this international Jewish plot can be connected up with the Civil War. Just keep on reading."

On Saturday the campers were ready to move on, but heavy rains kept them cooped up in their tents at Swallow Falls. Muddy roads on Sunday morning further delayed the trucks' departure, but the passenger cars were able to navigate through the muck for about fifty miles to Elkins, West Virginia, with several stops in towns along the way. In each they took time to speak with local press along with any wire service reporters who were present. In Oakland, Maryland, Ford discussed his hopes for Muscle Shoals, if Congress approved the sale. The region, the state of Alabama, even the entire South would enjoy an economic boom from the increased availability of expansive hydro-electric power and cheap fertilizers. Ford emphasized that he wasn't doing this for personal profit. The carmaker regretted that he couldn't go into more detail "while the proposition is still before Congress," but made clear, one wire story reported, "that his plans are . . . stupendous."

Edison also spoke with the press in Oakland. His topic was civilization, which the inventor defined as "a mere veneer . . . every man way down in his heart revolts at [it]. Turn a man loose in the woods and he won't want to come back after a while."

The reporters were surprised when a third member of the party asked to speak with them. Mina Edison was furious over the articles about her husband napping through much of President Harding's Licking Creek visit and ignoring Rev. Anderson's sermon. In particular, one wire story including the headline "Ha, Edison Exposed" had been reprinted in such geographically diverse newspapers as the *Portsmouth* (Ohio) *Daily Times* and *Albuquerque Journal.* Mina considered her husband too modest to complain and Ford too self-centered to address the printed insults on his friend's behalf, so she took it on herself to set the record straight. "Mr. Edison takes his sleep scientifically," Mina explained to the reporters. It was true, as he'd always said, that while at home in New Jersey and busy in his laboratory, Edison really did sleep only about four hours at night. But on vacations, which these camping trips were intended to be, "with sleep he rebuilds himself against the [next] rigorous spell of work . . . he has a most peculiar power of dropping into a heavy slumber instantly." And her husband meant no offense to Rev. Anderson when he read a paper during the minister's Sunday service at Licking Creek: "It is one of Mr. Edison's chief regrets that because of his poor hearing he cannot attend church services. He used to try, but he couldn't hear a word that was said. Nevertheless, his every instinct is Christian."

Mina asked Rev. Anderson to corroborate her statement, and the Reverend good-naturedly joked, "If I didn't know how deaf Mr. Edison is, I might charge myself with preaching him to sleep." She was undoubtedly gratified that many of the same papers that printed the "Edison Exposed" article ran follow-up stories with her explanation.

The group's plan was to camp by the Cheat River outside Elkins, but the equipment truck hadn't caught up when they arrived in town, so they spent the night in a hotel. The next day they set up their tents near the bank of the river, a mile or so removed from a Boy Scout camp. Two Scouts, Macon and Joseph Fry, decided to see the famous men for themselves. They later told reporters that Mr. Ford and Mr. Edison were "most affable." The inventor was pleased to learn that the brothers had their own "wireless outfit," and urged them to keep experimenting with it. Mr. Ford gestured toward the Scout knives hanging from the boys' belts, showed them his own pocketknife, and, according to the Fry brothers, "told how he was recently attacked by an infuriated deer and was forced to kill the deer with his knife to save himself."

Reporters also visited the Vagabonds at

Cheat River. None of them asked Ford to corroborate that he'd triumphed over a maddened deer in a battle to the death. Instead, they listened as Ford talked about his plans for Muscle Shoals, and the excellent potential of West Virginia rivers to provide statewide hydroelectric power. Ford declared, "This country is on the eve of a great wave of prosperity, if only we will grasp the opportunity." Harnessing the might of rivers and "pushing" an international disarmament plan was critical — "labor questions would settle themselves, factories would spring up in every section and the country blossom like a rose."

On Tuesday, August 2, the Vagabonds turned north toward home. They ended the day at the Summit Hotel in Uniontown, Pennsylvania, but on the way they stopped in or near several towns and spoke to the press. United Press wire reporter Karl A. Bickel was present outside Belington, West Virginia, when the group stopped to eat sandwiches and bacon cooked on a portable stove. This was the last time on the 1921 trip that Ford and Edison spoke with the media, and they persuaded Bickel and the other reporters that they were being allowed to listen in on a typical camp lunchtime conversation. Bickel described the scene:

> Edison leaned against the side of his car, Firestone sat upon the running board, Ford . . . moved restlessly about, sometimes reclining on the ground picking at the grass, or, if stirred by the talk, springing to his feet, making his point and then dropping to the ground again.

Their subject was Warren G. Harding, who, Edison warned, would have trouble "forc[ing] the military to accept a real disarmament." The president had promised the American people that he'd succeed, Edison emphasized, so if he failed, Harding would have to accept full responsibility: "It all rests on him."

Ford interjected that "the common people . . . are sick and tired of the claptrap talk. . . . Why, I have received as many as 2,500 letters in a single day about it. Letters from everywhere."

Firestone agreed that America currently had "great opportunity" for peace and prosperity, adding that "it all depends on the quality of American leadership." These leaders must realize that foes of the common people lurked everywhere, ready to wreak havoc "if they see the slightest inkling of indecision."

"The motives of men are unfathomable," Edison said, and Ford agreed: "You said it."

On Wednesday, as their trip ended in Pittsburgh, Bickel's wire story about Ford's, Edison's, and Firestone's remarks was printed in many newspapers. Besides the comments themselves, many of the accompanying headlines placed the president on notice ("Ford and Edison Put It Up to Harding to Block War" in the *Baltimore Sun*).

On Thursday, the *Chicago Tribune* wrote a new editorial about its old antagonist Henry Ford, its first major mention of him since the libel trial two years earlier. The editorial's tone reflected a lesson learned: This time the newspaper criticized Ford's recently expressed opinions without calling him names. Ford, Edison, and Firestone

are successful and rich. . . . Mr. Ford is incomparable in his vocation and has done a great service by the development and [sales distribution] of cheap automobiles. He has been rewarded for this service by a huge fortune amassed in a time bewilderingly short. But mental efficiency in one direction, knowledge and insight as to one range of facts or forces, gives no guarant[ee] of efficiency in other matters. . . . All of which ought to be a truism. Yet our American guilelessness goes on swallowing the utterances of men who are accepted, and esteem themselves, as authority on all subjects because they are authority on one.

The *Tribune* reminded its readers of Ford's opposition to the war, and how, once America entered the fray, "for a time his authority dwindled." But now he was back, holding forth "at the behest of his admirers on many matters as to which his opinions [are] valueless." This time, the editorial warned, Ford had a different goal — "running again for senate or presidency."

At least in an exploratory sense, he already was.

CHAPTER EIGHT:
INTERLUDE:
NOVEMBER 1921–JUNE 1923

In 1921 Henry Ford and Thomas Edison took another trip together, this one to Alabama. On November 23, the *New York Times* reported that the carmaker and the inventor would leave soon to "inspect" the dams and manufacturing facilities at Muscle Shoals. They hoped "to obtain data to convince the United States Government that Mr. Ford's offer for the nitrate and water power project is liberal." Members of Senate and congressional oversight committees had criticized what they considered Ford's paltry offer for the taxpayer-funded operations that had fallen into disrepair. Ford pledged an immediate $5 million, plus about $1.6 million annually for the duration of a one-hundred-year lease. But the original construction cost at Muscle Shoals was $85 million, and Ford wanted the government to spend another $68 million for repairs before he took over the properties. Legislators wanted Ford to assume most or all of the renovation costs. Otherwise, they stated publicly and often, the terms were overwhelmingly in Ford's favor, not the taxpayers'. Senator George W. Norris of Nebraska claimed that "No corporation ever [wanted] a more unconscionable contract." That impression ran counter to Ford's public image as a man of the people and the implacable enemy of financiers who exploited them. He could not allow the government's criticism to stand.

Ford's best recourse was to overwhelm the elected officials with widespread support for his Muscle Shoals acquisition. To ensure he had it, he enlisted Edison. The inventor remained among the most famous Americans, and perhaps the most trusted. No elected official ever suggested that Edison wished to exploit taxpayers for personal gain. Ford's publicity department stressed that while the automaker and the inventor would travel to Muscle Shoals together, they would conduct their inspections separately: They "will examine the project with a view to ascertaining how much water power may be developed and as to the cost [to Ford] of the development. [Then] conferences will be held between the two each evening during the inspection period." The "data obtained" would be forwarded to the secretary of war.

Ford and Edison left for Alabama by train on December 2. They made their studies and submitted their report, which unsurprisingly supported Ford's claim that the benefits to the regional economy would far outweigh any additional government investment. The *New York Times* also reported that Ford had increased his initial offer to $28 million. It didn't matter. Congressional debate about the proposal continued. Legislators were in no hurry.

Ford ordered his publicity department to conduct a Muscle Shoals publicity effort that resembled a political campaign. Farmers were the target — they would benefit first from hydroelectric power and cheap fertilizers. Ford paid for rallies where participants wore buttons proclaiming "I Want Ford to Get Muscle Shoals." Supporters were urged to write letters to President Harding. Robert Lacey writes in *Ford: The Men and the Machine,* his history of Ford Motor Company, that "Muscle Shoals became a national craze for a season, another California Gold Rush." Ford himself reiterated again and again that he pursued the purchase only "to do a certain thing that will benefit the whole world." And still the government remained unresponsive.

Mounting frustration fueled Ford's burgeoning political ambition. Above all things he hated layers of larded bureaucracy, time wasted when pared-down efficiency was required. Every moment of windy Washington debate delayed the blessings that he was prepared to bestow. Why couldn't a man make the government a reasonable offer and get an immediate answer back? For the first time, Ford began privately mentioning his intentions if elected president: "I'd . . . like to go down there for about six weeks and throw some monkey wrenches into the machinery." President Henry Ford wouldn't tolerate laggardly political processes; he'd trash the system and rebuild it in his own efficient business image. Exactly how that would be done didn't concern him — as with Ford Motor Company, he'd set the course, announce the goals, and then expect the people who worked for him — currently in Dearborn, soon in Washington — to make it all happen. If they didn't, he'd get rid of them and appoint people who could. But Ford would relish throwing the monkey wrenches. Otherwise, he espoused no further political philosophies. From Ford's previous actions and public statements, it could be generally assumed that as president he would avoid foreign entanglements of all kinds, abolish regulations on business, and champion the development of hydroelectric power. Beyond this, his beliefs and intentions were mysteries, and for disenchanted American voters, this was part of his allure. Since Ford declared no specific plans, they could assume that he'd do whatever they personally hoped that a president would.

There's no record that Ford gave much thought to how Ford Motor Company would operate in his absence. Edsel Ford still served as president, but his father could and did veto anything the son wanted that went against the older man's wishes. Edsel wanted to develop new cars to supplement the Model T, automobiles with different body styles, a few more embellishments, eye-pleasing Model T alternatives that offered traditional Ford automobile reliability at slightly higher prices. Ford wouldn't have it — the Model T had been and would continue being the perfect car for the masses. Sales bore him out. About 1.1 million Model Ts would be sold in 1922, more than in any previous year. Survey results varied, but all agreed that Model Ts comprised 40 to 50 percent of all cars driven in America. Many were ten years old, or more

— they were designed not to wear out. Ford didn't disdain high-end luxury cars. He sometimes drove them himself (and the Vagabonds rode in them on their summer trips). In February 1922 he acquired the Lincoln Motor Company. But utilitarian Model Ts remained the Ford Motor Company's trademark — and only — passenger car. Ford felt little concern for rival companies like General Motors, a conglomerate of brands including Buick, Oldsmobile, Cadillac, and Chevrolet. The continuing dominance of the Model T proved to Ford that he understood what consumers wanted better than any competitor.

By late 1921, politics and the *Dearborn Independent* claimed much of Ford's attention, as did his now numerous nonautomotive businesses. In 1923 the *New York Times* listed these as ore, timber, coal, property investment ("land"), railroads, "industrial activities," and banking. With the boss's attention so often diverted, Ford Motor Company officials had leeway to run their departments as they believed Ford wanted, carrying out new, sometimes draconian policies in his name. This was most evident in the long-standing company programs intended to support employees in low-level jobs.

Ford's employment philosophy had been not only to pay higher salaries than competitors, but to control employees' lives in a benevolent but firm manner — management, in Ford's opinion, always knew best. The famed $5 workday came with conditions. To qualify for this munificent income, employees had to allow company inspectors to visit their homes. There could be no evidence of liquor on the premises. The household must be tidy. Inspectors had to see evidence of financial prudence — the increased income must not be frittered away. If otherwise qualified employees had no bank accounts, they were expected to open them — the inspectors showed them how, and monitored them afterward to make certain it was done. Court records were checked — no employee with a history of domestic violence was eligible for the higher wage. Foreign-born workers, especially those with little or no command of English, were enrolled in company-underwritten classes that not only taught language but American history. There were regular, elaborate graduation ceremonies — students crossed stages draped with bunting to receive diplomas. The company had stores open to all, with arrays of quality products available at reasonable prices. These operations were collectively known as the Sociological Department.

But by 1921, opposing the spread of unions became one of Ford's public missions. He expected all workers, his own especially, to be appreciative of and loyal to their employers. Accepting a salary also meant accepting the responsibility of working as hard and efficiently as possible. Any attempt to form a union was in fact a declaration the employees intended that they rather than their employer would run things. Ford certainly wasn't going to allow any unions in his shops. He didn't doubt that some, perhaps many, of his workers read or heard about unions and were tempted to accept outside — *socialist* — help in organizing their own. This meant they didn't appreciate all that Ford Motor Company did for them. To protect his company from insidious outside influence, Ford toughened up on management and workers alike. The Sociological Department was eliminated. Assembly line supervisors, in part from management direction and often on their own, cracked down further. Factory atmosphere became oppressive, with more pressure than ever to turn out perfectly assembled cars *faster*. Previously, it had been considered lucky, even an honor, to work line jobs at Ford Motor Company. Not anymore. Robert Casey, a retired historian for the Ford Museum in Dearborn, says that "Working for Ford came with lots of stress. It translated all the way down the line. Ford Motor Company ultimately became a grim place to work, top to bottom."

Ford was more hands-on in January 1922 when he ordered that the *Dearborn Independent*'s ongoing series of antisemitic articles be immediately discontinued. Ford gave no explanation, but two reasons appear obvious. The first was financial. In late 1921 Model T sales remained strong, but there were dips in certain places, especially New York City, where the area sales manager believed that the *Independent*'s articles had sparked a Jewish boycott of Ford's signature vehicle. There were additional sales blips in other states and regions with a significant Jewish population. When the first articles appeared in 1920, Ford discounted the possibility of Jewish consumer backlash, but now it was fact rather than speculation.

The other cause was political. Presidential candidates were rarely elected without carrying the electoral-vote-heavy states of New

York and Ohio, both of which had significant Jewish populations. Most of the Midwestern and Western states, which comprised Ford's primary political base, had relatively few Jews, but they also had less heft in the all-important electoral college. Future events would prove that Ford retained his antisemitic beliefs, but for immediate political expediency he chose to mute them.

Ford was also preoccupied with his autobiography — those with presidential ambitions routinely published ghostwritten, highly sanitized memoirs that were often stilted and virtually unreadable. Ford predictably wanted a book that appealed to the same hardworking middle-class voters who'd made his Model T the standard in automobiles. Samuel Crowther, his ghostwriter, concocted a conversational tome, and in 1922 *My Life and Work* became a bestseller.

All these activities kept Ford so busy that he apparently did not suggest a Vagabonds trip in 1922. Even if he had, it's unlikely that Edison would have agreed. He, too, was otherwise engaged.

In early 1922, Edison was in regular touch with Ford's engineers about the proposed

351

electric truck. Edison and his assistants always had multiple experiments and product tests ongoing in their laboratory, but this project had the boss's particular attention. He believed they were close to perfecting a battery that would hold its charge long term, and sent on to the Ford engineering department a blueprint indicating that the battery should be placed under the seat. On February 21, Ford engineer "F. Allison" replied, congratulating Edison on his seventy-fifth birthday and explaining why the proposed positioning of the battery wouldn't do:

This looks very good but would suggest that the Motor and Control be put under the Hood and also undersling the battery at rear if possible so as to throw as much of this load on rear . . . as possible. We are all very busy at the present time getting the Lincoln Plant into operation but I expect to be in New York very shortly . . . will have some drawings on Ford Electric Truck with me for your inspection.

Edison responded, "Will await your arrival which I hope will be soon," before insisting that his placement of the battery must be followed. "One of the greatest things to make a success of a battery truck is to have battery under seat where it can be got at without trouble to the [driver]. If it is [placed inconveniently], they always neglect it [because] it is so unhandy. The life of the battery is 50% greater [under the seat.]"

Ultimately, the placement of the battery didn't matter because plans for the Ford electric truck were eventually abandoned. Edison wasn't much bothered. He'd learned during his long career that most experiments were unsuccessful — it was a matter of constantly trying lots of things, and making the most of those that panned out. Besides, a more important project dominated his thinking.

During 1922, and for the next few years, Edison spent considerable time reading rather than supervising work in the laboratory. He continued to be interested in rubber, specifically determining which latex-bearing plants could be grown in the U.S. in sufficient quantities. To do that successfully, Edison needed to study previous rubber-related research, and learn as much as possible about the rubber tree itself — why it wouldn't grow in America, which of the plant's properties might be artificially replicated in the laboratory. It would be foolish to attempt any experiments before he'd done his extensive homework. Edison was obsessed with the subject, as he'd been in his effort to develop a long-burning electric bulb suitable for homes and offices. That project took four years, from 1878 when Edison first focused on the problem to the late summer of 1882, when parts of New York City were lit with incandescent bulbs and Edison declared, "I have accomplished all I promised." Now the inventor was ready to dedicate another four years or even more to providing America with the means of supplying its own rubber. As he began what would surely become a drawn-out process, the aging inventor was too preoccupied for a summer car trip.

But if the Vagabonds didn't hit the road in 1922, many other Americans did. Summer automobile travel, much of it extended autocamping, was becoming integral in national culture. It certainly helped that roads were getting better — gasoline taxes paid for much of the upgrade. Only three years earlier, an article in the *Washington Evening Star* warned motorists to bring along at minimum a tow rope, a wrench, a file "for cleaning ignition points," a box of assorted nuts and bolts, a full set of spare tires, a chain, and a fire extinguisher. Now the roads were better, and if repairs were required there were garages in virtually every roadside town, and towing services available to haul autos out of ditches or gluey mud. A whole new industry had sprung up, too, dedicated to manufacturing products designed specifically for those traveling by car. Products like Coleman stoves (no need for campfires!) and trailers (why sleep in tents if it rained or was unseasonably chilly?) made autocamping far more comfortable. In just over another decade, *Fortune* magazine would conclude that accoutrements for road travel had grown into a $3 billion annual industry "based on the restlessness of the American people." Nineteen twenty-one saw the opening of the first drive-in restaurant — for those in a hurry, no need to waste additional drive time getting out of a car to go inside and eat. In 1924 Rand-McNally would publish its first extensive U.S. road maps. Five years after that, the first public parking garage was opened in Detroit, and when other cities soon followed the problem of downtown parking was lessened.

So many Americans were autocamping that the free autocamps proliferating only a few summers earlier became impractical.

Not everyone making use of them was on vacation. Migrant workers finding employment in the area set up shelters and stayed in place for weeks or even months, hoarding their earnings, not spending their travel money in surrounding businesses, which was the purpose of towns offering free camp space to tourists in the first place. Theft became a problem. Hoodlums posing as campers filched unguarded property at a frequently fearsome rate, and unless police were called in it was difficult getting unwelcome individuals to leave. Since the camps themselves didn't generate income, few towns were willing to pay for security guards. Because campers could stay at no cost, they often demonstrated little regard for the campgrounds, leaving piles of trash when they departed.

Beginning in 1922, the free camps were gradually replaced by pay camps, with travelers charged a dollar or two to stop and spend the night. The money generated paid for guards, which cut down considerably on theft and rowdy behavior. Rules regarding garbage were more strictly enforced. The problem remained of campers wanting to be up and out early, disturbing the sleep of others who were planning later departures — in another few years, the first pay facilities providing actual structures for overnight customers rather than empty camp space would gradually become the norm. Called "motor hotels" or "tourist courts," soon they were popularly known as "motels." Like their predecessor autocamps, the earliest of these were outside towns, but they eventually became downtown staples, too.

But in the early 1920s, another form of traffic became common on U.S. roads: an ongoing migration of young rural Americans into the cities. The country was continuing its transformation from an agrarian to an industrial economy. Farmers never fully recovered from the 1920 economic crash. While parents stayed on, trying desperately to retain their property, to eke out their living selling crops at prices barely above the accumulated cost of planting, nurturing, and harvesting, their children were increasingly unwilling to settle for such a marginal life. There were jobs to be had in the cities, and even the lowest-paying of these still exceeded the income that most farmers could expect for their sweaty labor. And, besides, the cities offered *fun* — restaurants, speakeasies, dance clubs, movies, things their mothers and fathers did without and often considered corrupters of youth. Rural

America remained mostly austere, lacking even that most basic of new luxuries, electric light — in 1923, just over 44 percent of American residences had electricity, but that fell to only 3 percent on farms. The Eighteenth Amendment had banned the sale of liquor except for certain medicinal purposes since 1920, but booze was always available to city folk in the know. The world was changing — throughout rural America, young people embraced the change, while their parents longed for a leader who would not only respect but somehow restore a sober, more sensible way of life. It was ironic that the man they believed would best represent them was in great part responsible for the cultural change they deplored. For Henry Ford's presidential aspirations, man and moment had come together.

Farmers felt they could trust Ford — he was the son of a farmer, and married to the daughter of a farmer besides. In public statements he constantly defended the interests of farmers. Those offended by sexually charged music like jazz had no doubt Ford was like-minded. It was widely known that he hired sound engineers to record symphony orchestras, then sent the recordings to friends so they would have an alternative to suggestive, discordant modern music. Big-city press might criticize Ford, but the majority of his followers mistrusted everything about big cities, so when their newspapers made fun of Henry Ford, the man who shared their values, then they felt that the media was mocking them, too. Mean-spirited articles and editorials only made them support Ford more. Ford's anti-semitism was widely shared in Middle America, where in some states even Catholics were considered exotic and suspicious. Ford's avowed opposition to drink was critical. Midwest country folk formed the backbone of the Prohibition movement. The anti-alcohol sentiment was so strong in these middle states that the Ku Klux Klan, driven for the time being from the South, found refuge there by urging support for the Eighteenth Amendment and improved public schools. There was no need for the KKK to emphasize its racist roots because in its new surroundings there were so few people of color. During 1922 alone, registered Klan membership in Indiana swelled from 445 to about 118,000.

Best of all, as an outspoken foe of Wall Street and the East Coast financial interests, Ford was deemed incorruptible. Though President Harding appeared personally uninvolved, in early 1923 there were the first exposures of corruption in his cabinet. The Senate began investigating complaints against Charles Forbes, head of the Veterans Bureau, who was accused of selling hospital supplies and cutting deals with shady contractors for substandard goods. Harding demanded Forbes's resignation, and got it only after his appointee put the president off for days, allowing the press time to write additional stories about the scandal. Then Jesse Smith, who occasionally joined the president in White House poker games, was accused of backdoor business deals with bootleggers, and committed suicide. Other old friends of the president were rumored to be illicitly enriching themselves through their White House connections. They were nicknamed the Ohio Gang by the press. Henry Ford's friends were Thomas Edison and Harvey Firestone. No one could imagine a Vagabonds Gang using their relationships with President Ford to fleece the public.

By the summer of 1923 it seemed possible that Ford could either seek the presidency as a Democrat or else wrest the 1924 Republican nomination from the incumbent president. Party affiliation meant nothing to Ford. But it would be difficult for leaders of either party to choose prickly, unpredictable

Henry Ford as a standard-bearer. As a result of his carping about American government in general, Ford wasn't esteemed by any of them, and the ongoing Muscle Shoals controversy only exacerbated the hard feelings. Senator Norris, the most outspoken opponent of Ford's offer, was one of the most popular members among his Senate peers. But if there was a widespread groundswell of public support for the man from Michigan and the Harding administration continued awash in scandal, both parties' reservations about Ford would pale beside their desire to control the White House. Gaining the Democratic or Republican nomination might be harder for Ford than winning the presidency. Even without him announcing his candidacy or a party adherence, "Ford for President" clubs began popping up, mostly in the Midwest. Media speculation about the 1924 election predicted Ford's path to the White House. He'd certainly lose the heavily populated Northeast in the national election, and also the West Coast, but he'd sweep all of Middle America and would probably win most Western states besides, prevailing in the electoral college even if he somehow lost the popular vote to whomever either the Democrats or Republicans put up against him.

■ ■ ■ ■

In July, Firestone began making preparations for another Vagabonds trip. This one would begin sometime in early August at Edison's birthplace of Milan, Ohio, where residents would host a celebration honoring the inventor. Then the travelers would drive to Michigan's Upper Peninsula, the same trip that was planned, then postponed, in 1921 to accommodate President Harding. Much of this trip's post-Milan stages would highlight the achievements of Henry Ford, including visits to properties he owned alternating with stops in small towns, daily reminders to America that this was a highly successful man who never lost the common touch. The media would be invited along — some of the time a few reporters might even ride in the Vagabonds' caravan. For two weeks, their stories of Ford and his stalwart friends would contrast with the latest revelations of Harding administration malfeasance. It seemed a foolproof plan.

And then, on August 2, President Warren G. Harding died.

CHAPTER NINE:
1923

Thomas and Mina Edison left West Orange by car on Wednesday, August 1. They planned to meet Harvey and Idabelle Firestone in Akron, stay a day or two visiting Mina's relatives in the area, and then meet the Fords and begin the Vagabonds' trip in Milan at the town's celebration of its most famous son. Firestone, undoubtedly aware that Mina hadn't enjoyed the 1921 excursion, was especially anxious that she have a good time on this one. In a July 19 letter, he urged Edison to bring his wife and be the Firestones' houseguests just before its outset: "We have a good-sized place and grounds where I think we could make you very comfortable." Edison was glad to get away from work for a while. He'd begun his first tentative experiments with potential sources of rubber, and initial results were discouraging. In mid-July, he'd sent a message to Ernest Liebold instructing him to "tell Ford that I have been experimenting a little with milk weed. . . . It is going to be a difficult matter to get a commercial process to get the latex out." Firestone, too, was eager for the trip. In July he wrote Edison that "the going in the tire business has been a little rough in the last few months and a week or two in the woods with you and Mr. Ford ought to clear up the cobwebs a little bit."

The press provided perhaps the most advance coverage of any Vagabonds trip. Some articles speculated about destination and duration ("The exact location has not been given out"; "Some place in Michigan or Wisconsin"; "Western New York, Pennsylvania and Ohio"; "Two weeks"; "About a month"). There were breathless headlines ("Wow! The World's Brains Goes [sic] Out for an Airing"; "Three Monarchs of Industry to Try Gypsy Life") and a few fawning small-town newspaper editorials ("They could surround themselves with every luxury . . . [but they choose to] get out in the open and live close to nature — simply"). Some wire service reports speculated that this trip was really intended as the kickoff of Ford's campaign for the presidency: "Politicians are worried lest Ford come out of the . . . wilderness with his mind made up to enter the presidential race. In his latest interview, published in *Collier's* last week . . . he said he could not foretell what would be in his mind a little later on. Politicians here have a hunch that Firestone and Edison may try to persuade Ford to become a candidate and will be successful."

Edison was in a fine mood on the afternoon of Thursday, August 2, as his chauffeur whisked him and Mina through Pennsylvania on the way to Ohio. Reporters in towns where they stopped made much of the automobile they rode in, a gleaming new Lincoln touring car given to them by Ford. Edison, apparently feeling especially warm toward Firestone, directed the journalists' attention to the wheels. Firestone had recently launched a brand of "balloon tires," which were inflated with more air to reduce jarring. "We came on balloons," Edison joked with a reporter in Reading. "This car is equipped with Firestone balloons, [his] new tire. It works like a charm." As usual, a crowd gathered around the inventor, and although Edison refused to give a speech, "with a smile that covered his entire face . . . rais[ed] his forearm to his hat . . . saluted and called back a pleasant good-bye."

The inventor was still cheery a few hours later when the Edisons checked in to the

Penn-Harris Hotel in Harrisburg. He and Mina took "a suite of rooms" on the second floor and settled in for the night. Soon afterward, Harding's death in San Francisco was announced, and reporters gathered in the Penn-Harris lobby, sending messages up to Edison's suite requesting that he come down and make a statement. Edison didn't appear all night. On Friday morning, an intrepid journalist bounded up the stairs and knocked on Edison's door. He was greeted by Mina, who said that she'd ask her husband if he would talk for a few minutes. Mina explained that Edison had been up all night, making and receiving phone calls about Harding's death. Edison granted the reporter a brief interview, making an official statement to be used by him and the rest of the assembled press. Beyond expressing his grief, Edison seemed to send a thinly veiled warning to Ford:

I was very much shocked and grieved at the news of President Harding's death. The last time I saw the President was about two years ago when we were camping near Hagerstown, Maryland. He was a wonderful man. The presidency seems to be a very dangerous position considering the history of our presidents.

366

Edison didn't mention that the last time he saw Harding was also the first time he met him, or that he and the other Vagabonds had found the president to be a less than wonderful man. So far as the general public was concerned, Harding's death immediately erased all the qualms about him — the corruption among his cabinet and cronies, the lack of any substantial legislative achievement during his two and a half years in office. There would be additional, more salacious Harding scandals made public in the years ahead: the Teapot Dome scandal (members of his administration selling oil leases in return for pieces of the financial returns), an illegitimate child, White House couplings with a lover that allegedly included a tryst in a closet while Secret Servicemen stood guard on the other side of the door. But for a period of time, beginning with the announcement of his death and extending into the foreseeable future, the president's demise transformed him into a near-faultless martyr who, in the overwrought words of Theodore Roosevelt Jr., "gave his life for the service of our country as truly as anyone in our history." In fact, Harding hadn't been well for some time, but insisted on an otherwise unnecessary trip to Alaska and the West Coast to bolster his shaky public image. As Francis Russell wrote in *The Shadow of Blooming Grove,* his epic biography of Harding, "As the first dismay at the news of Harding's death became absorbed by grief . . . ordinary Americans became suddenly aware — although they would soon forget — how much they loved their white-haired President with the face of a Roman senator." (Historians would conclude that Harding's chief attribute as president was how much he looked the part.) Ordinary Americans also comprised Henry Ford's political base. He'd planned to base his campaign on their dissatisfaction with the incumbent. So far as his presidential aspirations were concerned, Harding couldn't have died at a more inconvenient time.

For business reasons as well as preserving whatever remained of Ford's political hopes, the Vagabonds had no option other than to publicly demonstrate the same grief as the rest of America, and to a greater degree — after all, the suddenly saintly Warren G. Harding had been their personal friend and a boon camping companion. They offered no correction to stories claiming Harding had often joined them on their trips, or that the only reason he wasn't going on the current one was the administrative necessities that demanded him to make his ill-fated Western trip instead. Ford, Edison, and Firestone announced that they would postpone their 1923 excursion so that they could attend Harding's August 10 funeral in the late president's hometown of Marion, Ohio.

Florence Kling Harding was receiving friends at her home when the Vagabonds and their wives arrived in Marion. Edison, Ford, and Firestone called on her. Mina Edison, Clara Ford, and Idabelle Firestone apparently chose to remain at their hotel. The three men found the Harding home virtually buried under floral tributes — all of America, it seemed, had sent flowers. Later, two arrangements were singled out for special praise by the press, the flowers sent collectively by the Fords, Edisons, and Firestones, and a massive floral display from the Ku Klux Klan ("a six-foot, ornately contrived cross of flaming red flowers on which was worked in white 'K.K.K.' "). After offering their condolences to the former First Lady, the three men lounged awhile on the front porch made famous by Harding during the 1920 presidential campaign. He'd refused to campaign around the country, preferring to make occasional speeches there. Reporters noted the Vagabonds' attire — dark alpaca coat and light trousers for Edison, dark blue business suit for Firestone, and a gray business suit for Ford. They posed for pictures and chatted a bit with the media, sharing fond memories of their camp experience with the late president, and regretting that they would never be repeated. Reporters noted that in the background, long lines of "citizen mourners" waited to walk up the steps and file past Harding's casket on display in the parlor.

When the time arrived for the funeral procession to begin, the Vagabonds collected their wives and received an honored place on the processional drive to the cemetery. The service was lengthy — Rev. William F. Anderson, who'd also been at Camp Harding, offered one of the benedictions. Ford, Edison, Firestone, and their wives were placed among the most prominent mourners, just behind newly sworn-in president Calvin Coolidge and the previously much maligned Harding cabinet. Some funeral planner either oblivious to past news events or possessed of a keen sense of humor seated Ford next to General John J. Pershing, now chief of staff of the U.S. Army and former commander of the

Mexican expedition that had so aroused Ford's public fury several years earlier. In between singing hymns and bowing their heads during prayers for the departed chief executive, Ford and Pershing found something to talk about — wire services reported that they "chatted," but a reporter for the *Philadelphia Inquirer* wrote that "Ford, the pacifist, and General Pershing, the soldier, plunged into debate. The General shakes his finger and Ford is smiling."

After the service, Ford and Edison told reporters that they planned to immediately commence their Vagabonds trip. It would begin the next day in Milan, where residents of Edison's birthplace would honor him, and then proceed, Ford said, "wherever the spirit moves . . . we plan to get as far away from civilization as possible. We are seeking rest and recreation." Then, a wire service reported, "as an illustration of recreation Mr. Ford grabbed Mr. Firestone and gave him a jerk which nearly caused him to fall to the floor." The stories did not note Firestone's reaction, if any.

Ford spoke more seriously to a reporter from the *New York Times,* praising the same Washington officials he'd previously criticized, assuring the journalist and *Times* readers that Harding's death "will not have any effect on business or polices of the government as the administration at Washington is practically the same as when Mr. Harding was president." Ford told a *Wall Street Journal* reporter that the U.S. economy would continue flourishing: "Don't worry about foreign competition. Europe is too lazy to work." In the immediate wake of Harding's death, journalists were apparently too respectful to bring up Ford's presidential aspirations, and he made no mention of them.

While Ford talked about practical subjects, Edison was more philosophical. He mentioned that, at age seventy-six, he was experiencing constant sorrow as old friends passed away, and that he personally "was seeking after truth and had made much progress" determining what happens when "the soul after death takes flight." Though Edison "could not say . . . that men live after death," his studies so far convinced him that "there is a great directing head of things and people, a Supreme Being who looks after the destinies of the world . . . we know that the soul does exist after death."

The next day, birth rather than death was a much happier subject. Milan had not grown much from its five hundred or so residents when Edison was born in 1847 (his family moved when young Tom, then called Al, was seven), but everyone living there and most of those from neighboring towns turned out to pay the inventor tribute. Reporters estimated the crowd at four thousand. Edison refrained from making a lengthy speech, saying simply that it had taken him so long to return because he'd been busy. When Ford was introduced, the throng chanted, "There's our next president." The automaker didn't respond directly, but did hop off the grandstand "to shake hands, and to comment on how clean the village looked." Firestone agreed to speak, telling the crowd that "you citizens of Milan may well be proud of your distinguished son. Mr. Edison is unquestionably the greatest man of his generation." A brass band played "Yes! We Have No Bananas," supposedly one of Edison's favorite tunes, and then the inventor visited a house where one of his sisters had lived. Afterward the Vagabonds' group, which again included wives, drove on to the Fords' home in Dearborn. On August 14 they began their delayed Upper Michigan Peninsula trip.

From the beginning, it was far from Ford's description of "getting far away from civilization." Had that really been their intention, the Vagabonds could have camped in the Southwest, where in many areas only the most primitive roads bisected sweeping swaths of sand, cactus, and snakes. The Northwest woods still contained vast tracts of forest relatively untouched by auto-campers or industry. But in 1923 what Ford and Edison really wanted, with Firestone's automatic acquiescence, was something far more controlled — camping spots well-removed from other travelers, media-friendly visits to properties controlled by Ford, the better to avoid any on-camera stumbles or controversies, and an itinerary suitably civilized for the ladies. Edison's health was another consideration. At age seventy-six, his decades of squinting into microscopes, bending over trays on laboratory tables, and working odd hours while fueled by equally odd diets had caught up with him. In July his New Jersey physician had diagnosed neuritis, nerve inflammation in various extremities, and ordered the inventor to "keep away from the factory for a while." Like John Burroughs before him, Edison had reached a stage of late life where even the ordinary vicissitudes of daily driving and camping were a strain on his system.

So the trip was planned to give the appearance of roughing it without any of the inconveniences. From Dearborn they'd head north, staying in hotels on the drive up and then after arrival in the Upper Peninsula resting comfortably in cabins on land Ford owned. Several nights would be spent camped on an island reached not by car but via Ford's luxury yacht the *Sialia* — they could loll in their battery-lit tents, savor chef-prepared meals, and not concern themselves with disrespectful reporters describing all the costly amenities. They could take day trips from the island, sailing on the *Sialia* to different Upper Peninsula ports where their caravan of chauffeur-driven Lincolns and Fords would whisk them away to see various sights, many of them located at Ford industrial operations where, again, public and press access could be rigidly controlled.

They felt the perfect plan was in place, but from the moment they set out from Dearborn the weather didn't cooperate. Mid-August in Michigan is traditionally hot, sometimes uncomfortably so, but rarely cool and wet. This August, it was. On the departure date from Dearborn of Tuesday, August 14, Edison had already been away from home for two weeks. It had taken its toll, and the damp, slightly chilly weather didn't help. A cold settled in the inventor's chest almost before the first few miles passed. The illness was clearly slight; a few days' rest at home in New Jersey would undoubtedly have resulted in quick recovery. But Edison was a stubborn man. He was on a well-publicized vacation with his wife and friends, and entirely unwilling to have every newspaper in the nation inform readers that elderly Thomas Edison wasn't up to a little camping in the Upper Peninsula wilds.

Early on, they set a leisurely pace, three hundred miles in two or three days, motoring northeast toward Grand Rapids, then following an even more northerly route toward Traverse City on Lake Michigan's east coast, where the *Sialia* would take the travelers across to Escanaba on the lake's west coast in considerable comfort (the crew often numbered as many as thirty while ferries served for the cars, camp gear, and trip staff). Most of the press waited in Escanaba for the Vagabonds' arrival — the photo opportunities would be better there. A few reporters popped up along the way to Traverse City, mostly local journalists. The only substantial coverage came at the stop in Paris, where Ford, Edison, and their

376

wives met Jep Bisbee and the old fiddler played for them. Firestone's car got lost — the automaker, his wife, and son Russell caught up with the others in Traverse City. Edison's cold remained worrisome. While the others explored Traverse City, he stayed behind at the hotel. Because the press waited on the other side of Lake Michigan, Edison's absence wasn't widely noted. Instead, there was considerable media speculation on how long the Vagabonds would remain camped on the island — speculation ranged from two weeks to a month.

But Edison's illness caused a change in plans. They spent the night of August 18 aboard Ford's yacht, where the inventor could rest comfortably. Ford visited with the waiting media by himself in Escanaba. None of the reporters asked where Edison was; instead, they queried the carmaker about whether he was now prepared to formally announce a plan to seek the presidency.

It would have been a propitious moment — there was much national speculation about the kind of president Calvin Coolidge might prove to be, and whether he was up to the job. But Ford chose to laugh the questions off. Ford didn't say he wouldn't run, but stopped short of stating he would. The journalists couldn't pin him down. A wire service reported, Ford "inferred that he was not going after the presidency, but . . . would be willing to accept the honor if it were conferred upon him."

The next day, they drove from Escanaba to Iron Mountain near the Michigan-Wisconsin border. Ford had a lumber mill there, and the property offered several prime camping spots. The site chosen was described as "a grove" by the press, who were invited to visit but not stay long. The reporters were also allowed to trail along as Edward Kingsford, who ran the lumber operation there for Ford, took his boss and the rest of the Vagabonds party on a tour of the facilities. Edison felt well enough to come along. Ford lectured his guests and the media on the importance of putting every bit of material to some use. Even burned wood scraps were compressed into squarish briquets of charcoal, then packaged and sold as a fuel source for home heating and outdoor barbecues. Ford named the product "Kingsford Charcoal" in honor of his valued employee.

The campers remained at Iron Mountain through Monday, August 20. That day, Ford briefly spoke to the media again about the presidency, this time focusing not on himself but the new White House incumbent: "I hope that President Coolidge will follow closely in the footsteps of his illustrious predecessor, the late President Harding. I know nothing about President Coolidge. I was very intimately acquainted with the late President Harding as it was only two years ago that we were on a similar camping trip to this." Beyond his exaggerated claim of intimate acquaintance with a former president he'd only known and camped with for twenty-seven hours, Ford was being honest regarding Coolidge, who was relatively unknown to the country beyond his ending the Boston police strike while governor of Massachusetts and a reputation for taciturnity. (Supposedly a woman once told Coolidge, "I have a bet with friends that I can make you say three words." His reply: "You lose.")

If the new president was in Ford's thoughts, Coolidge and his advisors were just as aware of Ford. On August 21, there was a wire service report that "President Coolidge has set about building up the reputation in which he hopes to be returned to the White House for a full term." Coolidge, the story declared, would offer voters

"Yankee reticence and gumption — in other words, reserve and decision." For the present, at least, Coolidge and his team were more worried about challenges from within their Republican Party than anyone nominated by the Democrats. The man most feared by them was Senator Hiram Johnson of California, the voice of the more liberal Republican wing, and "of course Henry Ford looms big in all political speculation. . . . Every well-informed politician who is at all candid will admit that the sentiment for Ford is solid and widespread. The more candid will admit in addition that this sentiment is grounded not alone on admiration for the achievements of Henry Ford, but on disgust with the ways of all politicians of all parties." A second wire story a week later cited Ford's strength with voters in Middle America, the South, and West and concluded, "While Republican leaders appear to find amusement in the thought of Ford as a Republican presidential possibility, and emphatically [insist that] he could never secure [their party's nomination], they are far from confident."

If there was ever an opportunity for Henry Ford to declare for the presidency, this was it. Americans were uncertain about the new incumbent, and they already knew all about

Henry Ford. He had an indelible reputation, and if it was negative among party leaders it also inspired bone-deep devotion among Ford's many followers, who distrusted mainstream politicians as much as he did. Declaring his candidacy on the Vagabonds' 1923 trip, posed against a background of towering timber or a rippling Great Lake, joined by his famous friends Edison and Firestone (no crooked cronies here!), would have immediately established Ford as a valid contender for the White House, perhaps even the front-runner. The reporters and photographers following the Vagabonds around Michigan's Upper Peninsula were ready to relay the news throughout the land. Ford's sense of timing was keen. He surely realized that, if he really wanted to become president, the moment to announce it had come.

Yet Ford didn't. Instead, he and his party left Iron Mountain and traveled a few dozen miles north, where they set up camp again near Lake Michigamme, overrun as usual by summer visitors eager to enjoy sunshine and swimming in one of Michigan's most scenic settings. If the Vagabonds truly intended to stay as far from civilization as possible, stopping at the lake was an odd choice. Perhaps they needed some necessities available only there. A steady rain fell; once their staff had tents set up, the travelers took shelter under canvas, wives with husbands, private time for a while. When the rain let up, the entire party set off on a walk around town. Many other vacationers did the same, and there followed an incident brought about by the most unlikely of instigators.

In August 1923, Henry and Clara Ford had been married for thirty-five years. When they met at a country dance in 1886, Ford was twenty-three and Clara twenty. He was farming and hated it; she was a farmer's daughter and a dutiful child to her parents. The young couple fell almost immediately in love and were eager to marry, but when Clara's parents insisted on a lengthy engagement she obeyed. After they were finally allowed to wed in 1888, Ford supported his bride by cutting timber and operating a sawmill. When all the trees on that property were cut, the Fords moved to Detroit. Clara kept a small house while her husband took an engineering job at Edison Illuminating Company. She never complained when Ford spent most of his off-the-job hours trying to build a combustion engine in their kitchen. Clara encouraged Ford to pursue his dream of creating "a car for the great multitudes," remaining supportive when his first two companies failed, encouraging him during the difficult first years of Ford Motor Company, his third. As Ford became one of America's richest, most famous men, Clara the farm girl evolved into a genteel lady of means, running their expansive household, participating in charitable work, never forgetting that her chief responsibility remained being her husband's staunchest supporter. She forgave his obsession with work, accepted his constant certainty that whatever he thought had to be right, and even overlooked his extended affair with an employee that resulted in a child out of wedlock.

Ford, in turn, adored Clara. His affairs — there was probably more than one — to Ford's mind had nothing to do with his devotion to his wife. His nickname for Clara was "the Believer," and it was justified. If Ford listened to anyone, it was Clara — he knew she had only his best interests at heart. Ford didn't always agree with her — when Clara warned him not to sail with the Peace Ship, he did anyway. But she certainly expressed her opinion about Ford running for president, and may have raised the matter in their tent beside Lake Michigamme while they sheltered from the rain. When the storm abated and they emerged to walk toward town, Clara Ford committed perhaps the most uncharacteristic act of her entire life. In public, no matter what the circumstance, she always remained poised, soft-spoken, the epitome of a well-to-do lady. Now, perhaps upset by an intense discussion with Ford that may have escalated into a rare all-out argument, Clara briefly snapped.

By unfortunate coincidence, the Fords' stroll intersected a charging group of teen girls from Camp Cha-Ton-Ka, a popular Lake Michigamme summer retreat for young ladies. The teens were identically clad in somewhat abbreviated garb, shirts and cutoff overalls that ended slightly above the knee. As etiquette required, they also wore stockings, which, for comfort, the girls left rolled just below their overalls' shortened hems. They instantly recognized the famous Fords, and gathered around the couple. Several of them rummaged in pockets for scraps of paper and pencils, which they proffered to the Fords with requests for autographs. Ford obliged, but Clara waved the girls away. That was bad enough, but then she said, "You ladies and girls are showing very poor taste and worse judgment coming into town garbed as you are, without skirts or dresses. I do not want to sign my name for you and prefer not to look at you. I resent your idea of dress." One of the campers protested that Michigamme was a small town, they were on vacation there, and could wear what they liked. Clara flared at the impertinence: "Yes, Michigamme is small and that's all the more reason why you should dress properly, and not set a bad example for the young people."

An Associated Press correspondent walking behind the Fords heard and jotted down every word. The next day, all the "Will Ford Run for President" headlines were replaced by "Mrs. Ford Rebukes Women in Overalls and Short Stockings at Michigan Resort." Soon after that, there was a follow-up story. The *New York Times* sent a reporter to Michigamme, and was told by an unidentified Camp Cha-Ton-Ka director that "[our] girls' costumes are chosen for comfort and not style. They are like the cars in the Ford-Edison-Firestone caravan. We do not wish to enter into any controversy with Mrs. Ford or anyone else. We have the confidence of the girls' parents . . . and also their approval for [the girls] dress. It was an amusing incident."

The less-than-amused Vagabonds moved on

385

quickly from Lake Michigamme, driving a few dozen miles further north to Sidnaw, where Ford operated a series of lumber camps. One of the camps included guest cottages warmed by steam heat, which the travelers appreciated — the uncommonly cool August weather turned even colder as they reached one of the northernmost points in the U.S. Soon after she was comfortably ensconced in one of the cottages, Mina Edison composed another letter to her son Theodore. As usual, Mina was not enjoying herself, and wasn't hesitant telling Theodore why:

> This being [the] Fords' guests is all very nice but it is not our trip. All has been for Ford and his say from the time we reached Detroit until we get back again. Just looking over his possessions. [Mina underlined "his."] I hate to be owned by anyone and that is the feeling one has with Mr. and Mrs. Ford. Everything comfortable and luxurious but you have no say as to what you can do. . . . The Firestones are with us & I guess they feel the same way but have said nothing to me about it.

Mina even found fault with the Lincoln that Ford gave to the Edisons for the trip:

I guess [he] is going to give us a Lincoln limousine as well. I am rather hoping so if it will be one like Mrs. Ford's. I don't care for those [like the first one they received] that have no window between ourself and the driver.

Toward the end of the three-page letter, Mina mentioned the tension that might have led to Clara's uncharacteristic outburst in Michigamme — she was strongly encouraging her husband not to run for president, and Mina guessed that it was working:

[Ford] will never run for president as Mrs. Ford is bitterly opposed to it. I think he would have done it. She recognizes his limitations better than he does.

Clara Ford wasn't the only one among the traveling party who was against her husband running for president. Edison was strongly opposed, though he never directly told the carmaker so. Instead, he signaled his misgivings through the press. When reporters interviewed Edison in Akron, just prior to Harding's funeral, they led their stories with the inventor's comments about the late president. But a few also included Edison's brief observations regarding his best friend's interest in the White House. Edison told the correspondent for the United Press wire service that "I doubt if Henry Ford will run for president because he does not think that the people want him now." Asked by a reporter for the *Akron Beacon Journal* if "Mr. Ford will run for president," Edison replied that "I do not believe he will." Asked to elaborate, the inventor said, "I believe that Mr. Ford is merely glad to find out how he stands with the country." If Ford noticed these secondhand hints, he gave no sign. But his wife's privately expressed comments had the desired effect.

Two months after the August 1923 trip, when the inventor still considered Ford's candidacy to be a possibility, Edison made additional comments to a reporter from the *New York Times.* These were far more personal, though still not directly addressed to the carmaker: "I would hate to see Ford president because you would spoil a good man. He's more valuable where he is," expanding his business empire and creating jobs.

The Vagabonds spent two days at Sidnaw and then another at Ford's lumber operation in L'Anse, which was a few miles even further north. If the increasingly familiar sights bored Mina — how many times could anyone act, let alone really feel, interested in toppled trees and sawmills? — the press was even more frustrated. Their readers assuredly didn't know one lumber camp from another, or much care how many logs littered Ford's properties in Sidnaw or L'Anse. Ford said nothing about the presidency and, as colorful as the story of Mrs. Ford chastising inappropriately dressed girls might have been, that subject was exhausted. The reporters needed something new, something of significant interest, to write about, and Thomas Edison's sneezes served wonderfully.

The first stories ran on Wednesday, August 22, the same day the Vagabonds fetched up at the guest cabins in Sidnaw. Readers were informed that Edison "was not feeling well." The inventor stayed behind in his cabin while the rest of his party toured the Sidnaw facilities. At one point he "personally received" a United Press wire correspondent and assured him that he was fine. Still, his friends "expressed concern for him, if the weather continues damp and cold." The headlines expressed more urgency than the stories themselves: "Edison Taken Sick on Camping Trip in North," and "Edison Denies Rumor of Serious Illness."

On Thursday, the *New York Times* assured

readers that although "rumors concerning the health of Thomas Edison caused considerable commotion," he was "a little indisposed but not ill," even though, in addition to his cold, the elderly inventor had also somehow "suffered a slight injury to one finger." Other publications were less optimistic. The Ironwood, Michigan, *Daily Globe* reported that "Ford, Firestone and Edison Cancel Trip" because Edison "was not feeling well." Readers in Phoenix were informed by the *Arizona Republic* that "Thomas Edison Is Critically Ill on Michigan Vacation," and the *Fort Wayne Journal-Gazette* carried the story to an alarming extreme with an all-capital-letters headline, "EDISON HURTS FINGER, IS REPORTED DEAD." Edward Kingsford gathered reporters to assure them that Edison "simply did not feel well," and requested they "quiet the rumors" by informing their readers. But the rumors continued until Friday, when Edison finally emerged from the cabin and signed autographs before he and the rest of the Vagabonds drove from Sidnaw to L'Anse.

On Friday, August 24, the party toured Ford's lumber mill in L'Anse, and the next day indulged in an actual tourist experience by visiting a Chippewa reservation. Harvey Firestone hosted a luncheon in a nearby town, and then the Vagabonds returned to the *Sialia,* which cruised through the Sault Ste. Marie, Canada, locks separating Lake Superior and Lake Huron and down to Detroit, where the trip would end on August 27. At the Sault Ste. Marie locks, Ford obliged reporters hoping for a final story by remaining on the dock shaking hands with bystanders while the *Sialia* began pulling away. Just in time, the spry sixty-year-old automaker offered one last handclasp, turned, sprinted down the dock, and leaped aboard the yacht "like a boy," according to the Mattoon, Illinois, *Journal-Gazette.* A wrap-up story by the Associated Press assured readers that "Mr. Edison's cold, from which he suffered some on the trip, has disappeared and the inventor today was said to be in his usual health."

The remaining months of 1923 were momentous for Edison and Ford, not because of anything they did, but what they chose not to do.

On December 17, Firestone sent a chatty letter to Edison, who had taken an increasing interest in Firestone's business, offering advice on products and marketing. Firestone began his letter by thanking the inventor for "the note you wrote me several weeks ago urging me to get busy [on making and marketing] balloon tires. We have been busy and I am glad to say are selling all we can manufacture. I feel sure it is the coming tire."

Firestone assured Edison that his company was finally regaining the full financial footing it had lost during the economic crash of 1920: "We just closed our fiscal year and I am proud to enclose a copy of our Annual Statement. You will note that we still have some bank indebtedness but that we have made some material reductions in the past three years and if we have as good a year next year we will be entirely out of debt. Then you and Mr. Ford will have to find something to replace your joshing about my obligations to the bankers."

But the real purpose of Firestone's letter was to gently urge his friend to enter a new branch of business.

I was down on the [family] farm for a few days a short time ago and one of the boys brought down a radio. . . . Much to my surprise we heard distinctly addresses and music from all over the country. At dinner in the evening we usually tuned in to the

William Pitt Hotel in Pittsburgh for their dinner music. The thought occurred to me, why should not the Edison Phonograph Company go into the manufacture of these radios. Every home, especially in the country, should have and will have a radio and with your knowledge and experience I would like to see you go into the manufacture and sale of them. I would also like to see Mr. Ford interested with you, to give it his magic touch, not only for the money that you would make out of it but for the pleasure you would both get in doing one more great thing for the people.

Radio would have been a logical new field for Edison. He had brought electricity and light into American homes. His phonograph provided the first home electronic entertainment. His kinetoscope and flexible film were critical steps in creating the film industry that swept the country and entertained millions more. By December 1923, it seemed obvious that radio would be the next great entertainment innovation embraced by the public. It happened quickly. KDKA in Pittsburgh became the nation's first commercial radio station in 1920. Two years later, there were 30; a year after that, the same year Firestone urged Edison to get into radio, there were 556. One hundred thousand primitive radios were manufactured in 1922. A half-million were built in 1923.

Edison would not have been the inventor of the first radio, as he had been in 1877 with the phonograph. But he hadn't been the first to create electric light or movies, either — his inventive contribution had been to advance these technologies, making them more efficient and widely available. In December 1923, radios were still primitive — had Edison turned his genius to that field and product, all sorts of innovation might have been possible, and the inventor could have enjoyed a new, lucrative era late in his life and career.

But in his way, Edison was as stubborn as Ford, and as temperamentally bound to the supposed timelessness of his most famous products. Phonographs, which allowed people to choose the music and other audio entertainment that they wanted to hear at any particular moment, rather than relying on the whims of radio station programmers, in the inventor's opinion seemed certain to outlast ephemeral radio. In his return letter, he told Firestone so: "I shall not go into radio. When I have got my own factories & selling forces in a high state of efficiency my policy is to keep out of new things." Instead, Edison continued focusing on rubber-related research.

Radio flourished at such a rapid rate that less than a decade later, President Franklin D. Roosevelt chose radio broadcasts — his famous "Fireside Chats" — over formal press conferences to quell public panic during the darkest days of the Great Depression. FDR explained to aides that, in his opinion, over half of all Americans, especially in rural areas, relied on radios rather than newspapers for crucial information: "It seems to me that radio is . . . bringing to the ears of our people matters of interest concerning their country which they refused to consider in the daily press with their eyes."

It had seemed only months earlier that, besides radio, America's immediate future might also include President Henry Ford. But on December 19, just two days after Firestone sent his letter to Edison, Henry Ford issued a brief, formal announcement: He would not seek the presidency in 1924 because the United States was "safe with Coolidge." In *Henry Ford and the Jews,* historian Neil Baldwin describes a quid pro quo agreement between the men: "Ford . . .

would support Coolidge if he promised to enforce Prohibition. As a show of solidarity, Coolidge said he would not oppose Ford's bid to take over . . . Muscle Shoals." There were probably two more critical factors — Clara Ford's adamant opposition to her husband's candidacy, and Ford realizing that, if elected, his Muscle Shoals bid would become a blatant conflict of interest. Simply put, Ford decided that he wanted Clara's approval and the opportunity to own and harness vast hydroelectrical power more than he wanted to be president. That Coolidge's political sense was vastly superior to Ford's is indicated by the president's agreement not to *oppose* Ford's Muscle Shoals purchase. Coolidge never promised to *endorse* it. As later events would prove, the president got what he wanted, and Ford got nothing.

The carmaker was never seriously considered as a presidential candidate again.

CHAPTER TEN:
1924

Henry Ford was mostly disdainful of books and those who loved them. In his opinion, people "read to escape thinking." So far as Ford was concerned, being literary-minded was symptomatic of an escalating national softness, with far too many people content to lounge poring over pages instead of getting on their feet and *doing* something: "Book sickness is a modern ailment."

But in this as in almost everything else, Ford was contradictory. He had nothing against people reading the *right* books, starting with the beloved McGuffey readers of his own childhood (which influenced Ford's adult antisemitism) and extending to the works of certain authors and poets who, to Ford's mind, celebrated appropriate American qualities and history. Henry Wadsworth Longfellow was one of Ford's elect, and in October 1923 the carmaker was able to add a momentous Longfellow artifact to his growing collection of Americana memorabilia. This one couldn't be stored with the other collectibles in a Ford warehouse back home in Michigan. Rather than a first edition tome or an original manuscript, it was an endangered edifice — Sudbury, Massachusetts's, Wayside Inn, beloved of Longfellow and immortalized in his *Tales of a Wayside Inn,* which included the epic poem "Paul Revere's Ride," originally published in 1861 in *The Atlantic Monthly* and reintroduced as "The Landlord's Tale" by Longfellow in the *Wayside Inn* collection two years later. The inn opened in early Colonial America, survived the Revolutionary War, served generations of travelers heading in and out of Boston, and finally fell into apparently permanent disrepair in the early 1900s. Ford purchased it with the aim not only of restoring the inn, but of eventually surrounding it with authentic period structures (among them an old-fashioned schoolhouse and a gristmill). Then the property would, he hoped and believed, remind modern-day Americans of their tougher-minded forebears and rouse them from their current sloth.

The restoration process took many months. Money was no object. When a major road had to be rerouted to preserve the inn's intended Colonial-era atmosphere, Ford paid for it. The carmaker also built an additional first-floor living quarters for himself — he intended to stay there often. Ford fixated on even the smallest details. Over the years on his various journeys, the carmaker kept an undated, near-illegible series of pocket notes, brief stream-of-consciousness thoughts and reminders he jotted down in pencil on the pages of small notebooks. These ranged from the mundane ("1 lb. of sugar," "Pure play camping boys") to the philosophic ("Study what [a] young fellow knows," "Where does the money come from but the land") to the cryptic ("Mrs. Edison what station did you get kicked off at"). A few were frankly anti-semitic ("Who is behind the League of Jew?" "A republic is in competition with the J[ews]"). One was obviously scribbled during an early Ford inspection of his new property in Sudbury: "Way Side — every damn picture is crooked."

But by August 1924 the pictures were straightened, and Ford felt the Wayside Inn was sufficiently restored to host the Vaga-bonds on a summer trip that retained certain parameters but was altered in one significant way — they'd drive during the day, seeing interesting places and things, but utilize the inn as their nightly base. If they did find themselves too far afield to return to Sudbury, they'd overnight in some cozy hotel. Tents would no longer be involved — the wives had never been enthusiastic campers. When Ford and Firestone initially suggested a trip to the Rocky Mountains, Clara Ford said she "would not be up to it." Something less strenuous would appeal to her more — Clara's suggestion was the White Mountains of New Hampshire, and only if they would be "stopping at hotels." Firestone as usual was amenable to whatever the Fords wanted, and Edison found the proposed trip acceptable, too.

It's possible that Clara Ford made her excuse to avoid camping and suggested hotels instead because Edison wasn't up to a more strenuous trip. Firestone passed along the hotels-rather-than-camping suggestion to the inventor in a July 1 letter. Edison, as usual, sent back his opinion via a letter written by one of his secretaries. He scribbled his approval in the margin of Firestone's note: "This would suit me as I am not sure of my health." That specific message was meant for the secretary, not for Firestone or, especially, Ford. Edison was a proud man. The articles about his alleged serious illness or death came close to ruining the 1923 Michigan trip for everyone. A year later, he did not want the slightest hint of requiring special concessions because he really was in poor health, probably a recurrence of the neuralgia that periodically plagued him. A primary if unspoken rule in his close friendship with Ford was that neither should burden the other with admissions of uncertainty or weakness. They could, and did, rail in private conversation and correspondence about frustrations with outside sources — Jews, unions, greedy and mindless Washington politicians — but never about personal problems. When either had personal advice for the other, it was passed along via third parties, as when Edison's secretary wrote Ford's assistant that the inventor hoped Ford would drop his libel suit against the *Chicago Tribune,* or through some of Edison's comments to the press about his friend's presidential ambitions. (Their 1919 campfire conversation about Ford's race for the U.S. Senate was an aberration.)

Mina Edison remained fiercely protective of her husband, and she was certainly aware that his health was not robust during the summer of 1924. Mina understood Edison well, and realized he'd never make such an admission to Ford himself. She may have done the next best thing — passed information about the inventor's health to Clara Ford. Clara enjoyed ruddy good health, but claimed indisposition so that Edison could avoid both camping and admitting to Ford that he was the one not up to it.

Edison's pride was preserved, and alternate plans made. Instead of camps, they'd stay at the Wayside Inn in Sudbury, and, if the mood struck them, use it as a base for daily jaunts out into the New England countryside. Everyone would be spared nights on cots and bathing in streams. As a bonus, every news story mentioning the location would be free advertising for its restored period-piece rooms and dining facilities, all now available to the discerning modern-day New England traveler.

The new plan suited Edison perfectly. For the inventor, it was a much needed opportunity to escape creative frustrations. He'd spent much of 1924 trying to resuscitate his failing phonograph business. Preparations for intense rubber research took up additional time — it would require another two years of preliminary study before Edison felt he'd accumulated enough data to undertake full-scale experimentation, aiming to discover which latex-bearing plants would flourish properly in America as well as a cost-effective means of extracting the latex and refining it into rubber. It was a slack time for actual invention in his New Jersey laboratory. Over the course of his career, Edison applied for and received 1,093 patents, more than any other American. But the majority of these came before 1914; during the years that he made summer trips with Ford and Firestone, Edison managed just 55 patents, compared to 256 in the three years (January 1880 — December 1882) when the phonograph and incandescent bulb established him as the world's preeminent inventor. Many of the latter 55 involved Edison's storage battery, which never achieved marketability. Edison was beginning to be asked now in interviews just when he would unveil something new and wonderful to dazzle the public again. He had nothing specific to report.

Other than the purchase and renovation of the Wayside Inn, Ford had not had an especially productive 1924, either. Now that he was no longer running for president, he allowed the *Dearborn Independent* to resume its attacks on Jews; these often concentrated on alleged Jewish plots to take control of

American farming. Ford's personal attention was elsewhere. As the months passed, he was no closer to attaining ownership of the dams and properties at Muscle Shoals. As promised, President Coolidge had not opposed the proposed purchase, but Senator Norris of Nebraska, Coolidge's fellow Republican, still did, and his obstinacy influenced enough other senators to keep the matter tied up in committee limbo. Patience was never Ford's strength; he chafed at the ongoing delay. Every wasted moment delayed the beneficent bestowal of cheap hydroelectric power to the sprawling Tennessee Valley — Ford knew that he could make this fine thing happen quickly if only the government would get out of his way. The carmaker's place in U.S. history was already assured; in February 1924, a much discussed study by University of Michigan president M. L. Burton proclaimed Ford, Edison, Theodore Roosevelt, and Orville Wright the most outstanding men so far in the twentieth century, with Ford cited for "industrial development [of cars] leading to a new social order." (Edison was simply lauded for "his inventive genius.")

But Ford had no interest in laurel-resting. It seemed to him that Norris's opposition to the Muscle Shoals purchase might be swept away if only Coolidge came out forcefully in favor of the sale. Having already spoken out on behalf of the president's reelection, in July 1924 Ford took his support a step further. Every Ford dealer in the nation received from the Michigan home office a 9x13 "tinted halftone photograph" of Coolidge, and the *Houston Chronicle* reported that "the inference is drawn that the picture is to be placed in a conspicuous place." The gesture would surely remind the president that Ford was more than upholding his end of their informal bargain.

Ford would have served himself better by focusing on his car business instead. Though in 1924 there was no apparent obvious cause for concern — the Model T still dominated the market, with sales up as much as 25 percent from just a few years earlier — there were signs that indicated, to someone more observant, the competition was catching up.

In the sixteen years since 1908 when Ford first introduced his signature vehicle, competitors grudgingly came to accept that they could not match the Model T's utilitarian virtues and cheap price. Flat-out copying would do little good — the Model T had captured the minds and pocketbooks of a general public eager to get out on the roads in automobiles that had previously been the exclusive playthings of the rich. Having a car, albeit a bare-bones Model T, elevated its owner in personal prestige, proof of moving beyond the crushing cares of subsistence existence. There was exhilaration in being a *consumer.* Even better, ownership of a Model T virtually guaranteed almost indefinite four-wheeled mobility. The cars were built to last. In 1924, many early Model Ts still trundled their owners about, never flashy, in every way efficient, always dependable, much like the man whose company assembled them. And, just as Ford never saw any reason to change himself, he felt no pressure to change the Model T, either, or to augment it with flashier models. Ford ignored the urging of his son, Edsel, and company officers to give customers alternatives. To Ford's mind, what was good enough in 1908 was still good enough in 1924 and forever after that. At Ford Motor Company, his was the only opinion that ultimately counted.

Ford's stubbornness gave competitors the opening they needed. In particular, when Alfred Sloan took over General Motors in 1923, the new boss emphasized a marketing plan based on Americans wanting not just transportation, but selection. Enough people now owned cars so that ownership itself was no longer special. What was going to matter soon was driving a car that reflected the personality, the *specialness,* of the individual owner. That meant offering cars in colors spanning the rainbow, and models that changed every year or two, adding chrome, shifting bumper shape, allowing consumers the opportunity to showcase ownership of the very latest styles. There would always be certain makes and styles so costly that only the wealthy could afford them, like Cadillacs and Lincolns, but with the evolving need of rank-and-file car buyers to own something different, lower-end Chevrolets and Oldsmobiles could be and were spruced up as appealing alternatives to the dull Model Ts. Now that U.S. roads were being vastly improved at a rapid rate, the Model T's acclaimed smoother drive over rough surfaces no longer mattered. The Model T still cost less — but who wanted to appear cheap?

Had the Vagabonds ventured further afield on their 1924 trip, away from the relatively concentrated region of Sudbury and its Boston environs, they might have noticed that the Model T was no longer the near-exclusive vehicle of choice for autocampers. America's highway adventurers were increasingly out to see-and-be-seen in snappy, colorful cars, and this contributed in turn to the gradual demise of autocamps and the emergence of motels. After buying an attractive Chevy or Olds to drive in, few wanted to clutter the flashy image by cramming the car full of bulky camping gear. They wanted to stay in places that included some kind of convenient parking, and what the market demanded, savvy entrepreneurs were pleased to make available.

In 1924, Henry Ford acknowledged none of this. On June 4, the ten-millionth Ford vehicle — of course, a Model T — rolled off the assembly line and, with considerable fanfare and attendant press coverage, was driven cross-country from New York to San Francisco. Two months later, the Vagabonds' trip to Sudbury was announced, with a kickoff event planned that would simultaneously advertise the newly restored Wayside Inn and emphasize Ford's ongoing allegiance to American farmers, recently the core of his political support and still the most reliable purchasers of his Model Ts and tractors. It would be a Wednesday, August 13, gala on the inn's grounds, with spaces allocated for games (horseshoes, baseball, tug-of-war), exhibits (the latest Ford tractors, various demonstrations of plowing techniques they made possible), a band concert, a parade, and even, it was rumored, a speech by Mr. Ford himself. A nursery was set up so that mothers "could leave their offspring under expert care" and enjoy themselves accordingly. All members of the Middlesex County Farm Bureau and Extension Service were invited, and admission was free, though everyone was asked to provide their own picnic lunches. It would be, advance publicity declared, "a get-together of neighbors and fellow-workers [with] an emphasis on play rather than on work."

The gathering was hugely successful. Major newspapers sent reporters to describe the scene, and press accounts estimated between two thousand and three thousand farmers and their families came to Sudbury and enjoyed a rapturous time. Ford and Firestone circulated, shaking hands and chatting. The Edisons were detained in New Jersey (the inventor hosted a luncheon for his distributors the day before) and arrived in Massachusetts too late on the 13th to participate. Ford never made a formal speech; at one point he stepped up on a makeshift stage to say that "We'll restore the old inn. We want to make it pleasant here," adding that he hoped to shake hands and talk with as many attendees as possible. When Ford did, he warned about the dangers of coffee, tea, and tobacco, which he predicted would be "legislated out of existence, not by law but by common sense." The carmaker said that he, Edison, and Firestone planned "several jaunts" while in New England. The representative of a local boys club presented Ford with a 1790s hoe, and when he stumbled trying to offer just the right remarks, Ford graciously covered for him by saying he'd unsuccessfully scoured the state of Michigan for just such a relic.

The newspaper reports printed on Thursday were gratifying, and so was the rest of the week at Wayside Inn. For the first time on any of their trips, the Vagabonds didn't embark each day on photo-friendly visits to Ford-owned properties or various local attractions. They spent the next few mornings and afternoons strolling the inn grounds; Edison surely made suggestions about a location for the proposed gristmill. In the evenings there were tasty meals cooked in the inn's kitchen (Ford, having strong beliefs on proper diet, insisted on whole wheat bread), and after-dinner entertainment was provided by local dance instructor Benjamin Lovett, who taught the Fords and Edisons and Firestones dance steps popular with original New England colonists. Everyone had a good time. If they wished, they could have stayed for the entire duration of their vacation. For a change, the famous men and their wives enjoyed considerable privacy. Besides staff, they had the Wayside Inn to themselves. The press was gone; reporters for major newspapers and wire services who remained in the region were two hundred miles away, camped outside the tiny community of Plymouth Notch, Vermont, where President Calvin and First Lady Grace Coolidge were spending their own late-summer retreat.

It may have been the lure of additional publicity, and the desire of the other two Vagabonds to get their share of it — the stories about Ford's farmer-friendly picnic didn't help sell a single Edison phonograph or Firestone tire. All three Vagabonds surely sensed an opportunity to remind Americans (and, in Ford's case, legislators still debating his offer for Muscle Shoals) that they could speak to the president as peers, virtual equals — Coolidge, in turn, would certainly relish reiterations of their support for him in his November bid for reelection. And, probably, Ford, Edison, and Firestone grew bored after only a few days of strolling the grounds and dancing the nights away at the Wayside Inn. Relaxation was fine, but they were men who felt constantly compelled to *accomplish* something. A highly publicized call on the president and his wife in their quaint country surroundings would benefit everyone involved. Warm greetings on a front porch, a Coolidge-conducted tour of his birthplace, lunch at the Coolidge family table, a postprandial chat with the president, strolling nearby fields while photographers and reporters looked on from a respectful distance, a final late afternoon visit with the media when the Vagabonds would again pledge their political support . . . the president might even say a few words favoring Ford's purchase of Muscle Shoals. In any case, the headlines and stories would practically write themselves.

On Sunday, August 17, Firestone's son Russell drove to Plymouth, Vermont, where he met with Bascom Slemp, Coolidge's personal secretary. The entire population of Plymouth Notch numbered just under thirty. There were a few houses, a general store/post office, working farmland, and a cheese-making business. Presidential staff had to spend nights in nearby Plymouth. Coolidge's Secret Service detail slept in pup tents surrounding the Plymouth Notch house where the president and First Lady stayed. Details of Russell's conversation with Slemp were never made public, but Russell certainly made the case for a Plymouth Notch visit by the Vagabonds. Slemp, though cognizant of potential media coverage, would have found the president difficult to convince — the Coolidges had withdrawn in part to mourn the death of their son Calvin Jr. Just seven weeks earlier, the sixteen-year-old died in particularly devastating fashion. An apparently trifling blister raised on Calvin Jr.'s foot while playing tennis turned septic; he passed away a few days later.

Calvin Coolidge was not an especially sociable man. Besides dealing with the terrible grief wracking him and the First Lady, the president spent most of his supposed vacation days in Plymouth Notch meeting with advisors about various matters of national urgency. At the same time that Russell Firestone proposed that he host the Vagabonds, Coolidge was scheduled to discuss with staff potential means of containing the worrisome spread of Ku Klux Klan influence. Where Harding, his predecessor, craved publicity above all else, Coolidge's sense of it was more measured. He recognized the value of positive media coverage, especially in the months prior to the November 1924 presidential election, but not to the extent that he would gladly sacrifice valuable working and private time for the sake of a few stories and photographs. He already had the hovering press describing his every Plymouth Notch movement and meal — a recent breakfast was "country ham" fried by Grace Coolidge herself, according to the *Washington Post.*

Coolidge almost surely would have declined a Vagabonds meeting in Plymouth Notch except for a recent, thoughtful gesture toward the president and First Lady by Thomas Edison. The day after the death of Calvin Jr., the inventor sent a succinct, heartfelt telegram to Coolidge at the White House:

May I venture to intrude upon you to express my deep sympathy with you in the sorrow that has been laid upon you. Thomas A. Edison.

It would not have been lost on Coolidge

that, while a number of famous, influential Americans expressed sympathy following his namesake son's death, most did so in letters that they copied to the press or else by sending showy floral arrangements with the names of the senders prominently displayed. Edison's message of condolence was sent privately, parent to parent. It was the sort of plainspoken sentiment that Coolidge himself might have offered under similar circumstances. The meeting was arranged and announced to the press: The Vagabonds would call on the Coolidges in Plymouth Notch at 11 a.m. on Tuesday, August 19.

On Monday, Edison, Ford, and Harvey and Russell Firestone drove from Sudbury to Ludlow, Vermont, which was a dozen miles from Plymouth Notch. Mina Edison, Clara Ford, and Idabelle Firestone didn't accompany them — the ladies may have remembered Florence Harding's 1921 snubbing of them in Maryland and didn't care to risk a second rebuff from a First Lady. Instead, the women went off to visit scenic New England coastal locales, arranging to meet their husbands in Portsmouth, New Hampshire, on Wednesday.

The men had dinner and spent Monday

415

night in a Ludlow hotel. A few reporters left Plymouth Notch to see what the Vagabonds were up to, which wasn't much. Ford and Firestone took an evening walk around town. Edison stayed in the hotel lobby, where he smoked a cigar. But on Tuesday morning, the inventor was the first out of bed, banging on the Fords' and Firestones' doors, urging them to be up and about. After breakfast they spent some time at Ludlow's "Home Town Coolidge Club," visiting with organizers there and purchasing the president's modestly sized campaign buttons. With these pinned to their suit lapels, they drove on to Plymouth Notch, maneuvering their car through the media horde at the foot of the narrow road leading up to the house where the Coolidges waited to receive them.

After handshakes all around, the president invited his guests to sit with him and the First Lady on the porch of their summer retreat, which served as the year-round residence of his father, Col. John Coolidge. There weren't enough chairs on the porch to accommodate everyone, so Grace Coolidge went inside to fetch a few more. Even so, Ford and Coolidge had to perch on a hammock. It was pleasantly informal. Edison, whose deafness usually put him at a disadvantage in casual conversation with new acquaintances, sat next to the First Lady. He was delighted by her ability to easily communicate with him — she had once worked as a teacher for the deaf, and was adept at speaking slowly and clearly. While the others chatted about the local weather (cooler than usual), Edison and Grace Coolidge joshed about Secret Service protection. Edison recalled that during his World War I government service, his every step had been guarded by four agents. Mrs. Coolidge said she had only one agent assigned to her because "one is all I can stand."

Down at the foot of the road, the press clamored to come up. Coolidge suggested that he, Grace, and their guests move to a sunlit spot on the lawn where photographers could snap the best pictures. Col. John Coolidge joined the party — everyone picked up their chairs and moved them to the designated place. Two additional chairs were found for Ford and the president. When everyone was seated in an informal semicircle, the media was allowed to gather a few feet away. For the time being, questions were deferred — instead, the press witnessed the giving of a presidential gift. Coolidge had been briefed on Ford's plans to use the Wayside Inn and its grounds as a means of re-creating the atmosphere of Colonial America. Now he presented the automaker with a family heirloom, a 125-year-old oaken "sugar bucket" used by four generations of Coolidges, including the president himself, during the traditional New England maple tree–tapping process. Ford was thrilled. He turned and remarked to Edison, "I've never received anything since I married Mrs. Ford that I appreciated so much." Edison grinned and nodded. Ford insisted that everyone sign the bucket. Besides his signature, Coolidge added a lengthy inscription: "Made for and used by John Coolidge, one of the original settlers of Plymouth, Vermont. Died 1822. Used also by Calvin Coolidge in sugar lot when he was a boy at home." Ford noted to the reporters that the bucket symbolized the admirable Colonial work ethic — an implement so well-made that it had lasted more than a century. He promised it would be exhibited in a place of honor at the Wayside Inn.

The mood was so merry that Edison took over a cinematographer's camera and filmed the scene himself. Besides the press, some locals had joined the crowd around Coolidge and his guests. Ford spotted nine-year-old George Chalmers and called the boy over. The carmaker dug in his pocket and took out a watch. He gave it to the youngster, saying, "That's something for you, sonny." Ford then hurried to pose for more photos with the president. Several reporters asked young George how it felt to receive a gift from such a famous man. He had no comment. Ford darted back to inform the press, "I buy watches by the gross. I like to give them to youngsters. I found that last one in my grip this morning." Then Ford gave Coolidge a compass for the president's surviving son, John, who wasn't present. Ford told the president, "It's the kind that we always use on our trips about the country." Coolidge replied that John would certainly appreciate the gift.

The press was pleased when the president proposed a short stroll — he wanted to show his guests Plymouth Notch's small cheese factory just up the road. Off the Coolidges and Vagabonds went, with reporters and photographers trailing behind. The visitors were offered samples not only of cheese, but also whey and curd. They ate it all. Col. John Coolidge suggested that they sprinkle salt on some of the fare. The president paused between his own unsalted bites to comment, "I like it just the way it is." Edison also drank some of the fresh milk brought to the factory earlier in the morning by local farmers. The inventor joked that it was a mistake showing Ford around the facility; the carmaker would think of ways to run the process more efficiently and "first thing you know, he'll be making cheese himself."

One reporter described the cheese factory scene as jolly: "The President's callers acted like a group of boys out on a lark." In his memoir, Firestone recalled it differently — or, at least, the aftermath some hours later: Coolidge "explained every process of cheese-making, and we all tasted cheese in various stages — with the result that Mr. Edison, Mr. Ford and my son Russell nursed stomachaches that night and developed an aversion to cheese factories!"

When the factory tour was complete, reporters were finally allowed to ask questions of the visitors. The media apparently had been briefed by Coolidge's aides prior to the Vagabonds' arrival, because their queries exclusively focused on predictions for the November election. As the president looked on, Ford said that the other candidates — former West Virginia congressman John W. Davis for the Democrats, Wisconsin senator Robert M. La Follette for the third-party Progressives — didn't matter: "The only issue in this campaign is Calvin Coolidge. There is no other. The people as a whole have implicit confidence in him." Ford said he personally supported Coolidge because "he stands for law and order and that is what the country needs. There is too much lawlessness and too much disregard for the things that have made America the greatest nation in the world."

Edison touted Coolidge as the best person to clean up government corruption: "A great majority . . . know that he is honest. They are convinced that he will not wink at graft in or out of the White House." The inventor added that it would be wrong to hold Coolidge responsible for Harding's mistakes: "Whatever others may have done, nobody believes [Coolidge] to be a part of any wrongdoing in Washington."

Firestone was even more laudatory: "I regard President Coolidge as the best-fitted candidate for president and I shall do all I can to help elect him. I believe that his election is a foregone conclusion."

With that, Coolidge gestured for his guests and the press to exit the factory and walk back toward Plymouth Notch's few houses and general store. Their mood remained upbeat. Grace Coolidge walked beside Edison, and referred to the watch Ford had given nine-year-old George Chalmers. "I've been told that you never get to bed and don't need a watch," she teased. "Mr. Coolidge goes to bed early, and gets lots of sleep." Edison laughed.

It seemed an exceptionally congenial moment. Ford, Edison, and Firestone were ready for more. Though there wasn't much else in Plymouth Notch itself to see, the tiny hamlet had additional attractions for them. There was no indoor plumbing or electricity; Edison, if asked, would have sketched out a workable generator on the spot, and brought electric light to Coolidge's birthplace just as he already had for half of America. Ford would have enjoyed a president-led tour of the surrounding farms, noting with his keen eye where Ford's tractors might lend themselves to more efficient plowing, planting, and harvesting. Ford might even have pressed a tractor or two upon locals as gifts. And a walk around the fields, perhaps to work up prelunch appetites, could have afforded him an opportunity to remind Coolidge about the abundant benefits awaiting the Tennessee Valley region, if only the president would enthusiastically endorse Ford's long-delayed purchase offer. Firestone as usual was up for anything. Perhaps he looked forward to a restful hour or two seated on the president's porch, taking in the spectacular mountains that ringed the tiny town, with a good chance of glimpsing a heavy-antlered moose or two lolling below the treeline. Lunch would no doubt be tasty, and healthy enough to suit Ford and Edison besides — all those farm-fresh vegetables. Then, in the late afternoon or early evening, there might well be an invitation for the guests to stay the night, in rather cramped quarters, perhaps, but cozy ones, a welcome extension of what was already such an enjoyable first meeting.

But it became apparent, as they all stood outside Col. John Coolidge's house, kitty-corner from the general store, that the president and First Lady were saying *goodbye*. Whatever further hospitality Edison, Ford, and Firestone might have anticipated, so far as the Coolidges were concerned, their hosting duties were done. There was nothing rude or abrupt in their manner as they thanked their guests for stopping by and wished them a pleasant journey to their next destination, but there was also no mistaking a certain underlying firmness. The Vagabonds expected a lengthy visit among equals; the president allocated a small portion of his day for a photo opportunity and endorsements of his candidacy by three prominent men. Firestone wrote later that "we talked of nothing in particular — with the motion-picture cameras and the reporters we indeed had little time for talk." In this instance, as in all things, Calvin Coolidge was precise. They were the president's guests for exactly one hour.

There was nothing for the three visitors to do but gamely shake hands, climb into their car, and drive down past the throng of reporters and cinematographers to the main road, where they turned east in the direction of Portsmouth on the New Hampshire coast. No media followed them. The Vagabonds all were hungry — it would be several more hours before the Plymouth Notch cheese worked its evil on their digestive systems — so they stopped at a hotel in Woodstock, Vermont. There was much scrambling among the hotel's restaurant staff, who hadn't been expecting a request for lunch from three celebrities. Woodstock was one of the loveliest towns in Vermont, meaning it ranked among the loveliest in the nation, but the travelers were in no mood to linger. They weren't expected in Portsmouth until the next morning, but the *Sialia* was scheduled to dock there sometime that night, so they could bunk in comfort on the boat.

The Vagabonds arrived in Portsmouth late Tuesday night and joined their wives aboard the *Sialia*. Ford emerged early Wednesday morning to greet the local press. The reporters wanted to know about the visit with the president. Ford spoke instead of how impressed he was by the beauty of Portsmouth, and in particular with its profusion of antique shops. Ford stressed that, given his choice, he would have "been greatly pleased" to spend more of his vacation there, but "previous plans interfered . . . I will try to come here again." Only then did he mention Coolidge, and his praise seemed more directed at the region than the president. The *Portsmouth Herald* wrote that Ford declared "the greatest need at the present time is to have a man of old New England stock like Calvin Coolidge at the head of the nation for the next four years."

The *Herald*'s headline — "Ford Is Pleased with Portsmouth" — and story emphasized the carmaker's compliments for the city rather than Coolidge. Virtually every other newspaper around the nation featured stories about the Vagabonds' Plymouth Notch visit. By an overwhelming majority, their headlines confirmed that Henry Ford was now preeminent among the trio: "Coolidge Is Host to Ford Party" (Wisconsin Rapids *Daily Tribune*); "Henry Ford Is Caller on Coolidge" (Santa Ana, California, *Register*); "Henry Ford Pays Visit to Coolidge" (Dunkirk, New York, *Evening Observer*). A September 2 editorial in the *Arizona Daily Star* declared that "of the three, Ford is far the most important. He is a social force, a modifier of society as well as a mechanical genius. The others have invented machines and tires. Ford . . . has invented a new kind of man."

Those few newspapers like the *Boston Morning Globe* ("Coolidge Election Forecast by Edison, Ford and Firestone") that placed Edison's name in their headlines ahead of Ford's (Firestone was rarely included at all, and always third) usually did so because their stories featured a joke the inventor told reporters in Plymouth Notch. Edison wanted to illustrate how voters would prefer taciturn Coolidge over his much more loquacious rivals:

Politicians who [talk] so much remind me of a story of the reformer who went to Sing Sing to address the inmates. He talked a long time. A colored prisoner interrupted

426

him and otherwise disturbed the meeting. A jailer hit the colored man over the head with a club and he was quiet and senseless for a while. When he came to, he called out to the jailer, "Hit me again, boss. I kin still hear him talking."

Around eleven on Wednesday morning, Thomas and Mina Edison drove off from Portsmouth to spend a few more days in Vermont. Harvey and Russell Firestone went home to Akron by train, and the Fords sailed off for Maine in the *Sialia,* where they joined their son, Edsel, and his wife on a voyage to Montreal and then Detroit. For several weeks, movie theaters around the country showed film clips of the Vagabonds' visit with the Coolidges, but none of the carmaker, Edison, and Firestone on their 1924 trip in any place other than Plymouth Notch.

As the fall progressed, it became increasingly obvious that Calvin Coolidge would be reelected. Edison refused to take it for granted. He'd pledged his wholehearted support of the president during the Plymouth Rock visit, and felt obligated to follow through. In particular, Edison sent written statements endorsing Coolidge and

Charles G. Dawes, his running mate, to the Republican National Committee. These were reprinted in many newspapers. Edison declared that he would "vote for Coolidge and Dawes because I believe both men are practical, will get results and throw a bomb into that enormous expense account we have down in Washington known as the bureaucracy."

Ford didn't withdraw his Plymouth Notch praise of Coolidge, but he didn't seek out further opportunities to proclaim it. Ford's energetic backing probably made the difference in Woodrow Wilson's narrow 1916 reelection, but eight years later his endorsement — and Edison's, and Firestone's — was helpful rather than critical for Coolidge, who during his reelection campaign remained notably adverse about allowing even the perception of favoritism toward influential supporters. Without the president speaking out on its behalf, Ford's Muscle Shoals bid continued languishing in Congress. In October 1924 Ford bowed to the inevitable and withdrew his purchase offer. It was a terrible blow to him — Ford had not been so determined to make a personal vision come true since the time, now decades past, when he pledged to create a car for the great multitudes. The Model T brought about all the benefits Ford promised, and more. But his vision of Muscle Shoals never would bear fruit. Instead, the glory of its benefits to the public would be delivered nine years later by President Franklin D. Roosevelt when he signed the Tennessee Valley Authority Act. This act retained all the Muscle Shoals properties as quasi-public entities, and ultimately led to the Rural Electrification Act of 1936 that proved to be a key component of Roosevelt's New Deal. Ford had been correct in predicting the potential of Muscle Shoals, but his foresight brought him no joy.

In November 1924, voters returned Calvin Coolidge to the White House by a substantial margin. For decades afterward, magazine articles about the Vagabonds' trips and most biographies of Ford and Edison included descriptions of their meeting with Coolidge in Plymouth Notch. The visit went unmentioned in Coolidge's memoir.

Chapter Eleven:
Jep Bisbee Is Famous

The Vagabonds' summer car trips ended for good on August 20, 1924, when they went their separate ways from Portsmouth, New Hampshire. At the time, Ford and Firestone didn't realize it. Edison probably did.

A year later, Firestone called on Edison in New Jersey to tell the inventor it was time to plan the Vagabonds' 1925 outing. He said that Ford had in mind a driving and camping trip "in the western mountains." But as Firestone wrote to Ford immediately afterward, the seventy-eight-year-old Edison responded that "he didn't believe he could this year." The inventor cited mild stomach ailments and concerns "about the sales end of his business." Firestone tried to change his mind: "I told him that we must not take too long as he was getting older and would not enjoy [camping] as much later."

Firestone and Ford could have gone by themselves. In 1916, Edison and Firestone camped without Ford. But both Firestone and Ford recognized that, without Edison's cheerful, comforting presence, a crucial element of the Vagabonds' communal spirit would be missing. The more they thought about it, Ford and Firestone apparently understood that their road adventures were over.

In 1926 Firestone published a memoir, *Men and Rubber.* In it, he declared that the Vagabonds had mutually decided to end their formal summer trips. Edison's refusal to go wasn't mentioned. Instead, Firestone explained that the reluctant decision was forced on them by insatiable public interest in what were intended by the three participants as relaxing private getaways:

While Mr. Edison and Mr. Ford are as much disposed as ever for the outdoors and would like to go as we used to go, the publicity which the trips began to gather around them eliminated their object and charm. We were never free. Instead of a simple, gipsy-minded fortnight on the road, we found ourselves in the midst of motion-picture operators, reporters and curiosity seekers. We became a kind of traveling circus and, although all of us were ac-

customed to a degree of publicity, it became tiresome to be utterly without privacy.

In fact, the opposite was true. On every
trip, from their pre-departure announce-
ments to their media-friendly stops, the
Vagabonds welcomed and actively sought
publicity. Some of the "motion-picture
operators" worked for Ford. During their
first outings, car travel and camping were
sufficiently unusual that famous men doing
it together commanded daily coverage.
Ford, Edison, and Firestone were media-
savvy enough to offer small, endearing
scenarios to capture press — and public —
attention, like Ford chopping trees, Firestone buying eggs and milk at a remote
farmhouse, or Edison napping by the campfire. Then, as autocamping became more
common, it was necessary for the Vagabonds
to stage major events if they wanted substantial national coverage of their summer
adventures — inviting Harding to join them
in 1921, Ford hosting a farmers' picnic at
Wayside Inn, or visiting Coolidge in Vermont. But the possibilities for these special
moments were limited — they certainly
couldn't be staged every day for two weeks
— and the three learned at Camp Harding

and Plymouth Notch that when presidents were involved, the Vagabonds didn't dominate headlines or control schedules.

By 1925, Ford, Edison, and Firestone also found themselves in undeclared but constant competition for headlines with a whole new generation of American celebrities. In an era where entertainment possibilities, previously limited to modest amusements like local dances, church socials, and reading by oil lamp or candlelight, were vastly enhanced by movies and radio, the number of famous people increased exponentially. Public fascination was no longer limited to political, military, and business leaders along with a few writers and stage performers. Silent films created vast followings for Charlie Chaplin, Clara Bow, Mary Pickford, and Douglas Fairbanks, and the "talkies" that debuted in 1927 further expanded the movie star ranks. Radio broadcasts of sports events besotted listeners with Babe Ruth, Jack Dempsey, Red Grange, and a horse named Man o' War. Few if any outsiders could identify even one of Edison's laboratory assistants, but untold thousands of Americans could name the entire regular starting lineup of the 1927 New York Yankees.

Fans wanted to know everything about

virtually anything that this exciting new generation of national idols did, on and off the screen or playing field, and newspapers and theater newsreels obliged. By the time Firestone published *Men and Rubber,* there was no longer anything deemed special enough about three friends, even such well-known men, driving and camping to warrant national attention. While there was still considerable interest in Ford and Edison as individuals, widespread public appeal of their summer trips with Firestone had run its course. A contributing factor to the end of the trips wasn't the Vagabonds' expectation of too much attention being paid to them, but too little.

The three men still saw a great deal of each other, at their Florida estates during the winter, and in New York whenever business took Ford and Firestone there. Edison curtailed his travel, sticking close to his laboratories in Fort Myers and New Jersey. The inventor was immersed in research. As biographer Neil Baldwin wrote in *Edison: Inventing the Century,* "Patriot to the end, he wanted to find a plant that would produce 'prolific' supplies . . . as a contingency against the danger of curtailed foreign rubber flow due to crop disease or wartime." In 1927 he marked his eightieth birthday by announcing the Edison Botanic Research Corporation, dedicated entirely to the discovery of latex-bearing plants that would flourish in America, and a means of extracting the latex to produce rubber at a reasonable cost. Ford and Firestone agreed to jointly underwrite the project. There is some discrepancy regarding the amounts to which they both committed. Some sources suggest $250,000 and others $50,000, with payments spread over several years, presumably to allow Edison the time necessary to achieve his goals. The press hailed Edison, who set to work, using nine acres in Fort Myers to test approximately seventeen thousand plants. Eventually Edison declared that goldenrod was the best latex source, but try as he and his assistants might, Edison couldn't invent a cost-efficient method of extracting latex from it. That wasn't the inventor's only disappointment.

With the advent of the Great Depression in 1929, Harvey Firestone informed Edison that business setbacks prevented him from honoring his financial commitment. Edison, furious, called Firestone "a goddamned lightweight." The inventor soon resumed his friendship with the tire maker, probably because Ford stepped in to make up the difference. Ultimately, Edison's rubber research didn't result in any definitive breakthroughs. It was not until 1942, with Edison long since deceased and World War II well under way, that American industry produced significant amounts of rubber — the Firestone Company and other major U.S. tire manufacturers were key contributors to the process.

Ford also faced challenges. These were of his own making. For several years, he'd ignored warnings from Edsel and other Ford Motor Company executives that the Model T must be replaced — competitors were making sales headway with more colorful, eye-pleasing cars. In 1925, for the first time since its 1908 introduction, the Model T began losing overall market share. Competitors would have been thrilled to offer any model car that still commanded 40 percent of all sales, but that represented as much as a 15 percent dropoff from 1924, with even more precipitous decline imminent. Where cars were concerned, Americans previously wanted affordable, reliable transportation. Now they craved *choice*. Reluctantly, Ford bowed to the inevitable. He ordered that a new model Ford — only one, another car for the great multitudes — be designed, and in early 1927 Ford shut down Model T production at all his factories. Sixty thousand employees were laid off while assembly lines were rejiggered to produce a mystery car. No details were announced, and the lack of advance information fueled intense press speculation and public interest. One popular, erroneous rumor had Ford naming his new automobile "The Edison." On November 30 there was a press preview in Detroit, on December 2 showrooms opened, and Americans were finally introduced to the Model A. Ford had used the name before — there were several "alphabet" Fords before the Model T — but A, the first letter among twenty-six, was deemed appropriate to describe an automobile intended in 1927 to reassert Ford market dominance.

The Model A was faster than the Model T (top speed of 65 mph), glitzier (several different styles), more comfortable and safer (hydraulic shock absorbers, brakes on all four wheels, laminated safety glass windshields), and even came in a choice of four colors (Niagara Blue, Arabian Sand, Dawn Gray, and Gunmetal Blue). It was also more expensive. Late-era Model Ts sold for as little as $260. Model As ranged in price from about $500 to $1,200. Consumers didn't care. Four hundred thousand were ordered within two weeks. For a while the Model A dominated car sales to the same lopsided extent as its predecessor, but by 1931 its appeal slackened sufficiently for Ford to shut down its production and, like competing car manufacturers, begin offering a variety of models that changed on an annual basis.

Around the same time that he reluctantly shelved his beloved Model T, Ford also parted ways with the *Dearborn Independent.* That process began in February 1925, when Aaron Sapiro filed a libel suit against Ford and Dearborn Publishing Company. Sapiro requested $1 million for defamation of character in a series of *Independent* articles claiming he was part of a larger Jewish conspiracy to gain control over American farmers. (Sapiro served on the council and as a spokesman of the American Farm Bureau Federation, which represented the interests of some sixty cooperative farm associations.) Depositions took some time, and the case finally reached the court in March 1927. That resulted in a mistrial — Ford's attorneys claimed Jews tried to bribe a juror to vote in Sapiro's favor — but before a second trial set for September could begin, Ford capitulated. His attorneys surely advised him that he was likely to lose, and all of Ford's attention was needed back at his assembly plants, where the first Model As were soon going into production. His settlement with Sapiro included an unspecified amount of cash and a public apology. Handing over the money was far less painful than the apology, which was released to the press on July 8. In it, Ford described himself as "deeply mortified" by his newspaper's "resurrecting exploded fictions," and pledged to [ask Jews'] forgiveness for the harm I have unintentionally committed by retracting so far as lies within my power the offensive charges laid at their door." Including "unintentionally" was Ford's face-saving excuse. He claimed that he'd been entirely unaware of any antisemitic articles printed in the *Independent.* Now that he knew about them, he'd see that such offensive sentiments were never expressed on its pages again.

In general, his apology was accepted. There were a few holdouts. Broadway impresario Billy Rose, born William Samuel Rosenberg, composed a biting ditty:

I was sad and I was blue
But now I'm just as good as you
Since Henry Ford apologized to me

439

I've thrown away my little Chevrolet
And bought myself a Ford coupe
Since Henry Ford apologized to me.

Ford didn't tolerate the source of his humiliation long. On December 31, 1927, he officially shut down the *Dearborn Independent.* During the eight years he owned it, Ford lost $5 million on the weekly — and, ultimately, significant personal pride.

The Model A's instant success helped raise Ford's spirits, and by mid-1928 he had another idea that might further expunge his Sapiro capitulation from public memory. The Vagabonds should drive together again.

In July, Ford tasked Firestone to recruit Edison. Unlike three years earlier, Firestone chose not to risk a turndown in person. Instead he wrote the inventor a chatty letter that began with a report on the tire maker's recent business trip to the West Coast: "I met and talked with over one thousand Firestone dealers and had occasion to tell them of . . . the time you were spending in research work to find and develop a rubber plant that would produce rubber in the United States, and I am sure it would please you to know the interest people take in your work. The newspapers gave considerable

440

space to my reference to your work in the rubber field."

As it happened, Firestone continued, his trip also took him to Yellowstone National Park. "It is wonderful. If you have never been there it would be very interesting to you." If Edison didn't find that destination appealing — Firestone acknowledged that "it gets pretty hot traveling through certain sections of the west" — he still "wish[ed] that we might have an outing this year, some place where it would be convenient and you and Mrs. Edison would like to go . . . [perhaps] go over our old trip down in Virginia, or in that section. I think that would be a good trip, or up in Maine." Firestone emphasized that Mr. Ford was eager for the Vagabonds to regroup: He "suggested that we arrange something for the last of August." But it was left to Edison to pick the time and destination — "I shall be pleased with any plan you suggest and will try to do my part to make the trip as comfortable and enjoyable as possible."

Firestone closed by telling Edison, "Mr. Ford said he was going to Orange to see you this week and talk to you about it."

A few days later, Edison scribbled his response in the margins of Firestone's letter. He instructed his secretary Meadow-

441

croft to write that "I don't see how I can possibly make the auto trip this year." It's unclear whether Edison said the same to Ford when the carmaker called on him in New Jersey, or even if Ford discussed a Vagabonds trip with the inventor at all. Instead, Firestone was to be told that "Ford was here today, he says he wants me to lay [the] cornerstone of his museum in Dearborn." With the introduction of the Model A behind him and the *Dearborn Independent* shuttered, a new project dominated Henry Ford's thoughts, even at the expense of another Vagabonds trip. He'd once promised a Ford car for the multitudes. Now he'd give the American people a Ford museum of *real* national history, one where Thomas Edison was celebrated above all others.

Ford had been collecting Americana for well over a decade, items that to him reflected the best of the nation's history — farm implements, one-room schoolhouse desks and writing materials, water wheels and horse harnesses, and other objects that reminded Ford of the honest ambition and hard work that made modern America possible. He'd mostly stored these in overflowing warehouses on business properties. A small percentage graced shelves at the Wayside Inn. Now Ford wished to share his entire collection, or at least most of it, with the public. In 1926, Ford selected a site in Dearborn adjacent to Ford Motor Company and hired an architect to build a singular, eye-catching structure fronted by an exact replica of Independence Hall in Philadelphia. The massive building was to be filled with memorabilia already in Ford's collection and many more items to be acquired. An enclosed museum was only half of his plan. An additional 255 acres was designated as "Greenfield Village" (named for Clara Ford's girlhood home), a site harking back to the late nineteenth and very early twentieth centuries with everything authentic. Visitors could literally stroll through American history, because Ford purchased such historic buildings as the Wright brothers' bicycle shop and Logan County Courthouse, where Abraham Lincoln demonstrated his skills as a lawyer. There were sawmills, gristmills, steam engines, plows, and a working farm. Ford eventually included his own birthplace, buildings from the Firestone family farm, and Edison's Menlo Park, New Jersey, laboratory. All the structures were torn down on their original sites, transported in pieces to Dearborn, and reassembled with obsessive care. Ford insisted that every detail must be exact, down to chair styles and brands of nails.

The formal name of the museum was the Edison Institute, and in September 1928 Edison laid the cornerstone, scribbling his signature in wet cement. It was Ford's intention that the museum and Greenfield Village officially open on October 21, 1929, the fiftieth anniversary of Edison's breakthrough discovery of the incandescent bulb. Construction wasn't complete — the opening would be delayed until 1933 — but enough was in place to host a gala event. Edison was guest of honor. Attendees included Will Rogers, Madame Curie, and President Herbert Hoover, elected in 1928 after Calvin Coolidge declined to seek another term. There was a grand dinner, and after it a program broadcast nationally on radio. Speakers praised Edison, and finally the eighty-two-year-old inventor made some brief remarks. In them, he gave public credit for the first time to all the laboratory assistants who'd been at his side: "When you honor me, you are also honoring the vast army of workers but for whom my work would have gone for nothing." It was gracious, if overdue. The evening concluded with Edison connecting two wires and "lighting up" the Menlo Park laboratory just as he had fifty years earlier. The crowd applauded, and, high in the tower of the ersatz Independence Hall, a replica Liberty Bell clanged in the night.

There was to be no official Edison memoir — years earlier, the inventor and Samuel Clemens discussed collaborating on one, but couldn't agree on whose name should come first on the cover. Edison's respect for Ford was such that he would allow the carmaker top billing, but so far as the inventor was concerned, no one else, even the author renowned as Mark Twain, merited that privilege. Edison felt too poorly to attempt writing the book on his own. The inventor blamed "gases formed during digestion" for uncharacteristic listlessness and, for the last few years of his life and at his own insistence, subsisted entirely on milk, at first a pint every three hours, later seven glasses a day. Kidney failure hastened the end. Edison died on October 18, 1931, and by President Hoover's request, on October 21, the day of his burial, at 10 p.m. the nation turned off its electric lights for one minute.

Edison's family held a lingering grudge against the surviving Vagabonds. Mina Edison always believed that Ford took advantage of her trusting husband, and Edison's daughter Madeleine, who was along on the aborted 1914 excursion into the Everglades, declared in a 1972 interview (she was by then in her eighties) that the inventor never wanted to go on the subsequent Vagabonds trips: "He would let himself be taken on these things." While her mother resented Ford, Madeleine specifically accused Firestone, claiming that the tire maker organized the summer trips as personal "publicity stunts." It was a particularly unjust charge. As dozens of letters and telegrams at the Benson Ford Research Center and Thomas Edison National Historical Park make clear, Firestone was the organizer but never the initiator of the Vagabonds' trips. In every instance, either Edison (the earliest years) or Ford (the later ones) suggested a trip; then it fell to Firestone to contact the other one to gauge interest, agree on a destination, and coordinate dates convenient to Ford's and Edison's schedules. During the trips, Firestone was responsible for purchasing supplies, soothing John Burroughs during the cranky old naturalist's frequent tantrums, and serving as a constant buffer for Ford and Edison with townspeople and the media. He did this by sublimating his own ego; Firestone was eminently successful in his own right. Ford gave America a car for the multitudes, but Firestone was among several innovative manufacturers who developed the tires that allowed Model Ts and other cars to travel further with fewer blowouts and much smoother rides. As a member of the Vagabonds, he uncomplainingly accepted his secondary role, respecting two friends who were greater, though not necessarily better, men. On February 7, 1938, sixty-nine-year-old Harvey Firestone suffered a coronary thrombosis and died in his sleep.

Henry Ford lived to be eighty-four, and his last years were difficult. Ford's opposition to unions and his employees' increasing dissatisfaction with company work rules (no talking or sitting, only one fifteen-minute break each work shift that must be used for lunch, increasing verbal and occasional physical harassment by supervisors) inevitably led to conflict, culminating in a 1933 clash between police, recently laid-off workers, and outside agitators that left several men dead and dozens injured. The media described the bloody melee as "the Dearborn Massacre." It took another eight years before Ford reluctantly allowed employees to unionize, and then only after the U.S. courts ruled that workers could not be fired for participating in union activities.

Ford's antisemitic past continued haunting him. Adolf Hitler praised Ford in his polemical *Mein Kampf* (a title that translates to *My Struggle*): "Every year [the Jews] manage to become increasingly the controlling masters of [America]; one great man, Ford, to their exasperation still holds out." On July 30, 1938, his seventy-fifth birthday, Henry Ford became the first American recipient of the Grand Service Cross of the Supreme Order of the Golden Eagle, an award invented by Hitler to honor distinguished foreigners. In January 1940, just months after the Nazi blitzkrieg across Europe, Ford privately considered sending personal emissaries to Hitler with a request to halt hostilities. "I think I just may have [Hitler's] respect [and] the door may be open," he told future biographer James Newton. But Ford never followed through, and during World War II, as he had during the earlier world war, he converted his factories to the manufacture of war matériel. Ford's reputation as an antisemite still lingers. In 2014, the mayor of Fort Myers withdrew a proposal to name a city bridge for Ford when the director of a local Jewish organization protested.

Ford's last few years were especially difficult. Frustrated by being allowed only a figurehead role by his father in running Ford Motor Company, Edsel Ford planned to resign. Before he could, he was stricken with cancer and died on May 26, 1943. Henry and Edsel Ford had not been close — the father considered the son to be too soft — but Ford was devastated by Edsel's death all the same. Ford named himself as his son's replacement; that apparently meant no real change, since Ford already controlled the company anyway. But Ford's physicians detected signs of dementia in him, and in September 1945 an increasingly impaired Ford resigned in favor of his grandson Henry Ford II. With no company to run, and with few real friends remaining after the deaths of Edison and Firestone, Ford spent hours wandering Greenfield Village, increasingly unable to distinguish between past and present. One observer recalled Ford "standing in the middle of [Edison's] laboratory floor, with a wan smile on his lips, like a lost child, and a faraway expression in his eyes." The end came from a cerebral hemorrhage. With Clara by his side, Henry Ford died at home on April 7, 1947.

The Vagabonds are remembered to this day. Although the company he founded in 1900 was acquired by Bridgestone Corporation of Japan eighty-eight years later, Firestone tires remain one of the best-selling brands. In the 1960s and '70s, Firestone's name became familiar to a new generation thanks to a popular advertising jingle:

Wherever wheels are rolling,
No matter what the load,
The name that's known is Firestone
Where the rubber meets the road.

Harvey Firestone would have considered it a fitting epitaph.

Nearly fourteen decades after he invented incandescent bulbs and the power grid systems to efficiently and economically light them, Thomas Edison remains one of the most iconic and beloved figures in American history. At Thomas Edison National Historical Park in New Jersey, visitors can tour his former office and living quarters and, under supervision, immerse themselves in a collection of his letters and other papers. Rutgers University also boasts an exceptional collection of Edison material, much of which is available for viewing online.

Henry Ford's legacy is more complicated. The antisemitic taint may never be entirely expunged, and when his political ambitions are recalled at all, they are usually dismissed as the delusions of a crackpot. In fact, if Warren G. Harding hadn't died unexpectedly in 1923, Ford might well have become America's thirtieth president. But the Model T still reigns as perhaps the most famous, and certainly most popular, car in American automobile history. Ford Motor Company remains a major industry entity, and the justly renowned Greenfield Village and the Henry Ford Museum in Dearborn are among the most popular historical attractions in America. Ford would have liked that, though he would be less pleased that the museum he named for Edison is now popularly known by his own name instead. (It still is listed on official business forms as the Edison Institute.) Even long after his death, Ford dominates relationships.

As individuals, Edison, Ford, and Firestone created the means for the "great multitudes" to enjoy leisure entertainment far beyond what was previously imagined. As the Vagabonds, their summer car and camping trips exemplified what they had helped make possible: See what we're doing? You can do it, too. Eventually their own participation, for a time so newsworthy, became unremarkable. But that is inevitable for the most successful trend-setters. By their example, the Vagabonds encouraged countless ordinary Americans to pursue their own dreams. This was especially true in the case of Jep Bisbee, the elderly fiddler who encountered the Vagabonds in his tiny, remote hometown of Paris, Michigan, during August 1923.

It had been nearly two months since the Vagabonds made their surprise call at Jep's modest home, promising the obscure country musician a trip to New York, a recording session, and a new car. Jep, a shoemaker who fiddled at local dances less for the dollar or so he earned than for the love of playing traditional folk tunes, never previously aspired to or even imagined anything so grand. Now he did. But as weeks passed with no further word from his famous visitors, Jep and the rest of Paris's few hundred residents began believing that the rich men had either forgotten or never meant to keep their magnificent promises.

Then on October 10, 1923, Jep responded

to a knock on his front door and there stood Henry Ford and his uniformed chauffeur. Ford presented Jep's wife, Sarah, with a box of chocolates, and her stunned husband with a shiny new Model T parked in front of the house. Ford proposed that Jep use his barn as a garage, and instructed the chauffeur to move the car in there. When the barn door proved too low and narrow for the Model T to fit through, Ford and the chauffeur took off their coats, borrowed Jep's axes and hammers, and, in their shirtsleeves, tore down the old door, widened the frame, and built a new door along with a ramp so the car could be driven in easily. When the sweaty work was done and the old musician was invited to move the Model T into its new home, Jep had to admit that he didn't know how to drive.

The best way Jep could thank Mr. Ford for the car was to invite his benefactor in and play fiddle for him again. After tapping his foot to a few tunes, Mr. Ford said he had to go, but he'd be back in another month or so to personally escort Jep, Sarah, and any of their extended family they wanted to invite all the way by train to West Orange, New Jersey. There the Bisbees would be guests of Thomas and Mina Edison while Jep recorded songs in Mr. Edison's own studio. Then the recordings would be released on Mr. Edison's label. Every August promise would be kept.

It turned out that Mr. Ford got detained and couldn't go east with the Bisbees after all, but things worked out well anyway. The Bisbees were met at the West Orange station by Mr. Edison himself, who had in tow seemingly more reporters than there were people living in Paris, Michigan. Jep did his best to answer all the questions that they fired at him. The response that made most of the next day's papers was Jep's honest reply when asked what tunes he planned to record: "Oh, anything that happens to come into my old head."

Jep made his recordings, so many that afterward Mr. Edison told the press it was the most anyone had ever made in a single day. Then, after some New York City sightseeing, the Bisbees went home. But Jep's life was never the same, and in the best of ways. He chose not to use all the stories about him as the basis for a national concert tour — he felt he was too old and settled for that. But Jep, whose previous performances were limited to barn dances and other small local events, now accepted invitations to play in auditoriums all around Michigan. Where he'd once been thrilled to earn $5 a show, he now commanded ten times that amount, and collectors gladly paid handsome sums for his handmade fiddles. Jep kept on performing for almost a dozen years, and when he died in 1935 at age ninety-three, his obituary appeared in the *New York Times*. His wonderful late-life success was due to the Vagabonds, and Jep never forgot it. Though barely literate, he wrote to Henry Ford that "onley for you & Mr. Edison they would of forgotten me but now they all Know me."

If they'd never taken their summer trips, all of America would still have known of Henry Ford, Thomas Edison, and Harvey Firestone. But their adventures as the Vagabonds helped usher in a new national lifestyle, and that should be remembered, too. The country's fascination with their travels was expressed in "The Refreshing Trio," an uncredited poem printed in the *Oakland Tribune* just after the Vagabonds' final trip in 1924:

Whenever the news is too grewsome or
    dull,
Whenever the reader feels bored,
There come to the rescue those three
    worthy pals,

Edison, Firestone and Ford.

We turn from a murder or cyclone or flood
Or the stock broker's marks on the board,
To read what these three coots are up to
   again,
Edison, Firestone and Ford.

They picnic, they camp, they fish and
   they hike,
They talk and we all thank the Lord,
That no matter what things other fellows
   may do,
We have Edison, Firestone and Ford.

NOTES

As a point of general information, from fall 2016 through summer 2018 I drove every surviving road followed by the Vagabonds during their trips. Where those roads no longer existed, I used the modern ones that most closely paralleled them. In every instance, the scenery was spectacular, and if you decide you'd like to spend some vacation days traveling where the Vagabonds did, I'm sure you'll have a good time. I certainly did.

Prologue: Paris, Michigan — Mid-August 1923

The date of this prologue is deliberately vague. Newspaper accounts of the Vagabonds' visit to Jep Bisbee in Paris, Michigan, began appearing on August 18 (in the *Battle Creek Enquirer*) and then in other newspapers around the country for about two more weeks. Most of the papers ran the same story, which was written by a correspondent for the Associated Press. The August 18 story in the Battle Creek paper makes it likely that Ford and Edison's Paris stop came on August 17. And in his privately published *There to Breathe the Beauty,* which includes the only extensive record of where the Vagabonds drove and stopped on every night of their numerous summer trips, Norman Brauer has them visiting Jep in Paris on that date. But Brauer also places Jep and Paris in Michigan's Upper Peninsula, well removed from the actual town in Mecosta County far to the southeast on the other side of Lake Michigan. If they were in the Upper Peninsula on the 17th then they couldn't have seen Jep on the same day, road conditions and driving times being what they were. That would suggest they were in Paris on August 16. In the grand scheme of things, the date isn't really that important — what matters is that they met Jep Bisbee and made dazzling promises to him. But given the uncertainty of the date, I'm describing it as "mid-August."

Much of my description of 1923 Paris comes from on-site interviews with local officials Jim Chapman, Dave Basch, and Janet Clark. The town remains unincorporated.

Unseasonably cool temperatures combined with near-constant rain: Newspaper accounts of the Vagabonds' 1923 trip all cite this inclement weather.

If most of Michigan eerily resembled a palm-down left hand: I'm aware it can also be compared to a palm-up right hand. Either way, the "lowest joint of the ring finger" still applies.

In only two decades, the number of automobiles in Americas had swelled: Dayton Duncan and Ken Burns, *Horatio's Drive,* pp. 15–16.

Lincolns and Cadillacs and two other vehicles: St. Louis Post-Dispatch, August 10, 1923.

from them emerged strapping young men outfitted in matching khaki uniforms: Most of this scene is based on the *Battle Creek Enquirer* story published August 18, 1923. I also gleaned information from Norman Brauer, *There to Breathe the Beauty,* p. 197.

Town newspapers throughout the region were full of wishful speculation: An August 10, 1923, article in the *Green Bay Press-Gazette* is a good example.

he was in the early stages of a nasty cold: Associated Press wire story first published on August 18, 1923.

Firestone and his family, traveling in yet

another fine car: Brauer, pp. 192–93.

eighty-one-year-old Jep was the closest thing tiny Paris had: In the Winter 2004–2005 edition of *The Old-Time Herald: A Magazine Dedicated to Old-Time Music,* Paul Gifford contributes an absolutely delightful story titled "Jasper E. 'Jep' Bisbee — Old-Time Michigan Dance Fiddler" that tells all about Jep's background and briefly describes his August 1923 visit with the Fords and Edisons. I relied on some of that information here, and also on the Associated Press article that ran in newspapers all over the country.

It was well-known among Ford associates: Henry Ford *loathed* "modern" music, especially jazz. He also detested dances like the Charleston, which he considered lewd. Ford thought such things corrupted America's youth. Martin Gilbert, *A History of the Twentieth Century, Vol. I, 1900–1993,* p. 699; Bill Bryson, *One Summer: America 1927,* p. 239; James Newton, *Uncommon Friends: Life with Thomas Edison, Henry Ford, Harvey Firestone, Alexis Carrel & Charles Lindbergh,* p. 103.

Ford himself enjoyed sawing away: David L. Lewis, *The Public Image of Henry Ford: An*

460

American Folk Hero and His Company, p. 227.
Charlie Montague couldn't stop crowing: Battle Creek Enquirer, August 18, 1923.

Chapter One: 1914

Most of the studies of the Vagabonds present their epic car trips as beginning in 1915 in California. I believe that's because this was the year that newspapers began reporting on their stops along the way, entertaining readers with accounts and photos of the nation's greatest men picking their way along rugged roads and camping by streams just as many rank-and-file American car owners had begun to do. But Edison, Ford, and Burroughs took automobile vacations well before that — Edison and his family toured Europe and New England by car, and Ford and Burroughs took their 1913 driving trip to New England. I cite the abbreviated 1914 Everglades excursion as the first *Vagabonds* trip because Ford, Edison, and Burroughs were on it together, with the intent of seeing interesting sights without a specific daily agenda. No reporters went along, which was just as well, since Ford and Edison would not have appreciated the rest of the U.S. learning how they looked half-drowned in swamp water. But Ford,

461

Edison, and Burroughs thought, all in all, that it had been fun despite all that went wrong. In the future they'd factor in weather, proper camp locations, the necessity of at least rudimentary roads, and places to replenish supplies or buy necessities they either forgot to bring or learned that they would need along the way. Nineteen fourteen in the Everglades was the time where the soon-to-be-dubbed Vagabonds learned all the things *not* to do on their subsequent car trips.

It was especially challenging to research this chapter. In all other years, the Vagabonds' excursions were extensively covered by the press — accounts that appeared on national newswires and stories by local reporters and made it relatively easy to track day-to-day progress. There are no such helpful articles describing the two-day debacle in the Everglades.

Fortunately, there were other sources. Staff at the Benson Ford Research Center (part of the Henry Ford Museum in Dearborn, Michigan), Paul Israel at Rutgers University, Leonard DeGraaf at Thomas Edison National Historical Park, and Brent Newman of the Edison and Ford Winter Estates in Fort Myers were all exceptionally well-informed and immensely helpful. I also enjoyed a lengthy visit with members of the Southwest Florida Historical Society in Fort Myers — Glenn Miller, Genevieve Bowen, Ralph Ireland, Randy Briggs, Helen Farrell, Woody Hansen, and Pat Mann. (For brevity's sake, in specific notes their contributions will be collectively cited as "SWFLHS.") The 1914 plat map in the society's library made it possible to gauge almost exactly where the five-car Vagabonds caravan entered the Everglades, and to follow their swampy route toward Big Lake. Over a century later, it was still hard going, and there were plenty of opportunities to observe alligators at uncomfortably close range.

Finally, four books contain excellent descriptions of Fort Myers in 1914 and the Vagabonds' adventures there and in the Everglades that year. If you want every conceivable detail, I recommend *The Story of Fort Myers* by Karl H. Grismer, *Edison and Ford in Florida* by Mike Cosden, Brent Newman, and Chris Pendleton, and, most of all, *The Florida Life of Thomas Edison* by Michele Wehrwein Albion and *The Edisons of Fort Myers: Discoveries of the Heart* by Tom Smoot.

two thousand people swarmed around the

train depot: Michele Wehrwein Albion, *The Florida Life of Thomas Edison,* pp. 74–75.

An Oldsmobile Model S tipped the scales: Christopher Wells, *Car Country: An Environmental History,* pp. 46–48.

Fort Myers itself was mostly populated: My description of the town, and of Edison's arrival and property purchase there, is derived from several sources. Tom Smoot, *The Edisons of Fort Myers: Discoveries of the Heart,* pp. 1–27; Mike Cosden, Brent Newman, and Chris Pendleton, *Edison and Ford in Florida,* pp. 7–35; Karl H. Grismer, *The Story of Fort Myers,* p. 114; Albion, *The Florida Life of Thomas Edison,* p. xvii; Brent Newman interview; SWFLHS interviews.

Edison soon made an announcement: Brent Newman and SWFLHS interviews; Albion, pp. 42–50; Smoot, p. 41; Grismer, pp. 115–16.

Edison pledged to buy the trees: Smoot, pp. 81–86; Albion, pp. 67–69; SWFLHS interviews.

The train was late: Smoot, pp. 112–14; Albion, pp. 74–77.

In April 1911, one of Edison's business offices: Benson Ford Research Center, Acc. 1630, Box 2; Robert Conot, *Thomas A.*

Edison: A Streak of Luck, pp. 381–83; Randall Stross, *The Wizard of Menlo Park: How Thomas Alva Edison Invented the Modern World,* pp. 235–38, 250–53; Neil Baldwin, *Edison: Inventing the Century,* pp. 321–23.

Later, Edison followed up the meeting: Benson Ford Research Center, Acc. 1630, Box 3.

Ford announced that he and Edison were collaborating: New York Times, 1/11/1914.

Ford's friendship with John Burroughs: Robert Casey interview; Robert Kreipke interview; Edward Renehan Jr., *John Burroughs: An American Naturalist,* pp. 23–27; Ford R. Bryan, *Friends, Families & Forays: Scenes from the Life and Times of Henry Ford,* pp. 44–46; Shannon Wianecki, "When America's Titans of Industry and Innovation Went Road-Tripping Together," *Smithsonian Magazine,* January 2016.

Ford convinced Burroughs to take a car trip: Renehan, p. 273.

he told the New York Times: *New York Times,* 1/22/1914.

he'd suffered a breakdown: Conot, p. 406.

Edison lounged inside, listening to music: New York Times, 3/7/1914.

It wasn't that simple: SWFLHS and Brent

Newman interviews.

Mina Edison was an educated, opinionated woman: Brent Newman and SWFLHS interviews.

Early on Saturday morning: Photographer Ralph Lauer and I, aided by a 1914 plat map, approximately followed the Vagabonds' trail from Fort Myers into the Everglades. With the exception of some decent roads in (though not along some of the Vagabonds' route!) and areas cordoned off by park services, conditions are essentially unchanged. So some of the physical descriptions of the Everglades in this chapter come from firsthand observation. Otherwise, everything I write about the two-day trip in February 1914 comes from interviews with Brent Newman, the SWFLHS, and, above all, the excellent books by Mike Cosden, Brent Newman, and Chris Pendleton (pp. 62–64); Michele Wehrwein Albion (pp. 74–81); and Tom Smoot (pp. 116–27). If you're intrigued by this chapter, I urge you to track down and read their work. Publishing information for all three books can be found in the bibliography here.

Only Charles Edison and Burroughs wanted to stay: As will be demonstrated in subsequent chapters, John Burroughs was a world-class griper on the Vagabonds' trips. In camps far more luxurious than the soggy stop in the Everglades, Burroughs whined about everything from the mattress on his cot to the chilliness of summer winds everyone else found warm and soothing. There is absolutely no way he was a good sport and willing to stay soaked in the Everglades. I suspect that, among all the campers on this trip, Burroughs was the most determined to get back to Fort Myers at all possible speed, and that he voted along with Charles Edison to stick it out only after he was certain the majority would vote to leave. Of course, he was quite elderly by 1914. One imagines that he was tougher in his younger years.

Ford also had a request: Benson Ford Research Center, Acc. 1630, Box 3; *New York Times,* 5/11/1914; Smoot, pp. 127–28; Stross, pp. 239–41; Steven Watts, *The People's Tycoon: Henry Ford and the American Century,* pp. 327–28; *New York Times,* 5/12/14.

An advertising agent employed by Philip Morris Cigarettes: Pittsburgh Leader, 7/9/1914, courtesy of the Edison collection at Rutgers University.

Edison routinely employed smokers: Stross, p. 240.

Then, in early December: Paul Israel, *Edison: A Life of Invention,* p. 432; Leonard DeGraaf, *Edison and the Rise of Innovation,* p. 195; Newton, 16; Stross, p. 231; Watts, pp. 335–36. It's important to note that although James Newton writes that he was personally told by Edison that Ford's on-the-spot loan was $750,000, other historians believe it to have been $100,000. Since Ford was estimated to have a personal fortune of $100 million (approximately $1.8 billion in modern-day dollars), he could easily have afforded either sum.

Robert Conot offers a plausible suggestion: Conot, p. 407.

In one undated, handwritten memorandum: Benson Ford Research Center, Acc. 1630, Box 3.

Chapter Two: 1915

Anytime I write about history taking place in California, I always begin my research at the amazing California Historical Society on Mission Street in San Francisco. The staff there is incredibly knowledgeable and helpful. Rebecca Baker, archivist at the Luther Burbank Home and Gardens in

Santa Rosa, went out of her way to meet with me and provide critical background on Burbank and the Vagabonds' visit to him there. Kevin Hallaran, former archivist at the Riverside Metropolitan Museum, had valuable insights to offer. At Mission Basilica San Diego de Alcalá, Tony Falcon was a walking history book. Brian Butko, director of publications for the Senator John Heinz History Center in Pittsburgh, proved to be an invaluable resource regarding early roads in America. And in this chapter and every other in the book, assistance and advice from the staff at the Henry Ford Museum's Benson Ford Research Center was critical.

As a useful gauge of national interest in all things Edison and Ford, note the number of newspapers cited that carried wire-service stories about them at the expositions and in Los Angeles and Santa Rosa.

Thomas Edison set off by train: New York Times, 10/12 and 10/15/1915; *Bellingham* (Washington) News, 10/15/1915.

it was delightfully beyond the imaginations of most: Stross, pp. 1–2, 44–45.

Their telegram read: Benson Ford Research Center, Acc. 1630, Box 4.

A frenzied public greeting for the inventor: Aberdeen (North Dakota) Daily News, 10/

18/1915; *San Jose Mercury Herald,* 10/19/1915.

they were ensconced at the Inside Inn: San Jose Mercury Herald, 10/19/1915.

The smallest details of their day made print: Morning Oregonian, 10/20/1915; *Los Angeles Times,* 10/20/1915; *San Francisco Chronicle,* 10/20/1915.

San Francisco's telegraph operators hosted a dinner: Idaho Daily Statesman, 10/20/1915; *Nevada State Journal,* 10/20/1915.

While Edison toured the ship: San Francisco Chronicle, 10/21/1915.

He especially disdained anyone identified as an expert: Bryson, p. 251.

What wasn't written about: Benson Ford Research Center, Acc. 423, Box 1; Douglas Brinkley, *Wheels for the World,* pp. 165–69; Watts, pp. 179–198.

Ford had long believed: Watts, pp. 225–27; Brinkley, pp. 191–92; Neil Baldwin, *Henry Ford and the Jews: The Mass Production of Hate,* pp. 45–52.

In contrast, two weeks after the Lusitania *sinking:* Baldwin, *Edison: Inventing the Century,* p. 344.

a company magazine distributed to employees: Lewis, pp. 48–50.

Ford gloried in that freedom: San Francisco

Chronicle, 10/21/1915.

Edison Day on Thursday: San Francisco Chronicle, 10/21 and 10/22/1915; *Los Angeles Times,* 10/20/15; *San Jose Mercury Herald,* 10/24/1915.

Edison, Ford, and Firestone took a late morning train: Rebecca Baker interview; *Cleburne* (Texas) *Morning Review,* 10/23/1915; *Dallas Morning News,* 10/23/1915.

Edison wasn't as lucky: San Jose Mercury Herald, 10/24/1915; *San Jose Evening News,* 10/25/1915.

Edison's seminal contribution to the motion picture industry: Baldwin, *Edison: Inventing the Century,* p. 297; Conot, p. 394.

When the party arrived at the studio: Brauer, p. 28.

there were very few cars: Duncan and Burns, pp. 15–16.

Inconveniently for motorists: James J. Flink, *America Adopts the Automobile, 1895–1910,* p. 179, 183, 185.

For those whose cars boasted speedometers: Ibid., p. 188; David LaChance, *Hemmings Motor News,* September 2010.

or even the number or name of the roads themselves: Brian Butko interview; Duncan and Burns, p. 31.

a persuasive description of why travelers

471

should stop: Touring San Diego County, Automobile Club of Southern California, 1915.

As soon as word of their arrival reached the Exposition: The San Diego newspapers of the era covered Edison Day with comprehensive zeal. This section is mostly based on stories in the *San Diego Union,* 10/29 and 10/30/1915. The exception is noted next.

"You may know all about a flivver car": San Diego Sun, 10/20/1915.

That night, Firestone hosted a dinner: Brauer, p. 30.

Before Edison left, he had a suggestion: Ibid.

They would be "the Vagabonds": If there is a definitive record of when they chose this nickname, I've been unable to find it. That's why I write "then or not long after."

Chapter Three: 1916

he agreed to a visit from Rosika Schwimmer: Paul Israel and Leonard DeGraaf interviews; Brinkley, pp. 194–98; Smoot, pp. 130–31; Renehan, p. 285; Clara Barrus, ed., *The Heart of Burroughs's Journals,* p. 286; Frank Ernest Hill and Allan Nevins, "Henry Ford and His Peace Ship," *American Heritage,* February 1958; Benson

Ford Research Center, Acc. 1157, Box 1.

In March 1916 Ford was nettled: Benson Ford Research Center, Acc. 1630, Box 5.

Though he proclaimed himself uninterested: Baldwin, *Henry Ford and the Jews,* p. 68; Watts, pp. 240–43.

The great newspapers of the Midwest: John Tebbel, *An American Dynasty,* pp. 92–100; Robert Lacey, *Ford: The Men and the Machine,* pp. 197–99.

On July 15, one of Ford's assistants: Benson Ford Research Center, Acc. 1630, Box 5.

Ford's publicity gift was an instinctive knack: David Halberstam, *The Reckoning,* p. 68.

Edison understood the press: Paul Israel interview; DeGraaf, pp. xxvii–xviii; Baldwin, pp. 28–31; Conot, pp. 8–10; Stross, p. 4.

A ubiquitous wire story found Edison emphasizing: Boston Post, 8/28/1916.

he wired a last-minute appeal: Benson Ford Research Center, Acc. 1630, Box 5.

Firestone's staff began setting up camp: Brauer, p. 37.

even the best roads were poorly marked: Brian Butko interview.

Farmers whose acres included pleasant roadside: Warren James Belasco, *Americans on the Road: From Autocamp to Motel,* pp. 74–76.

he was even less pleased to see them: New York Times, 8/30 and 9/24/1916.

their crotchety host stood to the side: Barrus, ed., p. 295.

he'd decided not to go: Harvey S. Firestone with Samuel Crowther, *Men and Rubber: The Story of Business,* p. 196.

A telegram from Ford's assistant Ernest Liebold followed: Benson Ford Research Center, Acc. 1630, Box 5.

A wire service story reported: New York Times, 9/1/1916.

Burroughs's mood was good enough: Firestone with Crowther, p. 200.

Firestone stayed at the hotel, too: Ibid., p. 198.

But what awaited them instead was a telegram: Benson Ford Research Center, Acc. 1630, Box 5.

but reserved all public credit for himself: Israel, p. 195.

Instead, he offered a ringing political endorsement: Detroit Free Press, 9/4/1916.

There was a ferry ride: Brauer, p. 53.

Burroughs learned that his wife, Ursula, had died: Renehan, pp. 290–91.

he'd accept no personal profit: Lacey, p. 156. But Lacey later points out in *Ford: The Men and the Machine* that it seems likely that Ford did earn substantial personal profit from war-related manufacturing. *Rather than restate Edison's message in a typed letter:* Benson Ford Research Center, Acc. 1630, Box 5.

Chapter Four: 1918

It's interesting to contrast the accounts of the 1918 trip kept by John Burroughs and Harvey Firestone. Both mostly accentuate the positive, though Burroughs is open about his dislike of the South. But they still offer day-to-day descriptions of the journey, particularly the crowds that routinely gathered and sometimes proved troublesome. I relied a great deal on both trip journals in writing this chapter, and rather than cite each a hundred times over and extend these chapter notes by way too many pages, I'll note that with one exception, every otherwise unattributed quote comes from either the Burroughs or the Firestone manuscript. (The exception is Burroughs's quote that "Millionaires add to the health and well-being of all," which is found on page 199 of Edward J. Renehan Jr.'s excellent *John Burroughs: An American Naturalist.*)

Edison approached his Naval Advisory Board responsibilities: Albion, pp. 99–102; Conot, pp. 414–18; Israel, pp. 450–51;

Stross, pp. 259–60.

the best-known and most direct of which was the Lincoln Highway: Brian Butko interview.

Henry Ford understood the publicity potential: Lewis, 223. There are several excellent Ford biographies, and as various chapter notes indicate I've made use of them all in my research. But Lewis's is my favorite by far.

he granted an interview to the city press: Pittsburgh Press, 8/17, 18, and 19/1918; *Pittsburgh Post-Gazette,* 8/18 and 19/1918.

The rest of the camp was up around eight: Brauer, pp. 61–101. As with all other of the Vagabonds' trips (with the exception of the Everglades debacle in 1914, which he chose not to include), Norman Brauer's *There to Breathe the Beauty* account of 1918 includes helpful day-to-day summaries of how far the travelers drove, where they stopped, when they got up the next morning, and other bits of information all apparently gleaned from the same Burroughs and Firestone 1918 trip diaries that I found so helpful. (Brauer's source notes are limited to a bibliography.) I'm noting the Brauer chapters here rather than list individual page citations for purposes of brevity. *There to Breathe the Beauty* was published privately, and very few copies remain available at around $200–$300. If you want to own every word printed about the Vagabonds and their trips, it should be part of your collection.

since 1805, when millwright Oliver Evans attempted: Clay McShane, *Down the Asphalt Path: The Automobile and the American City,* pp. 81–82.

finding gasoline was a challenge: Flink, pp. 234–42; Daniel Yergin, *The Prize,* pp. 111, 209; Duncan and Burns, p. 77; Brinkley, pp. 57–58; Edmund Morris, *Theodore Rex,* p. 27; Wells, pp. 173–86.

The Summit Hotel was a wonder: Amanda Voithofer interview; the Voithofer family now owns the Summit Hotel. *Pittsburgh Post-Gazette,* 8/21/1918.

Firestone envisioned better, longer-lasting tires: Firestone's *Men and Rubber* includes lengthy, technical accounts of his efforts to design and market a better tire. There are too many pages and excerpts to cite list. The book is readily available.

Edison pointedly got out of his car: Ford wasn't about to snatch candy away from Edison.

There was a hiccup in Tazewell: Interview with Terry W. Mullins, regional historian and former Tazewell city official.

The first well-tended American roads were toll "turnpikes": Frederic J. Wood, *The Turnpikes of New England,* pp. 1–2, 191, 256–59.

These were popularly known as "shunpikes": Interview with Matthew Powers, director of the Woodstock, Vermont, Historical Society.

The questions from the press in Bristol were pointed: Washington Post, Concord (North Carolina) *Daily Tribune, Richmond Times-Dispatch, Charlotte Observer,* all 8/28/1918. Firestone's trip diary doesn't mention Ford and the Senate primary at all. Burroughs refers to it only once in his description of Ford and Edison musing about politics over a campfire.

Ford took further steps to separate himself: Lewis, p. 98.

Ford went to a factory where Camel cigarettes were packaged: Winston-Salem Journal, 8/30/1918. I have no idea why Ford, who hated smoking so much, deigned to visit a plant where cigarettes were made. Maybe he was pragmatic enough to realize that smokers bought cars, too.

Edison spent his early afternoon: Winston-

478

Salem Twin City Daily Sentinel, 8/30/1918.

First came the race for the Senate: Lewis, pp. 98–99.

he was determined to be the sole controlling voice: Ibid., pp. 102–3.

Ford never repaid it: Ibid., p. 96. Luckily for Ford, the government chose never to request the promised refund, and the press and public simply assumed that he'd done as he'd promised.

Chapter Five: 1919
Events in America during 1919 deserve an entire book, and fortunately there's a fine one on the subject. I highly recommend Ann Hagedorn's *Savage Peace: Hope and Fear in America, 1919.*

Even the 1918 flu pandemic: John M. Barry, *The Great Influenza,* pp. 5–6, 170, 208.

Beginning in Seattle in early February: Hagedorn, p. 86.

Race-related riots erupted: Ibid., pp. 314–22.

American women determined to gain: Ibid., p. 126.

It was not in the nature of Thomas Edison and Henry Ford's friendship: Benson Ford Research Center, Acc. 1630, Box 5.

a Rochester, New York, attorney named

George B. Selden: Hiram Percy Maxim, *Horseless Carriage Days,* p. 3; Watts, pp. 161–63, 166–69, 172; Miller, pp. 61–65, 249–50, 284–86; Brinkley, pp. 142–44; Benson Ford Research Center, Acc. 423, Box 1.

It began with the trial's venue: Tebbel, pp. 92–100; Reynold M. Wik, "Henry Ford and the Agricultural Depression of 1920–1921, *Agricultural History,* January 1955; Watts, pp. 265–71; Lewis, pp. 104–8; Robert Kreipke, *Faces of Henry Ford,* p. 75; Bryan, pp. 25–26; Brinkley, pp. 244–48; *Fort Wayne News-Sentinel,* 7/22/1919; Lexington *Kentucky Herald,* 7/23/1919; *San Jose Mercury Herald,* 7/25/1919; Benson Ford Research Center, Acc. 1117, Box 1.

Edison received a telegram from Ernest Liebold: Thomas Edison National Historical Park archive.

Out of the inky blackness: Oregon Daily Journal, 8/9/1919.

Firestone recalled it in his memoir: Firestone with Crowther, pp. 224–27; Albion, p. 114; Smoot, pp. 167–71.

Press speculation pegged the overall value: New York Times, 6/24/23.

not much of that accrued to the inventor himself: Stross, pp. 181–83, 187, 189–93,

276–77; Firestone with Crowther, p. 3; DeGraaf, p. 86, 100–108, 118–19, 122–45, 148–61; Peter Carlson, "Fat Cats and Vagabonds," *American History Magazine,* August 2013.

Ford ordered the camp cooks: Brauer, p. 119.

Firestone responded by bedecking: Carlson, "Fat Cats and Vagabonds."

Burroughs, as usual, was the grumpiest: Barrus, ed., pp. 326–27; Renehan, pp. 274–75.

But one night's 1919 campfire conversation: Carlson, "Fat Cats and Vagabonds"; Renehan, pp. 275–76.

historians have tried to determine its root cause: Baldwin, *Henry Ford and the Jews,* pp. 27–35, 327, 341–44, 376–90; Israel, pp. 444–45; Robert Casey interview.

they were racist as well as antisemitic: Conot, p. 310.

Edison attempted to qualify his mistrust of Jews: Baldwin, *Edison: Inventing the Century,* p. 334.

The celebrated travelers spoke in favor of the proposed League of Nations: Houston Chronicle, 8/10/1919.

Chapter Six: 1920
Warren James Belasco's *Americans on the Road* is one of the most interesting books

I've come across in years. Don't let the frequent insertion of lists and individual facts and figures put you off. Among those I've read — and in researching this book, I read dozens — no one does a better job than Belasco capturing America's headlong rush into a car-centric culture.

Before hostilities commenced in Europe: Wik, "Henry Ford and the Agricultural Depression of 1920–1921"; Jeff Guinn, *Go Down Together,* p. 18.

Burroughs was least affected: Barrus, ed., pp. 330–33.

"We could not keep up with demand:" Firestone with Crowther, pp. 246–52.

Thomas Edison endeavored to remove himself: Paul Israel and Leonard DeGraaf interviews; Israel, pp. 454–55; Stross, p. 273.

Ford was distracted by sagging sales: Brinkley, pp. 257–62; Watts, pp. 273–75, p. 377; Benson Ford Research Center, Acc. 1117, Box 1; Lewis, pp. 136–38; Baldwin, *Henry Ford and the Jews,* pp. 95–107; Sheldon M. Novick, *Honorable Justice: The Life of Oliver Wendell Holmes,* pp. 132–33.

In this description of the *Independent*'s antisemitic series, I chose not to include specific examples. The content was frankly offensive. For those who want to see for themselves, the articles are collected in *The International Jew: The World's Foremost Problem,* which is available at several sites online.

Meadowcroft sent an apologetic note: Thomas Edison National Historical Park archive.

The economic slump of 1920 could not have come at a worse time: Lewis, pp. 108–12; Brinkley, pp. 264–72.

As the number of car trips increased: Belasco, pp. 72–79; Paul S. Sutter, *Driven Wild: How the Fight Against Automobiles Sparked the Modern Wilderness Movement,* p. 30; Brian Butko interview.

Ford had Liebold write and inquire: Benson Ford Research Center, Acc. 1630, Box 5.

Burroughs recognized this himself: Renehan, p. 309.

the gist was generally the same: After the Vagabonds' 1924 visit with the president, the last line of the joke was reworked to, "And next you're going to tell me that the little guy in the back seat is Calvin Coolidge."

she disliked Ford: Brent Newman interview.

she took advantage of opportunities to torment Ford: Thomas Edison National Historical Park archive; Benson Ford Research Center, Acc. 1630, Box 5.

On October 29, Meadowcroft wrote: Benson Ford Research Center, Acc. 1630, Box 5.

On Tuesday, reporters and photographers received word: San Antonio Express, 11/17/1920; *Kingston* (New York) *Daily Forum,* 11/15/1920; *Oregon Daily Journal,* 11/16/1920; *Washington Times,* 11/18/1920; Firestone with Crowther, p. 227; Brauer, pp. 132–33.

Burroughs was a genial host: Firestone with Crowther, pp. 227–28; Brauer, p. 140.

Ford saw Burroughs again: Pittsburg (Kansas) *Sun,* 12/5/1920, article reprinted from the *Toledo Times.*

Barrus tried taking Burroughs home: Renehan, pp. 312–13.

The Republican ticket advocated tax cuts: Hagedorn, pp. 427–28.

The country was now led by a president: Novick, pp. 334–35.

Chapter Seven: 1921

Warren G. Harding was a terrible president, but a master of publicity. On the first part of this trip, he completely outmaneuvered the Vagabonds. But afterward they got even.

I'm especially grateful to Leonard De-Graaf at Thomas Edison National Historical Park for his help in locating documents used as references for the first portion of this chapter.

Thomas Edison received an unwelcome letter: Thomas Edison National Historical Park archives.

Edison's response was disingenuous: Ibid.

he sent a warm note of thanks to Ford: Benson Ford Research Center, Acc. 1630, Box 5.

Edison fired off a congratulatory telegram: Thomas Edison National Historical Park archives.

Firestone wrote "Mr. Ford": Ibid.

Edison developed a 146-question test: After the *New York Times* published the questions, some of them were replaced by new ones. But many of these new questions were still bizarre. Edison never explained why he chose the original questions, or the replacements, either.

all Edison would say was, "Maybe": New York Telegram, 4/10/1921.

His proposal in 1921: Thomas Edison National Historical Park archives.

Harvey Firestone described a surefire one: Ibid.

a four-page typed report: Ibid.

Edison found them all unacceptable: Ibid.

Meadowcroft made a written request: Ibid.

he used a chummy, informal greeting: Ibid.
the president's typed, tone-deaf reply: Ibid.
This was reflected in his formally worded letter: Ibid.
Ford made a formal purchase offer: Wik, "Henry Ford and the Agricultural Depression of 1920–1921"; Preston J. Hubbard, pp. 195–212; *Tennessee Historical Quarterly 18,* no. 3 (September 1959).
Firestone found himself far more preoccupied: Firestone with Crowther, p. 229.
Harding would permanently replace Burroughs among them: Santa Ana (California) *Register,* 7/22/1921.
Clara Ford was appalled: Brauer, p. 153.
President Harding and his entourage: My description of Harding's sojourn with the Vagabonds is drawn from many newspapers. The diverse locations of the newspapers confirm the breadth of coverage. I list here only those newspapers that I used for reference among the several hundred available. Publications include: *Gettysburg Times,* 7/23/1921; *Bridgeport* (Connecticut) *Post,* 7/24/1921; *Kansas City Post,* 7/24/1921; *New York Times,* 7/24, 25, 29, and 31/1921; *New York Telegraph,* 7/24 and 7/25/1921; *Baltimore Sun* 7/24 and 7/25/1921; *Washington Post,* 7/24/1921; *Washington Herald,* 7/24/1921; *Charlotte*

Sunday Observer, 7/24/1921; *Charlotte News*, 7/24/1921; *St. Louis Star and Times*, 7/24/1921; *Memphis Journal-Appeal*, 7/24/1921; *Pittsburgh Press*, 7/24/1921; *Palm Beach* (Florida) *Post*, 7/24/1921; *Oregon Daily Journal*, 7/24/1921; *Chicago Tribune*, 7/24/1921; *Fitchburg* (Massachusetts) *Sentinel*, 7/24–25/1921; *Kansas City Times*, 7/25/1921; *Newark Star-Eagle*, 7/25/1921; *Des Moines Register*, 7/25/1921; *Harrisburg* (Pennsylvania) *Evening News*, 7/25/1921; *Minneapolis Tribune*, 7/25/1921; *Houston Post*, 7/25/1921; *Boston Telegram*, 7/25/1921; *Akron Beacon Journal*, 7/25/1921; *Utica* (New York) *Press*, 7/25/1921; *Albuquerque Journal* 7/25/1921; *Bridgeport* (Connecticut) *Telegram*, 7/25/1921; (Wilmington, Delaware) *Morning News*, 7/26/1921; *Wheeling News*, 7/29/1921; *Wilkes-Barre Journal* 7/29/1921; Mattoon, Illinois, *Journal-Gazette*, 7/30/1921; *Philadelphia Inquirer*, 7/28/1921; *Oakland* (California) *Tribune*, 7/28/1921; *Atlanta Constitution* 7/31/1921; *Brooklyn Citizen* 8/7/1921.

Ford loathed alcohol: Halberstam, p. 69.

Firestone wrote: Firestone with Crowther, pp. 230–31. In his memoir, Firestone specifically noted that "Mr. Ford had already made his offer for Muscle Shoals [to Congress], but that we did not talk about — we kept away from everything personal."

Clara Ford, Mina Edison, and Idabelle Firestone received a typed, polite message: Thomas Edison National Historical Park archives.

They'd been invited to camp: My description of the Swallow Falls camp and the Vagabonds' experiences there is drawn from "Edison, Ford and Firestone Travel Through Allegany County in the Summer of 1921," an excellent eight-part series by Francis Champ Zumbrun posted on the Maryland Department of Natural Resources website (dnr.maryland.gov). I also interviewed Zumbrun in person.

Mina Edison wrote a letter to her son: Thomas Edison National Historical Park archives.

Ford discussed his hopes for Muscle Shoals: St. Paul News, 7/29/1921; Boston Herald, 7/29/1921.

Edison also spoke with the press in Oakland: Bismarck Tribune, 8/4/1921; Portland (Maine) Herald, 8/8/1921.

a third member of the party asked to speak with them: Paterson (New Jersey) *Press-Guardian,* 8/1/1921; *Freeport* (Illinois) *Journal-Standard,* 8/1/1921; *Portsmouth*

(Ohio) *Daily Times,* 8/4/1921.
Two Scouts, Macon and Joseph Fry, decided to see: Uniontown, Pennsylvania, *Morning Herald,* 8/6/1921.
Bickel described the scene: Baltimore Sun, 8/2/1921; *Franklin* (Pennsylvania) *News-Herald,* 8/2/1921.
The Chicago Tribune *wrote a new editorial about its old antagonist: Chicago Tribune,* 8/4/1921.

Chapter Eight: Interlude: November 1921–June 1923

I found intriguing information about Ford's bid for Muscle Shoals, and his interest in the presidency, in *Ford: The Men and the Machine* by Robert Lacey. I recommend it to everyone interested in Henry Ford.

I'm aware that this chapter is almost entirely Ford-centric, with Edison only briefly mentioned and Firestone just once. But in this interlude between the 1921 and 1923 trips, Ford was the most active.

Henry Ford and Thomas Edison took another trip together: New York Times, 11/23/1921, 12/3/1921.
Ford ordered his publicity department to conduct: Lacey, pp. 211–13.
Ford began privately mentioning his inten-

tions: Ibid., p. 213.

Ford's employment philosophy had been: Robert Casey interview; Watts, pp. 199–214; Baldwin, *Henry Ford and the Jews,* pp. 36–43; Bryan, pp. 27–81; Brinkley, pp. 169–75; Benson Ford Research Center, Acc. 423, Box 1.

Ford was more hands-on: Baldwin, *Henry Ford and the Jews,* pp. 164–65.

Ford was also preoccupied: Lacey, pp. 210–11.

Edison was in regular touch: Thomas Edison National Historical Park archives.

Edison spent considerable time: Benson Ford Research Center, Acc. 1630, Box 5; Israel, pp. 457–59; DeGraaf, pp. 207–9; interviews with Leonard DeGraaf and Paul Israel.

Only three years earlier: Pete Davies, *American Road: The Story of an Epic Transcontinental Journey at the Dawn of the Motor Age,* p. 2.

Products like Coleman stoves: Sutter, *Driven Wild,* pp. 32–33.

Fortune *magazine would conclude:* Ibid., p. 37.

Beginning in 1922, the free camps: Belasco, pp. 105–13.

another form of traffic became common: Guinn, pp. 18–19.

just over 44 percent of American residences had electricity: Historical Statistics of the United States, p. 510.

registered Klan membership in Indiana: Leonard J. Moore, *Citizen Klansman: The Ku Klux Klan in Indiana, 1921–1928,* p. 27; James H. Madison, *A Lynching in the Heartland: Race and Memory in America,* pp. 38–39.

in early 1923 there were the first exposures: John Dean, *Warren G. Harding,* pp. 138–44.

Even without him announcing his candidacy: Albion, p. 108; Russell, p. 564; Baldwin, *Henry Ford and the Jews,* p. 165.

Chapter Nine: 1923

Much of this chapter is based on newspaper articles. If the dates of some stories follow by several days (or even more) the events being described, bear in mind that wire service reports were often received and printed by far-flung publications as late as a week after being initially written and filed by correspondents. I also drove the Vagabonds' route in Michigan's Upper Peninsula, and can vouch that the weather there in August is usually blisteringly hot. From President Harding's death to the unseasonably rainy, chilly weather, everything seemed

491

to go against them on this, their next-to-last trip.

In a July 19 letter, he urged Edison: Thomas Edison National Historical Park archives.

Some articles speculated about destination and duration: Harrisburg, Pennsylvania, *Evening News,* 7/31/1923; Lancaster, Ohio, *Eagle-Gazette,* 7/31/1923; *Washington Post,* 8/1/1923; *St. Louis Star and Times,* 8/1/1923.

Some wire service reports speculated: Akron, Ohio, *Beacon Journal,* 8/4/1923.

Edison was in a fine mood: Reading (Pennsylvania) *Times,* 8/3/1923.

The inventor was still cheery: Harrisburg, Pennsylvania, *Evening News,* 8/3/1923; *Harrisburg* (Pennsylvania) *Telegraph,* 8/3/1923.

"As the first dismay at the news": Francis Russell, *The Shadow of Blooming Grove: Warren G. Harding in His Times,* p. 594.

Florence Kling Harding was receiving friends: Pittsburgh Press, 8/8/1923; *Modesto* (California) *Evening News,* 8/8/1923; *Logansport* (Indiana) *Pharos-Tribune,* 8/10/1923; *Detroit Free Press,* 8/10/1923; *Lincoln Evening Journal,* 8/10/1923; *Belvidere* (Illinois) *Daily Republican,* 8/10/1923; *Waxahachie* (Texas) *Daily Light,*

8/10/1923; *St. Louis Post-Dispatch,* 8/11/ 1923; *Philadelphia Inquirer,* 8/11/1923; *Louisville Courier-Journal,* 8/11/1923.

Ford spoke more seriously to a reporter: New York Times, 8/11/1923; *Franklin* (Pennsylvania) *News-Herald,* 8/11/1923; *New Castle* (Pennsylvania) *News,* 8/11/1923; *Wall Street Journal,* 8/13/1923.

Edison was more philosophical: Battle Creek Enquirer, 8/11/1923; *New York Times,* 8/11/1923; *Pittsburgh Post-Gazette,* 8/11/ 1923.

The next day, birth rather than death: Cincinnati Enquirer, 8/12/1923; *New York Times,* 8/12/1923; Port Huron, Michigan, *Times Herald,* 8/13/1923.

it was far from Ford's description: Hamilton, Ohio, *Journal News,* 8/10/1923.

Ford didn't say he wouldn't run: Rochester, New York, *Democrat and Chronicle,* 8/19/ 1923; Alexandria, Louisiana, *Weekly Town Talk,* 8/25/1923.

Ford briefly spoke to the media again: Decatur (Illinois) *Herald,* 8/21/1923.

Coolidge and his advisors were just as aware of Ford: St. Louis Post-Dispatch, 8/21/ 1923; Helena, Montana, *Independent Record,* 8/22/1923; *Waco* (Texas) *News Tribune,* 8/27/1923.

His nickname for Clara was "the Believer": Benson Ford Research Center, Acc. 1117, Box 1.

Clara waved the girls away: Oshkosh (Wisconsin) *Daily Northwestern,* 8/21/1923; *Washington Post,* 8/22/1923; *New York Times,* 8/22/1923; *Indianapolis Star,* 8/22/1923; *Battle Creek Enquirer,* 8/22/1923.

there was a follow-up story: New York Times, 8/25/1923.

Mina Edison composed another letter: Thomas Edison National Historical Park archives.

Edison's brief observations about his best friend's interest: Akron Beacon Journal, 8/9/1923; *Detroit Free Press,* 8/10/1923.

Two months after the August 1923 trip: New York Times, 10/18/1923.

The headlines expressed more urgency: Battle Creek Enquirer, 8/22/1923; *Santa Ana* (California) *Register,* 8/22/1923.

On Thursday, the New York Times *assured readers: New York Times,* 8/23/1923.

Other publications were less optimistic: Ironwood (Michigan) *Daily Globe,* 8/23/1923; *Arizona Republic,* 8/23/1923; *Fort Wayne* (Indiana) *Journal-Gazette,* 8/23/1923.

On Friday, August 24, the party toured Ford's lumber mill: Lebanon (Pennsylvania) *Semi-*

Weekly News, 8/23/1923; Brauer, pp. 205–6.

At the Sault Ste. Marie locks: Mattoon, Illinois, *Journal-Gazette,* 8/27/1923; *Detroit Free Press,* 8/27/1923; *Los Angeles Times,* 8/27/1923.

Firestone sent a chatty letter to Edison: Thomas Edison National Historical Park.

It happened quickly: DeGraaf, pp. 118–19.

In his return letter, he told Firestone so: Thomas Edison National Historical Park.

Radio flourished at such a rapid rate: Robert Dallek, *Franklin D. Roosevelt: A Political Life,* pp. 102–3.

He would not seek the presidency: Baldwin, *Henry Ford and the Jews,* p. 185; Amity Shlaes, *Coolidge,* p. 274. Shlaes writes that Ford's decision disappointed the Democrats, who hoped to match him against Coolidge. I believe that if Ford had run for president in 1924, he would have done so as a Republican.

Chapter Ten: 1924

Again, newspapers account for the majority of the information in this chapter, but those stories are supplemented by interviews with William Jenney, director of the President Calvin Coolidge Historic Site at Plymouth Notch, Vermont; Matthew Powers, director of the Woodstock Historical Society in Woodstock, Vermont; and Richard Candee, director of the Portsmouth Historical Society in Portsmouth, New Hampshire. One additional observation — after visiting the town, I *really* want to live in Woodstock.

Henry Ford was mostly disdainful of books: Halberstam, p. 72.

Ford fixated on even the smallest details: I learned of Ford's pocket notes during my interview with Ford Motor Company historian Robert Kreipke. I subsequently found them in an apparently unnumbered file folder at the Benson Ford Research Center. If you ask to see them, the very efficient staff there will locate them for you.

Clara Ford said she "would not be up to it": Edison Research Park archives.

He scribbled his approval in the margin: Ibid.

Edison applied for and received 1,093 patents: edison.rutgers.edu/patents.htm.

in February 1924, a much discussed study: New York Times, 2/17/1924.

Every Ford dealer in the nation received: Houston Chronicle, 7/18/1924.

Ford's stubbornness gave competitors: Brinkley, pp. 339–43; Robert Casey interview; Watts, p. 246; Halberstam, p. 97.

the Model T was no longer the near-exclusive vehicle of choice: Belasco, pp. 113–19.

It would be a Wednesday, August 13, gala: Brauer, pp. 215–17; Firestone with Crowther, pp. 234–35.

The gathering was hugely successful: New York Times, 8/14/1924; *Detroit Free Press,* 8/14/1924.

after-dinner entertainment was provided: Firestone with Crowther, pp. 235–36.

Firestone's son Russell drove to Plymouth: William Jenney interview; *New York World,* 8/19/1924.

the worrisome spread of Ku Klux Klan influence: Ibid.

The inventor sent a succinct, heartfelt telegram: Edison Research Park archives.

On Monday, Edison, Ford, and Harvey and Russell Firestone drove: Brauer; pp. 218–19; Firestone, p. 236.

they drove on to Plymouth Notch: Detroit Free Press, 8/19, and 8/20/1924; Harrisburg, Pennsylvania, *Evening News,* 8/19/1924; *Brooklyn Daily Eagle,* 8/19 and 8/20/1924; Monroe, Louisiana, *News-Star,* 8/19/1924; Hamilton, Ohio, *Journal News,* 8/19/1924; *Los Angeles Times,* 8/19 and 8/20/1924; Wisconsin Rapids, *Wisconsin Daily Tribune,* 8/19 and 8/20/1924; Bryan, Texas, *Eagle,* 8/19/1924; *Arizona Daily*

Star, 8/19/1924; *Philadelphia Inquirer,* 8/19/1924; *Washington Post,* 8/19 and 8/20/1924; Corsicana, Texas, *Daily Sun,* 8/19/1924; Burlington, Vermont, *Free Press,* 8/19 and 8/20/1924; Dunkirk, New York, *Evening Observer,* 8/19/1924; Elwood, Indiana, *Call-Leader,* 8/19 and 8/20/1924; *Anniston* (Alabama) *Star,* 8/19/1924; *Cincinnati Enquirer,* 8/19 and 8/20/1924; *Chicago Daily Tribune,* 8/19 and 8/20/1924; *New York Times,* 8/19, 20, and 24/1924; Santa Ana, California, *Register,* 8/19/1924; Medford, Oregon, *Mail Tribune,* 8/19/1924; *Baltimore Sun,* 8/19/1924; *St. Louis Post-Dispatch,* 8/19–20, 22/1924; *Pittsburgh Daily Post,* 8/20/1924; *Boston Morning Globe,* 8/20/1924; *Wall Street Journal,* 8/20/1924; *Indianapolis News,* 8/23/1924; William Jenney interview; Novick, p. 358; Conot, p. 341; Shlaes, p. 307; Firestone with Crowther, pp. 236–37; Brauer, pp. 219–25. Brauer gives George Chalmers's age as twelve, but according to newspapers the boy was nine. The oaken sap bucket given to Ford by Coolidge was displayed for a time at the Wayside Inn. It is now part of the collection at the Henry Ford Museum in Dearborn.

they stopped at a hotel in Woodstock, Vermont: Matthew Powers interview.

They weren't expected in Portsmouth until the next morning: This is my personal opinion.

Ford spoke instead: Portsmouth Herald, 8/20/1924.

Around eleven on Wednesday morning: Brauer, p. 225.

the glory of its benefits: Hubbard, "Henry Ford and the Agricultural Depression of 1920–1921," pp. 195–212.

Chapter Eleven: Jep Bisbee Is Famous

Firestone called on Edison in New Jersey: Bryan, pp. 39–40.

In it he declared that the Vagabonds had mutually decided: Firestone with Crowther, p. 188.

There is some discrepancy regarding the amounts: Israel, pp. 451–52; Stross, pp. 378–79.

called Firestone "a goddamned lightweight": Stross.

for the first time since its 1908 introduction: Watts, p. 246; Halberstam, p. 97; H. W. Brands, *Reagan: The Life,* p. 16.

another car for the great multitudes: Watts, pp. 366–75; Brinkley, pp. 346–62; Baldwin, *Henry Ford and the Jews,* pp. 224–

26; Bryson, p. 251.

Ford also parted ways with the Dearborn Independent: Baldwin, *Henry Ford and the Jews,* pp. 214–22; Watts, pp. 390–97; Bryson, p. 242.

he wrote the inventor a chatty letter: Edison Research Park archives.

Ford selected a site in Dearborn: Brinkley, pp. 365–67; Watts, pp. 404–15.

Edison was guest of honor: Benson Ford Research Center, Acc. 1630, Box 6; De-Graaf, pp. 226–27; Stross, pp. 281–82.

he gave public credit for the first time: Conot, pp. 444–45.

There was to be no official Edison memoir: Ibid., p. 462.

Edison's family held a lingering grudge: Smoot, pp. 232–33; Stross, p. 257.

The media described the bloody melee: Watts, p. 444–46, 455; Brinkley, pp. 383, 390–92.

the mayor of Fort Myers withdrew a proposal: Washington Post, 10/10/2014.

Ford's physicians detected signs of dementia in him: Watts, p. 502.

One observer recalled Ford: Ibid., p. 528.

It had been nearly two months: Battle Creek Enquirer, 8/18 and 23/1923; Paul Gifford, "Jasper E. 'Jep' Bisbee — Old-Time Michigan Dance Fiddler," *The Old-Time Herald,*

Winter 2004–2005; *New York Times,* 10/13/1923, 8/11/1935; *Big Rapids* (Michigan) *Pioneer,* 11/22/1923.

Thanks to the internet, it is possible to listen to some of the 1923 recordings made by Jep Bisbee in Edison's New Jersey studio. As they once did for Henry Ford, these tunes will set your toes a'tappin'.

BIBLIOGRAPHY

Books

Albion, Michele Wehrwein. *The Florida Life of Thomas Edison.* University Press of Florida, 2008.

Amero, Richard W. *Balboa Park and the 1915 Exposition.* History Press, 2013.

Baldwin, Neil. *Edison: Inventing the Century.* Hyperion, 1995.

———. *Henry Ford and the Jews: The Mass Production of Hate.* PublicAffairs, 2008.

Barrus, Clara. *The Heart of Burroughs's Journals.* Kennikat Press, 1928.

Barry, John M. *The Great Influenza.* Penguin, 2009.

Belasco, Warren James. *Americans on the Road: From Autocamp to Motel.* MIT Press, 1979.

Berg, Scott. *Lindbergh.* Putnam, 1998.

Bliss, Carey S. *Autos Across America: A Bibliography of Transcontinental Automobile*

Travel, 1903–1940. Jenkins & Reese, 1982.

Blondheim, Menahem. *News Over the Wires*. Harvard University Press, 1994.

Brands, H.W. *Reagan: The Life*. Doubleday, 2015.

Brauer, Norman. *There to Breathe the Beauty: The Camping Trips of Henry Ford, Thomas Edison, John Burroughs*. Norman Brauer Publications, 1995.

Brinkley, Douglas. *Wheels for the World*. Viking, 2003.

Bryan, Ford R. *Friends, Families & Forays: Scenes from the Life and Times of Henry Ford*. Wayne State University Press, 2002.

Bryson, Bill. *One Summer: America, 1927*. Doubleday, 2013.

Burroughs, John. *Camping and Tramping with Roosevelt*. Public domain reprint.

————. *Under the Maples*. Public domain reprint.

Chernow, Ron. *Titan: The Life of John D. Rockefeller Sr.* Random House, 1998.

Conot, Robert. *Thomas A. Edison: A Streak of Luck*. Da Capo, 1979.

Coolidge, Calvin. *The Autobiography of Calvin Coolidge*. Cosmopolitan Book Corporation, 1929; reprint by National Notary Association, 1955.

Cooper, John Milton Jr. *Woodrow Wilson: A*

Biography. Alfred A. Knopf, 2009.

Cosden, Mike, Brent Newman, and Chris Pendleton. *Edison and Ford in Florida.* Arcadia Publishing, 2015.

Dallek, Robert. *Franklin D. Roosevelt: A Political Life.* Viking, 2017.

Dauphinais, Dean, and Peter M. Gareffa. *Car Crazy.* Visible Ink Press, 1996.

Davies, Pete. *American Road: The Story of an Epic Transcontinental Journey at the Dawn of the Motor Age.* Holt, 2002.

Davis, J. Allen. *The Friend to All Motorists: The Story of the Automobile Club of Southern California Through 65 Years, 1900–1965.* Auto Club/Southern California Press, 1967.

Dean, John. *Warren G. Harding.* Times Books, 2004.

DeGraaf, Leonard. *Edison and the Rise of Innovation.* Sterling Signature/Sterling Publishing, 2013.

DeLoach, R. J. H. *Rambles with John Burroughs.* Project Gutenberg eBook Series, 2011.

Dreyer, Peter. *A Gardener Touched with Genius: The Life of Luther Burbank.* Luther Burbank Home & Gardens, 1993.

Duncan, Dayton, and Ken Burns. *Horatio's Drive.* Alfred A. Knopf, 2003.

Emery, Edwin. *The Press in America*. Prentice-Hall, 1972.

Encyclopedia of Recreation and Leisure in America. Scribner, 2004.

Englund, Will. *March 1917: On the Brink of War and Revolution*. W. W. Norton, 2017.

Feldstein, Albert L. *Allegany County*. Arcadia Publishing, 2006.

———. *Garrett County*. Arcadia Publishing, 2006.

Firestone, Harvey S., with Samuel Crowther. *Men and Rubber: The Story of Business*. Doubleday, Page, 1926.

Flink, James J. *America Adopts the Automobile, 1895–1910*. MIT Press, 1970.

Giddens, Paul. *The Birth of the Oil Industry*. Ayer Co., 1972; reprint of original 1938 edition.

Gilbert, Martin. *A History of the Twentieth Century, Vol. I, 1900–1933*. William Morrow, 1997.

Glasscock, C. B. *The Gasoline Age*. Bobbs-Merrill, 1937.

Goldstone, Lawrence. *Drive!: Henry Ford, George Selden, and the Race to Invent the Auto Age*. Ballantine, 2016.

Grismer, Karl H. *The Story of Fort Myers*. The Island Press Publishers/A Southwest Florida Historical Society Book, 1982.

Guinn, Jeff. *Go Down Together: The True, Untold Story of Bonnie and Clyde.* Simon & Schuster, 2009.

Hagedorn, Ann. *Savage Peace: Hope and Fear in America, 1919.* Simon & Schuster, 2007.

Halberstam, David. *The Reckoning.* William Morrow, 1986.

Harris, Charles H., III, and Louis R. Sadler. *The Great Call-up: The Guard, the Border, and the Mexican Revolution.* University of Oklahoma Press, 2015.

Harvey, Catherine, and Neville A. Stanton. *Usability Evaluation for In-Vehicle Systems.* CRC Press, 2016.

Hyde, Charles K. *The Dodge Brothers: The Men, the Motor Cars, and the Legacy.* Wayne State University Press, 2005.

Ingrassia, Paul. *Engines of Change.* Simon & Schuster, 2012.

Israel, Paul. *Edison: A Life of Invention.* John Wiley & Sons, 1998.

Keegan, John. *The First World War.* Alfred A. Knopf, 1999.

Kreipke, Robert. *Faces of Henry Ford.* M.T. Publishing Company, 2013.

———. *Ford Motor Company: The First 100 Years.* Turner Publishing Company, 2003.

———. *The Model T.* M.T. Publishing Company, 2007.

Lacey, Robert. *Ford: The Men and the Machine.* Little, Brown, 1986.

Lewis, David L. *The Public Image of Henry Ford: An American Folk Hero and His Company.* Wayne State University Press, 1976.

Maconi, Carole J., with Barbara Deveneau. *Longfellow's Wayside Inn.* Yankee Colour Corporation/A Historama Booklet, 1975.

Madison, James H. *A Lynching in the Heartland: Race and Memory in America.* Palgrave Macmillan, 2001.

Maxim, Hiram Percy. *Horseless Carriage Days.* Harper & Brothers, 1937.

McCullough, David. *The Wright Brothers.* Simon & Schuster, 2015.

McGuinness, Marci Lynn. *Yesteryear at the Uniontown Speedway.* Shore Publications, 1996.

McShane, Clay. *Down the Asphalt Path: The Automobile and the American City.* Columbia University Press, 1995.

Miller, G. Wayne. *Car Crazy: The Battle for Supremacy Between Ford and Olds and the Dawn of the Automobile Age.* PublicAffairs, 2015.

Miller, Jeanine Head, with Judith E. Endelman, Donna R. Braden, and Nancy Villa Bryk. *Telling America's Story: A History of*

The Henry Ford. Donning Company Publishers, 2010.

Millner, Lyn. *The Allure of Immortality: An American Cult, a Florida Swamp, and a Renegade Prophet.* University Press of Florida, 2015.

Moore, Leonard J. *Citizen Klansman: The Ku Klux Klan in Indiana, 1921–1928.* University of North Carolina Press, 1997.

Morris, Edmund. *Colonel Roosevelt.* Random House, 2010.

———. *Theodore Rex.* Random House, 2001.

Mullins, Terry W., and Louise Leslie. *Ramey: A Southwest Virginia Success Story.* Tazewell County Historical Society, 2018.

Newton, James. *Uncommon Friends: Life with Thomas Edison, Henry Ford, Harvey Firestone, Alexis Carrel & Charles Lindbergh.* Harcourt, 1987.

Novick, Sheldon M. *Honorable Justice: The Life of Oliver Wendell Holmes.* Little, Brown, 1989.

O'Keefe, Kevin J. *A Thousand Deadlines: The New York City Press and American Neutrality, 1914–1917.* Martinus Nijhoff, 1972.

Peterson, Joyce Shaw. *American Automobile Workers, 1900–1933.* SUNY Press, 1987.

Raitz, Karl, ed. *The National Road.* Johns Hopkins University Press, 1996.

Renehan, Edward J., Jr. *John Burroughs: An American Naturalist.* Chelsea Green Publishing Company, 1992; paperback edition, Black Dome Press, 1998.

Roosevelt, Theodore. *Outdoor Pastimes of An American Hunter.* Charles Scribner's Sons, 1905.

Russell, Francis. *The Shadow of Blooming Grove: Warren G. Harding in His Times.* McGraw-Hill, 1968.

Shlaes, Amity. *Coolidge.* HarperCollins, 2013.

Skrabec, Quentin R. Jr. *Rubber: An American Industrial History.* McFarland, 2014.

Smoot, Tom. *The Edisons of Fort Myers: Discoveries of the Heart.* Pineapple Press, 2004.

Stross, Randall. *The Wizard of Menlo Park: How Thomas Alva Edison Invented the Modern World.* Crown, 2007.

Sutter, Paul S. *Driven Wild: How the Fight Against Automobiles Sparked the Modern Wilderness Movement.* University of Washington Press, 2002.

Tebbel, John. *An American Dynasty.* Doubleday, 1947.

Touring San Diego County. Automobile Club

Warren, James Perrin. *John Burroughs and the Place of Nature.* University of Georgia Press, 2006.

Watts, Steven. *The People's Tycoon: Henry Ford and the American Century.* Alfred A. Knopf, 2005.

Wells, Christopher W. *Car Country: An Environmental History.* University of Washington Press, 2012.

Wood, Frederic J. *The Turnpikes of New England.* Marshall Jones Company, 1919; paperback reprint by Ronald Dale Karr, Branch Line Press, 1997.

Yergin, Daniel. *The Prize.* Simon & Schuster, 1991.

Articles

"America on the Move." http://amhistory.si.edu./onthemove/themes/story_47_1.html.

Blodgett, Peter. "What It Means to Be American." http://www/whatitmeanstobe aamerican.org/journeys/how-americans -fell-in-love-with-the-open-road/.

Carlson, Peter. "Fat Cats and Vagabonds." *American History Magazine,* August 2013.

Cook, Kevin L. "Ike's Road Trip." *MHQ: The Quarterly Journal of Military History,*

Spring 2001.

DeGraaf, Leonard. "Confronting the Mass Market: Edison and the Entertainment Phonograph." *Business and Economic History,* Fall 1995.

Feldstein, Albert L. "Alleghany County, Maryland: Economic and Historical Development Overview and Highlights." Privately published.

———. "The Historic National Road (Alleghany, Garrett and Washington Counties)." Privately published.

Ford, Henry. Letters to the Editor. *The Automobile,* January 1907.

Gifford, Paul. "Jasper E. 'Jep' " Bisbee — Old-Time Michigan Dance Fiddler." *The Old-Time Herald,* Winter 2004–2005.

Hanson, W. Stanley, Jr. "My Early Days in Fort Myers, as I Remember Them." Lecture, September 12, 2002.

"Highway History — Eisenhower's Army Convoy Notes 11-3-1919." http://www .fhwa.dot.gov/infrastructure/convoy.cfm.

Hill, Frank Ernest, and Allan Nevins. "Henry Ford and His Peace Ship." *American Heritage* 9, no. 2 (February 1958).

Hubbard, Preston J. "The Muscle Shoals Controversy, 1920–1932." *Tennessee*

Historical Quarterly 18, no. 3 (September 1959).

Huyck, Dorothy Boyle. "Over Hill and Dale with Henry Ford and Famous Friends." *Smithsonian,* June 1978.

"Inventing Entertainment: The Early Motion Pictures and Sound Recordings of the Edison Companies." https://www.loc .gov/collections/edison-company-motion -pictures-and-sound-recordings/articles -and-essays/history-of-edison-sound -recordings/history-of-the-cylinder -phonograph/.

Johnson, Offutt, and Champ Zumbrun. "The Sines Family of Garrett County: Maryland's First Family of Forest Conservation." Privately published.

LaChance, David. *Hemmings Motor News,* September 2010.

Lewis, David L. "Defining Moments in Ford Motor Company History." Lecture, May 15, 2003.

———. "Ford's Public Image Tops During Heyday of Model T." *Model "T" Times,* May–June 1973.

———. "The Great Gestation of the Model A." *Public Relations Journal,* December 1971.

———. "A Survey of Ford Jokes." *The Horseless Carriage Gazette,* January–

February 1973.

"Mina Miller Edison: A Valuable Partner to Thomas Edison." http://www.edison muckers.org.

Neuerberg, Norman. "The Changing Face of Mission San Diego." *San Diego Historical Quarterly,* Winter 1986.

Slater, Dashka. "Who Made That Charcoal Briquette?" *New York Times Magazine,* December 26, 2014.

Tennessee Valley Authority. "A New Beginning for the Muscle Shoals Reservation." https://www.tvo.gov/About-TVA/Our -History/A-New-Beginning-for-the -Historic-Muscle-Shoals-Reservation/.

Watson, Jenna. "The Four Vagabonds." *Cobblestone,* December 2005.

Westgard, A. L. "Motor Routes to the California Expositions." *Motor Magazine,* March 1915.

Wianecki, Shannon. "When America's Titans of Industry and Innovation Went Road-Tripping Together." *Smithsonian,* January 2016.

Wik, Reynold M. "Henry Ford and the Agricultural Depression of 1920–1921." *Agricultural History,* January 1955.

Winslow, Caleb. "Henry Ford Camped Here." *Journal of the Alleghenies,* 1977.

Zumbrun, Francis Champ. "Edison, Ford

and Firestone Travel Through Allegany County in the Summer of 1921." *Cumberland Times News,* eight articles, November 2008; Maryland Department of Natural Resources, dnr.maryland.gov.

Government and Industry Reports
"Annual Passengers on All U.S. Scheduled Airlines (Domestic and International 2003–2017)." U.S. Bureau of Transportation.

A Chronicle of the Automotive Industry in America, 1893–1952. Automobile Manufacturers of America, Detroit.
Federal Highway Administration Reports. "The Object Lesson Road," Rickie Longfellow; "The National Road," Rickie Longfellow; "The Lincoln Highway," Richard Weingroff; "A Vast System of Interconnected Highways: Before the Interstate," Richard Weingroff.
"Gasoline Prices." Bureau of Labor Statistics. https://www.bls.gov/date/inflationcal culator.htm.
"Historical Statistics of the United States: Colonial Times to 1970 (Subject: Electricity in U.S. Homes)." U.S. Census Bureau.
"Passenger Traffic Report, January 17, 1935." Federal Coordinator of Transportation.

"Railroad Mileage, Equipment and Passenger Traffic and Revenue, 1890 to 1957." U.S. Census Series Q 44-72.

"Real Wages in Manufacturing, 1890–1914." National Bureau of Economic Research.

"Report on Motor Vehicle Industry." Federal Trade Commission. House Document No. 468, 76th Congress, 1st Session, 1939.

A Short History of U.S. Freight Railroads. American Association of Railroads.

Newspapers

Aberdeen (North Dakota) *Daily News* — October 16 and 19, 1915.

Abilene (Kansas) *Daily Chronicle* — December 11, 1920.

Adams County (Iowa) *Free Press* — November 24, 1920.

Akron Beacon Journal — August 31, 1916; July 22, 23, 25, and 29, 1921; August 4, 9, 10, 11, 18, 1923; August 25, 1924.

Akron Evening Times — August 8, 1919; July 16, 1920.

Albany (Georgia) *Evening Herald* — August 20, 1924.

Anniston (Alabama) *Star* — November 22, 1920; August 19, 1924.

(Phoenix) *Arizona Republic* — August 23, 1923; August 31, 1924.

(Tucson) *Arizona Daily Star* — August 19 and September 2, 1924.

Asbury Park (New Jersey) *Park Press* — July 26, 1921.

Asheville (North Carolina) *Citizen-Times* — August 28, 29, and September 2, 1918; November 21, 1920.

Atlanta Constitution — July 31, 1921.

Austin (Texas) *Statesman and Tribune* — October 15, 1915.

Bakersfield Californian — August 29, 1924.

Baltimore Sun — September 2, 1918; July 23, 24, and 25, August 2, 1921; August 19, 1924.

Battle Creek Enquirer — August 2, 11, 18, 20, 22, and 29, 1923.

Bellingham (Washington) *Herald* — October 15, 1915.

Belvedere (Illinois) *Daily Republican* — August 10 and 24, 1923; August 19, 1924.

Bennington (Vermont) *Banner* — July 15, 1921.

Big Rapids (Michigan) *Pioneer* — November 22, 1923.

Bisbee (Arizona) *Daily Review* — November 23, 1920.

Bismarck Tribune — July 22 and August 4, 1921.

Boston Herald — July 29, 1921.
Boston Morning Globe — August 20, 1924.
Boston Post — August 28 and 29, 1916; July 25, 1921.
Bridgeport (Connecticut) *Telegram* — July 25, 1921.
Brooklyn Daily Eagle — August 7 and 14, 1921; August 11, 19, 20, 27, and 29, 1924.
Burlington (Vermont) *Free Press* — August 30, 1916; August 14, 1919; July 25, 1921; August 18, 1923; August 19 and 20, 1924.
Johnsbury, Vermont, *Caledonian-Record* — August 11, 1919.
Elwood, Indiana, *Call-Leader* — August 19 and 20, 1924.
Charlotte Observer — October 30, 1915; August 27 and 30, 1918; July 24, 1921.
Charlotte News — July 24, 1921.
Chicago Daily Tribune — July 24 and August 4, 1921; August 10, 1923; August 19 and 20, 1924.
Chillicothe (Missouri) *Constitution-Tribune* — August 22, 1923.
Cincinnati Enquirer — August 12, 1923; August 19 and 20, 1924.
Cleburne (Texas) *Morning Review* — October 23, 1915.
Tazewell, Virginia, *Clinch Valley News* — August 30, 1918.
Coffeyville (Kansas) *Daily Journal* — July

23, 1921.

Columbus (Ohio) *Enquirer-Sun* — September 3, 1916.

Concord (North Carolina) *Daily Tribune* — August 27 and 29, 1918.

Corsicana (Texas) *Daily Sun* — July 23, 1921; August 19, 1924.

Coshocton (Ohio) *Tribune* — August 23, 1923.

Bridgeport, New Jersey, *Courier-News* — August 26, 1916; August 10, 1923.

Connellsville, Pennsylvania, *Daily Courier* — August 19 and 20, 1918.

Keokuk, Iowa, *Daily Gate City and Constitution-Democrat* — August 21, 1918.

Canonsburg, Pennsylvania, *Daily News* — July 25, 1921.

Wisconsin Rapids, Wisconsin, *Daily Tribune* — August 10, 1923; August 19 and 20, 1924.

Dallas Morning News — October 23, 1915.

Decatur (Illinois) *Herald* — July 24 and August 10, 1921; August 11 and 21, 1923; August 19, 1924.

Rochester, New York, *Democrat and Chronicle* — August 20, 1924.

Des Moines Register — July 25, 1921; August 25, 1923.

Detroit Free Press — January 5, 1914; August 26 and 28, September 4, 1916;

August 10, 1919; August 8, 10, 16, 22, 25, and 27, 1923; August 14, 19, and 20, 1924.

Duluth News-Tribune — July 23, 1919; August 20, 1918.

Dunkirk (New York) *Evening Observer* — July 22, 1921; August 17, 1923; August 19, 1924.

Bryan, Texas, *Eagle* — August 19, 1924.

El Paso Herald — July 23, 1921.

Philadelphia, Pennsylvania, *Evening Daily Ledger* — August 22, 1918.

Wilmington, *Evening Journal* — July 25 and August 12, 1921; August 20, 1924.

Wilkes-Barre *Evening News* — August 19, 1924.

Uniontown, Pennsylvania, *Evening Standard* — July 25 and August 2, 1921.

Hornell, New York, *Evening Tribune* — August 6, 1923.

New York *Evening World* — July 25, 1921.

Fitchburg (Massachusetts) *Sentinel* — July 25, 1921.

Fort Wayne Journal-Gazette — July 22, 1919; August 23, 1923.

Fort Wayne Sentinel — June 16, 1920.

Freeport (Illinois) *Journal-Standard* — August 1, 1921; August 19, 1924.

Gastonia (North Carolina) *Gazette* — August 4, 1921.

Gettysburg Times — July 22 and 23, 1921.

Green Bay Press-Gazette — August 10 and 11, 1923.

Greensboro (North Carolina) *Daily News* — August 28 and 29, 1918.

Hagerstown Herald Mail — July 2017.

Harrisburg (Pennsylvania) *Evening News* — July 25, 1921; July 31 and August 3, 1923; August 19 and September 4, 1924.

Harrisburg (Pennsylvania) *Telegraph* — July 22, 1921; August 3, 1923; August 22 and 23, 1924.

Houston Chronicle — August 10, 1919; July 18 and August 28, 1924.

Huntington (Indiana) *Press* — August 8, 22, and 23, 1923.

Idaho Daily Statesman — October 20, 1915.

Helena, Montana, *Independent Record* — August 22, 1923.

Greenwood, South Carolina, *Index-Journal* — August 18, 1923.

Indiana (Pennsylvania) *Gazette* — August 23, 1923.

Indianapolis News — August 7, 1923; August 22, 1924.

Indianapolis Star — August 22, 1923.

Iola (Kansas) *Register* — August 19, 1924.

Iowa City Press-Citizen — August 25, 1923.

Ironwood (Michigan) *Daily Globe* — August 23, 1923; August 19, 1924.

Mattoon, Illinois, *Journal Gazette* — July 30, 1921; August 27, 1923.

Hamilton, Ohio, *Journal News* — August 10, 1923; August 19, 1924.

Kansas City Times — August 15 and 26, 1919.

Kingston (New York) *Daily Freeman* — August 28 and September 2, 1916; November 15, 1920.

Lancaster (Ohio) *Eagle-Gazette* — July 31, August 7, 9, and 28, 1923; August 16 and 19, 1924.

Lansing (Michigan) *State Journal* — August 17, 18, and 23, 1923.

Leavenworth (Kansas) *Times* — November 24, 1920.

Lebanon (Pennsylvania) *Daily News* — August 17, 1923; August 19, 1924.

Lebanon (Pennsylvania) *Semi-Weekly News* — August 23, 1923.

Lexington (Kentucky) *Herald* — July 23, 1919.

Lincoln Evening Journal — July 23, 1921; August 10, 1923; August 19, 1924.

Logansport (Indiana) *Pharos-Tribune* — August 29, 1918; August 10, 1923; August 19, 1924.

Los Angeles Times — October 20, 28, and 30, 1915; August 23 and 27, 1923; August 19 and 20, 1924.

Louisville Courier-Journal — August 11 and 13, 1982.

Macon (Georgia) *Daily Telegraph* — September 3, 1916; August 31, 1919.

Manitowoc (Wisconsin) *Herald-Time* — November 19, 1920.

Medford (Oregon) *Mail Tribune* — August 19, 1924.

Middlesboro (Kentucky) *Daily News* — August 20, 1924.

Middletown (New York) *Times-Press* — August 29, 1916.

Modesto (California) *Daily News* — August 8, 1923.

Montrose (Pennsylvania) *Democrat* — August 23, 1923.

Monroe (Louisiana) *News-Star* — August 19, 1924.

Uniontown, Pennsylvania, *Morning Herald* — August 2 and 6, 1921.

Wilmington, *Morning News* — July 26, 1921; August 22, 1923.

Portland *Morning Oregonian* — October 20, 1915.

Yuma, Arizona, *Morning Sun* — August 7, 1923.

Muskogee (Oklahoma) *County Democrat* — July 28, 1921.

Nevada State Journal — October 20, 1915.

New Castle (Pennsylvania) *Herald* — August

3, 1921; September 6 and 12, 1923.

New Castle (Pennsylvania) *News* — August 11, 1923; August 21, 1924.

Franklin, Pennsylvania, *News-Herald* — July 23 and August 2, 1921; August 11, 1923; August 18, 1924.

Morgantown, North Carolina, *News-Herald* — September 5, 1918.

Wilmington *News Journal* — July 23, 1921; August 1 and 23, 1923; August 19 and 21, 1924.

New York Herald — September 5, 1920.

New York *Sun* — August 26, 1916.

New York Telegraph — July 25, 1921.

New York Times — January 18, 1903; January 5 and 11, February 22, March 7, and May 11, 1914; October 12, 1915; August 29 and 30, September 1, 9, 11, and 24, 1916; August 25, 1918; August 5, 1919; November 13 and 21, 1920; July 23, 24, 25, 29, and 31, 1921; August 5, 11, 12, 17, 22, 23, and 25, September 27, October 18, 1923; August 13, 14, 19, 20, and 24, 1924; February 7, 1925; February 11, July 31, and November 29, 1927.

New York Tribune — November 14, 16, and 21, 1920.

New York World — August 19, 1924.

Oakland (California) *Tribune* — November 7, 1915; November 21, 1920; July 26,

1921; August 23, 1924.

Ogden (Utah) *Standard-Examiner* — August 6, 1921.

Portland *Oregon Daily Journal* — August 16, 1918; August 9 and 12, 1919; November 16, 1920; July 24, 1921.

Oshkosh (Wisconsin) *Daily Northwestern* — August 10, 21, 22, and 23, 1923.

West *Palm Beach* (Florida) *Post* — July 24, 1921.

Bloomington, Illinois, *Pentagraph* — August 20, 1924.

Philadelphia Inquirer — October 16, 1915; July 28, 1921; August 11, 1923; August 19 and 21, 1924.

Pittsburgh Daily Post — August 18, 19, and 20, 1918; August 8 and 22, 1923; August 20, 1924.

Pittsburgh Post-Gazette — August 18, 19, and 21, 1918; July 23, 1921; August 11, 1923.

Pittsburgh Press — August 17, 18, and 19, 1918; July 24, 1921; August 8, 1923.

Portsmouth (Ohio) *Daily Times* — August 4, 1921; August 8, 1923.

Portsmouth (New Hampshire) *Herald* — August 20, 1924.

Columbus, Indiana, *Republic* — August 23, 1923.

Raleigh *State Journal* — September 6, 1918.

525

Reading (Pennsylvania) *Times* — September 3, 1918; August 3, 1923.

Riverside (California) *Daily Press* — November 2, 5, and 17, 1915.

Rochester, New York, *Democrat and Chronicle* — August 19, 1923.

Salinas (Kansas) *Daily Union* — July 23, 1921.

Salisbury (North Carolina) *Evening Post* — August 29, 1918.

San Antonio Express — November 17, 1920.

San Bernardino County (California) *Sun* — December 11, 1920.

San Diego Union — January 12, 1910; August 9, 1910; October 15, 1915; March 22, 1979.

Sandusky (Ohio) *Star-Journal* — August 25, 1916.

San Francisco Chronicle — October 20, 21, 22, and 30, 1915.

San Jose Evening News — October 25, 1915; July 26, 1921.

San Jose Mercury Herald — October 19, 20, 23, and 24, 1915; September 3, 1916; July 25, 1919.

Santa Ana (California) *Register* — July 22, 1921; August 22, 1923; August 19, 1924.

Scranton Republican — August 29, 1924.

St. Joseph (Missouri) *Observer* — August 1, 1924.

St. Louis Post-Dispatch — July 22, 1921; August 10, 11, 18, 19, 21, and 23, 1923; August 19, 20, and 22, 1924.

St. Louis Star and Times — July 23 and 24, 1921; August 1, 1923.

Pittsburg, Kansas, *Sun* — December 5, 1920.

Shreveport, *Times* — August 2, 1923.

Richmond, *Times Dispatch* — August 27, 1918.

Olean, New York, *Times Herald* — July 23, 1921; August 1, 1923; August 19, 1924.

Port Huron, Michigan, *Times Herald* — November 19, 1920; August 12, 1921; August 13 and 27, 1923.

Zanesville, Ohio, *Times Recorder* — August 19, 1924.

Winston-Salem, *Twin-City Daily Sentinel* — August 30 and 31, 1918.

Winston-Salem, *Union Republican* — September 5, 1918.

Vancouver (British Columbia) *World* — Undated article undoubtedly from August 1923.

Vicksburg (Mississippi) *Evening Post* — July 23, 1921.

Waco (Texas) *News-Tribune* — August 22 and 27, 1923.

Wall Street Journal — August 20, 1924.

Washington (D.C.) *Herald* — August 18, 1918.

Washington Post — August 27 and September 2, 1918; December 5, 1920; July 24, 1921; August 1, 5, 22, and 23, 1923; August 19 and 20, September 8, 1924.

Washington (D.C.) *Times* — August 30, 1916; August 9 and 11, 1919; November 18 and December 11, 1920; July 24, 1921.

Waxahachie (Texas) *Daily Light* — August 10, 1923.

Alexandria, Louisiana, *Weekly Town Talk* — August 25, 1923.

Wilkes-Barre Record — July 29, 1921.

Wilkes-Barre Times Leader Evening News — August 21, 1918; July 29, 1921; August 20, 1924.

Winston-Salem Journal — August 30, 1918.

ACKNOWLEDGMENTS

Jim Donovan, my agent, continues to have my back. I very much appreciate the ongoing support I enjoy at Simon & Schuster from Bob Bender, Johanna Li, Jon Karp, Stephen Bedford, and Elizabeth Gay, as well as elite copyeditor Fred Chase. The unmatched research team of Andrea Koos, Jim Fuquay, Anne E. Collier, and photographer Ralph Lauer remains intact, assisted this time around by Clara Herrera. In Dearborn, Michigan, I was aided by the student team of Ryan Brim, Paul Oliver, and Brian Aldaco, the latter two representing the amazing LEAP (Center for Law, Engagement and Politics) program at Sam Houston State University in Huntsville, Texas. Paul Oliver also helped with online newspaper archival research. Special thanks to Mike Yawn, who supervises LEAP. Carlton Stowers and James Ward Lee once again volunteered to read along as I wrote, making critical suggestions throughout.

I was fortunate to be granted interviews and ongoing support from both institutional staff members and area historians all along the Vagabonds' various routes. It began at the Henry Ford Museum and its Benson Ford Research Center with Matthew G. Anderson, J. Marc Greuther, Melanie Bazil, Nardina Main, Ryan Jelso, Cuong T. Nguyen, and many other helpful staff members, as well as retired staffer/historian Robert Casey. From there, the list includes Robert Kreipke of the Ford Motor Company; Leonard DeGraaf of the Thomas Edison National Historical Park; Paul Israel, director and general editor of the Thomas A. Edison Papers, Rutgers School of Arts and Sciences; Brent Newman, curator at Edison and Ford Winter Estates, Fort Myers, Florida; Brian Butko, director of publications for the Senator John Heinz History Center in Pittsburgh; Glenn Miller, Genevieve Bowen, Ralph Ireland, Randy Briggs, Helen Farrell, Woody Hansen, and Pat Mann of the Southwest Florida Historical Society in Fort Myers; Rebecca Baker at the Luther Burbank Home & Gardens in Santa Rosa, California; Marie Silva and many other staff members at the California Historical Society in San Francisco;

530

Amanda Voithofer of the Summit Inn; Anna R. Cueto, archivist and curator at the Washington County Historical Society in Hagerstown, Maryland; Joseph H. Weaver, executive vice president of the Alleghany Museum in Cumberland, Tennessee, along with local historians Albert Feldstein and Champ Zumbrun; Dr. Terry Mullins in Tazewell, Virginia; Ron Ripley and Craig Mohler in various parts of West Virginia; Nancy Sorrels of the Augusta County Historical Society in Staunton, Virginia; John A. Cuthbert, director of West Virginia University's West Virginia & Regional History Center; Richard Candee, architectural historian of the Portsmouth (New Hampshire) Athenaeum; Matthew Powers, director of the Woodstock (Vermont) Historical Society; William Jenney, regional historic site administrator at the President Calvin Coolidge State Historic Site in Plymouth, Vermont; Fredda Hankes of the Mecosta County Historical Society Museum in Big Rapids, Michigan; and Jim Chapman, Dave Basch, and Janet Clark in Green Charter Township, Michigan. In every instance, their comments and insights were helpful. Even those not specifically cited in individual chapter notes added to my overall understanding of the places visited by the

Vagabonds.

Thanks to Cash, who, as usual, was at my side throughout the writing and editing process.

Everything I write is always for Nora, Adam, Grant, and Harrison.

PHOTO CREDITS

Photos 1, 6, 7, 8, 9, 13: Thomas Edison
Research Park

Photos 2, 4, and 5: Courtesy of Edison &
Ford Winter Estates, Inc., Fort Myers, FL,
www.edisonfordwinterestates.org

Photos 3, 15, 23, 24, 25, 26, 27: Ralph
Lauer/24 Words

Photos 10, 11, 12, 14, 16, 17, 18, 19, 20,
21, 22: Image from the Collections of
The Henry Ford

ABOUT THE AUTHOR

Jeff Guinn is an award-winning former investigative journalist and the bestselling author of numerous books, including *Go Down Together: The True Untold Story of Bonnie and Clyde; The Last Gunfight: The Real Story of the Shootout at the O.K. Corral — And How It Changed the West; Manson: The Life and Times of Charles Manson;* and *The Road to Jonestown: Jim Jones and Peoples Temple.* Guinn lives in Fort Worth, Texas.

The employees of Thorndike Press hope you have enjoyed this Large Print book. All our Thorndike, Wheeler, and Kennebec Large Print titles are designed for easy reading, and all our books are made to last. Other Thorndike Press Large Print books are available at your library, through selected bookstores, or directly from us.

For information about titles, please call:
(800) 223-1244

or visit our website at:
gale.com/thorndike

To share your comments, please write:
Publisher
Thorndike Press
10 Water St., Suite 310
Waterville, ME 04901